A TIME OF FEAR

ALSO BY ALBERT MARRIN

Black Gold: The Story of Oil in Our Lives

FDR and the American Crisis

Flesh & Blood So Cheap: The Triangle Fire and Its Legacy
A National Book Award Finalist

Thomas Paine: Crusader for Liberty

Uprooted: The Japanese American Experience During World War II
A Sibert Honor Book

Very, Very, Very Dreadful: The Influenza Pandemic of 1918

A Volcano Beneath the Snow: John Brown's War Against Slavery

A Light in the Darkness: Janusz Korczak, His Orphans, and the Holocaust
A YALSA Award for Excellence in Nonfiction Finalist

A TIME OF FEAR

AMERICA IN THE ERA OF RED SCARES AND COLD WAR

ALBERT MARRIN

Alfred A. Knopf   New York

THIS IS A BORZOI BOOK PUBLISHED BY ALFRED A. KNOPF

Text copyright © 2021 by Albert Marrin
Jacket art used under license from Shutterstock.com

All rights reserved. Published in the United States by Alfred A. Knopf, an imprint of Random House Children's Books,
a division of Penguin Random House LLC, New York.

Knopf, Borzoi Books, and the colophon are registered trademarks of Penguin Random House LLC.

For picture credits, please see page 292.

Visit us on the Web! GetUnderlined.com

Educators and librarians, for a variety of teaching tools, visit us at
RHTeachersLibrarians.com

Library of Congress Cataloging-in-Publication Data is available upon request.
ISBN 978-0-525-64429-3 (trade) — ISBN 978-0-525-64430-9 (lib. bdg.) — ISBN 978-0-525-64432-3 (ebook)

The text of this book is set in 11.5-point Adobe Garamond Pro.

MANUFACTURED IN ITALY
March 2021
10 9 8 7 6 5 4 3 2 1

First Edition

Random House Children's Books supports the First Amendment and celebrates the right to read.

Penguin Random House LLC supports copyright. Copyright fuels creativity, encourages diverse voices,
promotes free speech, and creates a vibrant culture. Thank you for buying an authorized edition of this book
and for complying with copyright laws by not reproducing, scanning, or distributing any part in any form without permission.
You are supporting writers and allowing Penguin Random House to publish books for every reader.

For those who fought the good fight

I want you to listen to me very carefully, Harry. You're not a bad person. You're a very good person, who bad things have happened to. Besides, the world isn't split into good people and Death Eaters. We've all got both light and dark inside us. What matters is the part we choose to act on. That's who we really are.

—Sirius Black in *Harry Potter and the Order of the Phoenix* (2007)

Exactly the point. Fudge isn't in his right mind. It's been twisted and warped by fear. Now fear makes people do terrible things, Harry.

—Remus Lupin in *Harry Potter and the Order of the Phoenix* (2007)

CONTENTS

ABBREVIATIONS

ACLU—American Civil Liberties Union

CCNY—City College of New York

CIA—Central Intelligence Agency

CPSU—Communist Party of the Soviet Union

CPUSA—Communist Party of the United States of America

FBI—Federal Bureau of Investigation

HUAC—House Un-American Activities Committee

ILD—International Labor Defense

IWW—Industrial Workers of the World

KGB—Committee for State Security

KKK—Ku Klux Klan

NAACP—National Association for the Advancement of Colored People

NATO—North Atlantic Treaty Organization

NCSJRC—National Committee to Secure Justice in the Rosenberg Case

NKVD—People's Commissariat for Internal Affairs

NRA—National Recovery Administration

OWI—Office of War Information

PCF—French Communist Party

USSR—Union of Soviet Socialist Republics

VOA—Voice of America

YCL—Young Communist League

YP—Young Pioneers

LENIN'S JOURNEY

The worst of all despotisms is the heartless tyranny of ideas.
—Paul Johnson, *Intellectuals* (1988)

A young man, whom we may let stand for Everyman, wrote in his diary just days before he was killed in action: "Humanity is mad! It must be mad to do what it is doing. What a massacre! What scenes of horror and carnage! I cannot find words to translate my impressions. Hell cannot be so terrible. Men are mad!"[1]

It was the worst of times. The war that began in July 1914 had been raging for nearly three years. It was the most terrible, the most brutal and destructive conflict the world had ever known. Those who lived through the horror, civilians and fighters alike, called it the Great War or the World War, because it was waged worldwide, involving countries and colonies on every continent. Yet few could imagine that it would become the First World War, prelude to the more hideous Second World War, which would start within a generation. For the most part, the First World War was a struggle for supremacy in

Europe and for overseas colonies, pitting two alliances against each other. One alliance, known as the Central Powers, was led by the German Empire and included the Austro-Hungarian Empire and the Turkish (or Ottoman) Empire. Opposing them were the Allies: France, Belgium, the Russian Empire, Italy, Japan, the United Kingdom, Canada, Australia, New Zealand, South Africa, and India.

Almost from the first shots, the war bogged down on the major European fronts. Advances in weaponry—repeating rifles, machine guns, quick-firing artillery, tanks, airplanes, flamethrowers, poison gas—forced the adversaries to dig lines of deep trenches, zigzagging for hundreds of miles, to avoid the hail of explosives and metal flying overhead. From then on, the war settled into a relentless slugging match, with neither side able to deliver the knockout blow. Battles lasted days, even months, ending with little to show but hundreds of thousands of casualties. On average, 6,000 fighting men were killed every day of the war; before it ended, in November 1918, more than 9.5 million had lost their lives. Millions more were gravely wounded, hideously disfigured, or psychologically crippled. Added to this carnage were the 10 million civilians dead of wounds, star-

vation, and disease directly related to the conflict.

By early 1917, Germany had become desperate. Its leading generals and politicians realized that fighting on two fronts, against Russia and the Western Allies, must end in disaster. Their country simply lacked the manpower and material resources to wage war on such a gigantic scale for years on end. Unless things changed soon, Germany would have to yield, dooming the Central Powers. And so Berlin decided that its only hope lay in forcing Russia out of the war.

Though Russian forces vastly outnumbered the enemy's, they were poorly trained, clumsily led, and badly equipped. After many battles, Russian bodies lay so close together that one could walk on a carpet of flesh for hundreds of yards without setting foot on the ground. Russian morale—the will to fight—snapped. Frontline troops, seeing the war's futility, clamored to go home. Some units mutinied, shot their officers, and fled the trenches. Even in elegant Petrograd, the national capital, residents grew desperate. Through mismanagement and corruption, the civilian economy had collapsed. Russia's overworked railroad system broke down; a train might arrive days late, if it arrived at all. For lack of coal, people froze in their apartments, while necessities like food, medicine, and clothing ran short. To make matters worse, Czar Nicholas II, the reigning emperor, was an incompetent weakling, unfit to rule a nation in crisis. Ex-president Theodore Roosevelt thought him "a preposterous little creature" with an empty head and a backbone of jelly.[2]

Starting in Petrograd, factory workers and the soldiers and sailors of the military garrison elected "soviets" (from the Russian for "councils"). The soviets demanded reforms, issued bulletins to keep citizens up to date, and organized massive street protests. Slow-moving rivers of humanity chanted, "Down with the czar!" "Down with the war!" and always "Bread! Bread!" It was too much for the emperor. Unable to cope with the growing disorder, in February 1917, Nicholas II abdicated, giving up the throne and ending the monarchy. People welcomed the news with outpourings of joy and "smiles on all faces." The Provisional Government, led by Alexander Kerensky, a prominent lawyer and reformer, took over until national elections could be held for the Constituent Assembly to draw up a constitution. Meanwhile, the Provisional Government declared freedom of

Workers demonstrating in Petrograd. The banners read "Feed the children of the defenders of the Motherland" and "Increase payments to the soldiers' families—defenders of freedom and world peace." (1917)

speech, press, and assembly and abolished the Okhrana, the czar's dreaded secret police. To show his government's good faith, Kerensky promised to keep Russia in the war on the Allied side, a move bound to anger the war-weary population.

Germany's own leaders decided on what we today call "regime change"— toppling a hostile foreign government and putting a more pliant one in its place. To that end, they planned to ignite a second, more radical Russian Revolution. If all went well, the Provisional Government's successor would betray the Western Allies, taking Russia out of the war and allowing Germany to transfer masses of troops and equipment to the Western Front.

Berlin turned to a stocky little man, bald as an egg, with a reddish mustache and goatee. Born in 1870 to an inspector of district schools and his wife, Vladimir Ilyich Ulyanov, better known by the alias Lenin, led the Bolsheviks. The name means "majority party" in Russian, yet this tiny group of zealots was hardly that. But unlike the far larger political groups, the Bolsheviks were professional revolutionaries. Many, including Lenin, had never done a day's work for pay, living off their families, contributions from supporters, or outright theft; as a young man, Joseph

Vladimir Lenin. (c. 1920)

Stalin, who will play a key role in our story, ran a gang of bank robbers. Though educated as a lawyer, Lenin spent his time plotting to overthrow the czarist regime. Hunted by the Okhrana, he fled to Zurich, Switzerland, where he joined fellow exiles. For a decade, he and his wife, Nadezhda Krupskaya, a stolid, unsmiling woman, lived in a grimy tenement across from a slaughterhouse, awaiting a chance to return. They had no children. When the war began, Lenin called for Russia's defeat, expecting military disasters to trigger the longed-for revolution.

The powers that be in Berlin saw Lenin as a human wrecking ball. They promised to send him back to his homeland, provided he did his utmost to overthrow the Provisional Government and sue for peace on German terms. Thus, on April 8, 1917, the Bolshevik leader and thirty-one fellow exiles began an eight-day journey aboard a "sealed train," actually a single engine and a single carriage, from Zurich to Petrograd. Writing about these events years later, the English statesman Winston Churchill said the Germans had "turned upon Russia the most grisly of all weapons": they introduced a "plague bacillus," Lenin, into Russia's weakened body at precisely the moment it was most vulnerable.[3]

Shortly before midnight on April 16, the exiles' train steamed into Petrograd's Finland Station. As it rolled to a stop, a crowd of well-wishers met Lenin with a bouquet of red roses, red banners, a brass band, and a giant searchlight that sent silvery beams streaking into the black sky. Greeters ushered the grim-faced Lenin into the "Czar's Room," the waiting area reserved for the imperial family. The Bolshevik chief stood on a chair and began to speak. Listeners recalled that his words,

delivered in a harsh, gravelly voice, came "like a clap of thunder." "Dear comrades, soldiers, sailors, and workers," he said. "I am happy to . . . greet you as the vanguard of the worldwide proletarian army. . . . The Russian revolution accomplished by you . . . has prepared the way and opened a new epoch. Long live the worldwide socialist revolution!"[4]

Socialist revolution! To understand what Lenin meant by this, we must view him as a man possessed, a man captivated by the ideas of a dead German economist named Karl Marx (1818–1883). Co-author with his friend Friedrich Engels of *The Communist Manifesto* (1848) and author of *Capital* (1867), a book on economic theory, Marx was a radical socialist thinker whose works are still read, discussed, and debated.

"Socialism" is not easy to define, because those who used the term often disagreed on its meaning. Hence, there were many varieties of socialism, which needn't concern us. Despite their differences, however, socialists agreed on a basic principle: Selfishness is wrong. People should not think only of themselves, socialists insisted, prospering at the expense of others. Instead, they must put the interests of society ahead of those of any individual,

Painting by Mikhail G. Sokolov depicting Lenin speaking in favor of the revolution of October 1917. A young Joseph Stalin appears just behind him. (c. 1937)

family, group, or nation. Most socialist groups, such as the American Socialist Party, valued democracy and were committed to peaceful change; today they might be called "democratic socialists." Rather than resorting to violent revolution, they wished to improve the lot of working people by establishing trade unions and free elections and putting government in control of the "commanding heights" of the economy. This meant running key sectors—manufacturing, energy, transportation, communications, banks—not for private profit, but to benefit society as a whole. These socialists further believed that people should own their own small businesses, provided that they treated their employees fairly, and that farmers should have their own land, so long as they did not have vast estates worked by poor peasants.

Karl Marx was the founder of Marxism, or communism (from the Latin *communis,* "held in common" or "belonging to all"). Unlike other forms of socialism, Marxism is a rigid ideology. We normally think of an ideology as a belief system that people accept as true, just, and useful. For example, the monotheistic religions—

Judaism, Christianity, Islam—share the belief in one God and the moral principles flowing from that belief. In the United States, the dominant ideology since the days of the Founders has been freedom of thought, freedom of speech, free markets, free elections, and equality under the law. Yet "ideology" can mean a lot more. I use it to describe a system of ideas held as infallible science and thus as the key to understanding the "immutable laws" governing human affairs. In this sense, ideology makes seemingly unrelated facts fall into their proper place, like a thousand-piece jigsaw puzzle magically assembled in the blink of an eye. In doing so, it explains everything: all that has happened to humans in the past is happening today, and will inevitably happen in the future. Furthermore, an explain-all ideology dictates rules for the most basic and personal aspects of human existence: how to live, love, learn, labor, relate, read, create, relax, think, and believe. Ideologies are powerful mind shapers, inspiring true believers to sacrifice everything and everyone, including themselves, for the sake of their beliefs.

Oddly, such people are motivated not by a desire to do evil, but by just the opposite. Russian novelist and historian Aleksandr Solzhenitsyn learned this through painful experience. He wrote: "To do evil, a human being must first of all believe that what he's doing is good, or else that it's a well-considered act in conformity with natural law. . . . Ideology—that is what gives evildoing its long-sought justification and gives the evildoer the necessary steadfastness and determination. That is the social theory which helps to make his acts seem good instead of bad in his own and others' eyes." For the true believer, then, ideology can turn lying into an obligation, hatred into a virtue, and violence against "the Other" into a duty. Let's call this the evil effects of good intentions.[5]

The twentieth century saw the rise and fall of the two most oppressive—no, murderous—ideologies ever conceived. One, racism—which for centuries was used as a justification for slavery—is based on the lunatic idea that skin color and other physical traits determine a person's or, for that matter, an entire people's character and aptitudes. Thus, the most extreme form of racism, as preached by Adolf Hitler, portrayed the course of history as a savage struggle between "superior" and "inferior" races for world domination. To Hitler and his followers, the superior "Aryan" race, embodied in the purebred Germanic "superman," had the right to conquer, enslave, and exterminate its "inferiors" as if they were vermin. During World War II, Hitler's maniacal racism led to the Holocaust, a systematic effort to murder Europe's Jews.

By contrast, Marxist ideology explained nearly all human activity in economic terms. Through Marxism, a German Communist declared, "we know the fundamental answer to the riddle of the past, present, and future, for all nations and for all countries." This is a heady notion, giving believers the conviction of their own virtue, infallibility, and destiny.[6]

Marx despised capitalism, the system of privately owned businesses operated for profit. The economist held that businesspeople, called "capitalists" or "bourgeoisie," would always oppress the "proletariat," or wage earners. He believed that private property lay at the root of all evil, because desiring it bred greed and exploitation, tyranny and war. The solution was obvious—at least to him and Engels. "The theory of the Communists," says *The Communist Manifesto,* "may be summed up in the single sentence: Abolition of private property." To drive home the point, the authors told critics: "You reproach us with intending to do away with your prop-

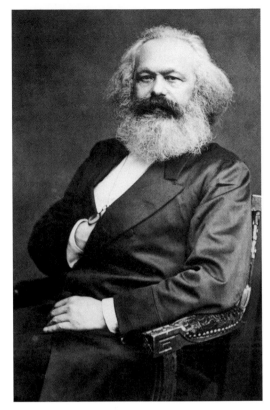

Karl Marx. (1875)

erty. Precisely so; that is what we intend." Thus, they rejected the age-old Western idea that private ownership of property is a natural right, essential to human existence. As stated in the Declaration of Independence, the right to "life, liberty and the pursuit of happiness" is given to humanity by a loving God. It follows that every person may use their talents to earn, acquire, keep, sell, and give away the fruits of their labor as they see fit.[7]

Marx and Engels thought capitalists

would never be swayed by reason. Therefore, they concluded *The Communist Manifesto* with a promise and a threat: "The Communists . . . openly declare that their ends can be attained only by the forcible overthrow of all existing social conditions." They predicted that the old order, if dedicated men and women struggled against it, would give way to the "dictatorship of the proletariat"—that is, the rule of the working class. Under the dictatorship, progress would logically come in two stages. At the outset, the victors would impose socialism, which, as we've seen, originally meant turning products and services into community property to be used for the common good. But according to Marxists, achieving socialism was merely a way station, a stage the new society would have to pass through to reach the second and final stage of development: communism. Under communism, workers would not receive wages but rather would get whatever they needed according to the maxim "From each according to his ability, to each according to his need." Since Marxists believed history was merely the record of injustice driven by greed, it followed that the advent of communism would signal the end of history. Heaven would descend to earth and humanity would enjoy everlasting peace and joy, harmony and prosperity.[8]

That was not to be, for the Marxist dream was just that—a dream. And with the victory of Lenin's Bolsheviks, it became a nightmare for millions of innocent people. Russia, a nation spanning one-sixth of the world's landmass and eleven time zones, was renamed the Union of Soviet Socialist Republics (USSR)—Soviet Union for short. The USSR's red flag—representing revolution, with its crossed hammer and sickle standing for the unity of industrial workers and peasants under communism—became the national symbol. The Bolshevik Party became the Communist Party of the Soviet Union. Though Petrograd was renamed Leningrad (today's St. Petersburg) in Lenin's honor, the nation's capital was moved to Moscow. From within the walls of the Kremlin (Russian for "fortress"), Lenin set in motion a horrific chain of events that continues to influence our world.

Though Lenin held human life cheap, blithely ordering executions, his successor, Joseph Stalin, was truly a monster, among the worst two or three humans who ever lived. Under Stalin's rule, the USSR became what historian Ralph Raico called "the worst reeking charnel house of the whole awful twentieth century, worse even than the one [Hitler] created." In time, the USSR aided and encouraged foreign Communists to seize power in Eastern Europe, China, Mongolia, North Korea, Vietnam, Laos, Cambodia, Afghanistan, and Cuba. This expansion came at an estimated cost of one hundred million lives, taken by man-made famines, wars, terror from secret police, torture, mass executions, wholesale deportations, and forced labor under inhumane conditions.[9]

The effects of the Bolshevik triumph would impact the United States as no foreign force since colonial times had done. Soviet leaders were determined to break "the backbone of the capitalist beast," as they called the world's leading industrial nation. To achieve that end, they hoped to transform their own country, economically backward in 1917, into a dynamic industrial and military titan capable of shaping global events. At the same time, they sought to undermine their enemy from within, by means of the Communist Party of the United States of America (CPUSA). We cannot, therefore, understand the Party apart from the development of the Soviet dictatorship from which it took its ideas, its marching orders, and much of its funding. While the CPUSA never came close

to succeeding, it aimed at sowing strife and division at every level of society. Even so, its activities were not altogether negative. In attempting to further Moscow's aims, the Party also championed causes worthy in themselves, notably aiding the unemployed, instituting Social Security, organizing workers, and protesting racial injustice.

For most of the twentieth century, the CPUSA had an impact on American life far out of proportion to its size. On balance, "the Communist menace," real or imagined, fostered a climate of fear and, occasionally, hysteria. People will do terrible things to avoid being ruled by those they believe hate them and mean them harm. America's time of fear saw two "Red Scares": the first was the Great Red Scare of 1919; the second was spawned by the Cold War—anxiety over the prospect of nuclear annihilation—and panic over Soviet spies in American government and industry. In response to the Great Red Scare, Congress created what became the Federal Bureau of Investigation (FBI) under the fanatical anti-Communist sleuth J. Edgar Hoover. The Second Red Scare saw bodies such as the House Un-American Activities Committee (HUAC) hold countless hearings, documented word for word in millions of pages of transcripts and congressional reports. These contain grim accounts of witnesses badgered to "name names" of fellow Communists or face crippling fines, long jail terms, and loss of livelihood. It was a time of "blacklists" and purges of the "disloyal" from government, education, radio, television, theater, and Hollywood's film industry. The pursuit of those responsible for stealing the "secret" of the atomic bomb led to the execution of Julius and Ethel Rosenberg—he a genuine Soviet spy; she convicted on tainted evidence. In the meantime, the name Joseph R. McCarthy became a byword for character assassination and abuse of civil liberties, as un-American as the alleged crimes the senator investigated.

The issues raised during America's time of fear remain with us. In an age of terrorism, when suicidal fanatics crash jetliners into New York's World Trade Center and blow themselves up amid crowds of peaceful shoppers in Middle Eastern cities, we still grapple with the same questions. How can we balance safety with the rights cherished by a free society? Are there limits to these rights in the face of clear dangers? If so, what are those limits? If there are no limits, do we risk more in the long run, gaining a tenuous feeling of safety at the expense of violating the core principles upon which our nation was founded?

FRIGHTENED VICTORS

The people are shivering in their boots over Bolshevism, and they are far more scared of Lenin than they ever were of the Kaiser [German emperor]. We seem to be the most frightened victors that the world ever saw.
—Walter Lippmann, American journalist (1919)

RED OCTOBER

Lenin bided his time. After arriving in Petrograd, he planned and plotted, aided by German money equal to $1 billion in today's dollars. Secret German funding was critical, enabling the Bolsheviks to buy a printing plant, publish newspapers, turn out protest signs reading "The Germans Are Our Brothers," and pay agitators to undermine morale in the army. "Lenin's entry into Russia successful," noted a German army intelligence report. "He is working exactly as we would wish."[1]

In October 1917—"Red October"—Lenin gave the word. Bands of armed Bolsheviks called Red Guards, joined by radicalized soldiers, sailors, and workers from the soviets, swung into action. In a series of swift moves, they stormed government buildings, taking control of the capital. But instead of allowing free elections, as millions had hoped, the Bolsheviks began to reshape Russian society. Ruthlessly tearing the economy from private hands, they ordered businesses and factories, buildings and land, seized and declared public property. Depositors could only withdraw a small amount from their bank accounts each month; safe-deposit boxes were broken open and valuables confiscated for "the people's use." An edict forbade hiring anyone for wages, because employing others in order to profit from their labor was deemed "class exploitation." Private trade, even for small-scale shopkeepers, was abolished.

To feed the newly created Red Army, "food brigades," teams of activists sent from the cities, forced peasants to turn over much, and in many cases all, of their crops. Infuriated peasants reacted by cutting open food thieves' bellies and filling them with grain as a sign of contempt. The Red Army retaliated, smothering rebels hiding in forests, including women and children, with poison gas.

For Lenin, there was no such thing as

A Red Guard unit, machine guns and all. (1917)

an honest difference of opinion. He was an aggressively intolerant man, whose nature didn't allow him to suffer "idiots." The Bolshevik leader, an aide noted, "didn't give a damn for the opinions of others." He saw no reason to, for Marxism was his absolute truth, beyond question or criticism; anyone who disagreed was by definition not only wrong, but evil. Lenin saw such people as scarcely human. To him, they were "slime and filth," "blockheads," "bastards," "prostitutes," "dirty scum," "shits," "cretins," "Russian fools," "windbags," "stupid hens," and "silly old maids." They deserved a bullet in the head, not the give-and-take of reasoned debate. Bullets were very useful things, in Lenin's view. He'd ask, in all sincerity, "How can you make a revolution without firing squads?" By its very nature, Bolshevik-style revolution meant unbridled violence.[2]

Lenin and his followers rejected traditional values and moral norms. For the vast majority of Europeans and Americans, these derived from the Ten Commandments and the Golden Rule, which tell us to act toward others as we would have them act toward us. Bolsheviks denounced these principles as "putrid" and silly. "Is there such a thing as communist morality?" Lenin asked a youth group. "Of course, there is. . . . Our morality stems from the interests of the class struggle of the proletariat. . . . We say: morality is what serves to destroy the old exploiting society and to unite all the working people around the proletariat, which is building up a new, communist society. . . . Communist morality is that which serves this struggle and unites the working people against all exploitation, against all petty private property." In practical terms, this meant that nothing was out of bounds, nothing innately immoral, if it served the Cause. Lenin explained: "We must be ready to employ trickery, deceit, lawbreaking and concealing truth. We can and must write in a language which sows among the masses hate, revulsion, scorn and the like, toward those who disagree with us." In short, Lenin held that the end justified the means—*any* means, including the murder of whole categories of human beings labeled "class enemies" and "counterrevolutionaries."[3]

Lenin further argued that Bolsheviks must always be "politically correct," an expression he used and may actually have invented. Nowadays, political incorrectness refers to language deemed offensive to others, often about race and gender. For Lenin's followers, however, political correctness meant that any position the Communist Party of the Soviet Union took was valid, because its ideology made it infallible. Yet a position could be instantly reversed, and without the slightest misgiving. For example, Lenin said that the politically correct way was not for the courts to put checks on violence, "but to substantiate it and legitimize it in principle," because "Marxists judge the results, not the methods." On the other hand, being "politically incorrect" meant believing or doing anything that harmed Soviet interests.[4]

Though trained as a lawyer, Lenin, as a Marxist revolutionary, rejected any notion of "Equal Justice Under the Law," the motto engraved on the front of the United States Supreme Court building in Washington, DC. In fact, he scorned the very idea of the rule of law. As understood in democracies, well-defined and enforceable laws protect citizens from government overreach, from officials driven by greed, passion, stupidity, and bigotry. Lenin, however, defined the dictatorship of the proletariat as "unrestrained, lawless power, based on force in the simplest sense of the word. It is nothing other than power totally unlimited by laws, absolutely unrestrained by regulations and based directly on the use of force." We cannot say it too

often: Bolsheviks deemed any action in the service of their ideology moral, regardless of the human costs.[5]

People from all walks of life, especially army officers still loyal to the former czar, rebelled against the new rulers. In the civil war that followed Red October (late 1917 to early 1922), a loose alliance of anti-Bolshevik forces known as the "Whites," aided by Great Britain and

Various images from the Russian Civil War. Note Leon Trotsky at bottom left. (c. 1920)

the United States, fought the Bolsheviks, or the "Reds." Both sides were merciless toward foes. The Bolsheviks, officially and stridently, unleashed the Red Terror. We must note that terrorism and terror are not the same. Terrorism is the weapon of the angry and weak against a stronger foe they have no chance of defeating in open battle. Its methods include assassination, hostage taking, and bombing specific targets.

Terror, however, is very different. It is government by fear—an organized system of violence by the state to create a climate of insecurity. In Russia, the Bolsheviks turned to terror, not democracy, to enable them to control the majority who yearned only for "peace, land, and bread." The aim of the Red Terror was to crush any and all opposition. Grigory Zinoviev, one of Lenin's favorite henchmen, excluded whole categories of the population from humanity. "We must," he said with all the conviction of the fanatic, "carry with us 90 million out of the 100 million of Soviet Russia's inhabitants. As for the rest, we have nothing to say to them. They must be annihilated." Yet Zinoviev was merely echoing his leader. In the infamous "Hanging Order," Lenin instructed Bolsheviks to "choke and strangle" hostages "in such a way that people for hundreds of miles around will see, tremble, know and scream out." In effect, snuffing out millions of human lives meant nothing when it came to gaining and securing Bolshevik power.[6]

The instrument of the Red Terror was the Cheka (a Russian acronym for the All-Russian Extraordinary Commission for Combating Counterrevolution and Sabotage). "Chekists" believed that their superior virtue and lofty intentions gave them license to kill with a clear conscience. For Chekists, their victims were not beings with God-given rights, but obstacles to progress. "Our humanity," declared their magazine, *The Red Sword*, "is absolute because it rests on a new ideal. *To us, everything is permitted*, for we are the first to raise the sword not to oppress races and reduce them to slavery, but to liberate humanity from its shackles. . . . Blood? Let blood flow like water! . . . For only through the death of the old world can we liberate ourselves."[7]

Lenin charged the Cheka with enforcing "revolutionary legality"—in reality, absolute lawlessness. Those who fell into the Cheka's hands were to be judged according to their social class. Cheka chief Martin Latsis ordered his men "not to look for evidence as proof that the accused has acted or spoken against the Soviets.

First you must ask him to what class he belongs, what his social origin is, his education and profession. These are the questions that must determine the fate of the accused. That is the meaning of the Red Terror." The head of the Soviet court system, Nikolai Krylenko, added: "We must execute not only the guilty. Execution of the innocent will impress the masses even more."[8]

Even under the most oppressive czars, such as Ivan the Terrible (who ruled from 1547 to 1584), Russia had never seen state killing on such a scale. Whereas the oppressive czars executed 6,321 people for capital crimes, primarily murder and treason, between 1825 and 1917, the Cheka shot some 15,000 "class enemies" and "counterrevolutionaries" in just a two-month period in 1918. The Red Terror also claimed the imperial family. On Lenin's orders, in July, Czar Nicholas II, his wife, his son, his four daughters, and four of his servants were shot. In the gruesome aftermath, their bodies were dismembered, ignited with gasoline, the larger bones dissolved in sulfuric acid, and the remainder thrown down an abandoned mine shaft.[9]

Calling themselves "engineers of the human soul," Bolsheviks believed they had the right to shape the minds and mold the lives of millions of ordinary people—people they had never met and knew nothing about. The word "spirit" did not exist in their vocabulary. As Karl Marx, their prophet, taught, humanity's spiritual aspect was a myth, and therefore so was religion. Marx reviled religion as "the opium of the people," because it supposedly dulled their wits, making them incapable of resisting injustice.

Lenin thought religion "the most dangerous baseness, the most vile infection . . . a poison which is as sweet as sugar-candy . . . but truly sickening." Guided by this belief, the Bolsheviks launched an all-out war on organized religion. They began by seizing all the lands and buildings of the Russian Orthodox Church, until then the official state church, and removing all schools from its control. This was followed by unspeakable atrocities committed against priests, monks, and nuns. Tens of thousands were shot, nailed to doors, thrown into cauldrons of boiling tar, scalped, buried alive, and drowned. Lenin relished these outrages, demanding to be informed "on a daily basis" how many priests had been killed. During the 1920s, Bolsheviks formed the League of the Militant Godless, a mass organization claiming 5.5 million members, to spread hatred of religion along with atheism, disbelief in the existence of God and his moral law.[10]

The Bolshevik Revolution and Russian Civil War claimed the lives of an estimated thirteen million people—killed in battle, died of wounds, murdered by the Cheka, starved to death—and forced two million Russians into exile, an immense brain drain from which the USSR would suffer for decades. Among the exiles were some of the nation's best minds: painters, dramatists, dancers, musicians, philosophers, linguists, scientists, mathematicians, and religious thinkers. In decades to come, these exiles and the young people they trained and inspired would enrich Western scholarship, culture, and spiritual life. Lenin, however, had only contempt for "those smart little intellectuals . . . who fancy themselves the nation's brains. In point of fact, they are not the brains, but shit."[11]

Lenin and his followers believed that getting rid of these "former people" was but the first step in a grand and glorious design. Bolsheviks regarded humans as nothing special, merely aspects of nature, like water and rocks and lice. Purely material beings, as Lenin explained, humans had no innate dignity or aspirations, but only their five senses: sight, hearing, touch, smell, and taste. This made them merely "raw material," malleable as wax, and therefore capable of being "processed" by the state. By changing the environment, Lenin declared, the Communist state could shape people according to Marxist principles. He said, "Man can be corrected. Man can be made what we want him to be." Thus, communism promised to create a higher, healthier, happier type of humanity. Called *Homo sovieticus*—Latin for "Soviet man"—this new man would be a selfless creature who lived only to serve the community, content to be a cog in the wheel of a great machine, or a worker ant instinctively sacrificing for its colony. Bolsheviks had absolute faith in their ability and right to remake human nature. It was not up to ordinary, "flawed" human beings to decide their fate, but to their enlightened masters. If need be, said Lenin, "we will drive mankind to happiness by force!"[12]

Leon Trotsky, the father of the Red Army, was ecstatic at the thought of the paradise sure to emerge with the remaking of human nature. Guided by the Communist Party of the Soviet Union (CPSU), Trotsky wrote, people everywhere would change physically and mentally, developing into beings more

Leon Trotsky, father of the Red Army. (c. 1924)

handsome, intelligent, and creative than had ever existed.

> Man at last will begin to harmonize himself in earnest. . . . He will try to master first the semiconscious and then the subconscious processes of his own organism, such as breathing, the circulation of the blood, digestion, reproduction, and, within necessary limits, he will try to subordinate them to the control of reason and will. . . . Man will make it his purpose to master his own feelings, to raise his instincts to the heights of consciousness, to make them transparent . . . and thereby to raise himself to a new plane, to create a higher social biologic type, or, if you please, a superman. . . . Man will become immeasurably stronger, wiser and subtler; his body will become more harmonized, his movements more rhythmic, his voice more musical. . . . The average human type will rise to the heights of . . . a Marx.[13]

We note that there is no mention of freedom for the new man, not a word about one's right to think one's own thoughts, go one's own way, and act according to one's own desires. For Russia's new masters did not think in terms of freedom for the individual. That sort of freedom, for them, was merely a "bourgeois prejudice," incapable of bringing humanity to happiness. Only the dictatorship of the Communist elite could do that.

Russia's Communist rulers were determined not only to transform humanity in their own country, but to spread "the Revolution," for them a sacred phrase uttered with awe. They meant, in Lenin's words, to use the USSR as a springboard from which to "conquer the whole world." Communism and capitalism were as fire and water;

Lenin thought it inevitable that one would destroy the other. And the most advanced capitalist nation was the United States of America.[14]

AMERICA GOES TO WAR

The United States was partially responsible for the German decision to send Lenin back to Russia. When the war began in 1914, Great Britain, the world's premier naval power, blockaded Germany, clearing the seas of its merchantmen; only German submarines, called U-boats (for *Unterseeboot*), were able to put to sea undetected. The blockade succeeded in cutting Germany off from the outside world; even supplies of food and medicine were kept from entering its ports. As a result, hunger and disease stalked the land, killing thousands of civilians each month, including young children. From time to time, the army itself, always short of rations, endured bouts of near starvation.

Though German U-boats had targeted Allied shipping from the moment the war began, in February 1917 the high command declared "unrestricted submarine warfare." This meant that *any* vessel, including merchantmen and passenger liners from neutral countries, found in the frigid waters surrounding the British Isles would be sunk without warning. When American vessels ignored the threat, claiming "freedom of the seas" for peaceful neutrals, the Germans acted. Almost certain death awaited those aboard a torpedoed ship. Even if the Germans had wanted to, they could not have rescued survivors; U-boats were tiny, with no room for anyone other than their crews. Those cast into the sea were left to their fate.

German submarines, called U-boats, were the only vessels capable of traveling undetected after Great Britain blockaded Germany. The text reads "Boats out!" (1917)

The sinkings put America in a difficult position. President Woodrow Wilson, like the public at large, thought it a blessing that the Atlantic Ocean lay between his country and the Old World's madness. The supposedly advanced nations, the *New York Times* declared, "have reverted to the condition of savage tribes roaming the forests and falling upon each other in a fury of blood and carnage to achieve the ambitious designs of chieftains clad in skins and drunk on mead." Since Europe's quarrels had no bearing on the American nation's true interests, it seemed best to remain neutral "in fact as well as in name," as Wilson advised.[15]

Neutrality made sense. About a third of America's 106 million citizens had been born in Europe, or had at least one close relative born there, so going to war seemed a bad idea. People of Irish and English, French and German, Italian and Austrian, Polish and Russian descent had grievances, carryovers from the old country, which might tear the nation apart if it took sides. Moreover, neutrality was immensely profitable. America stood ready to trade with anyone, including savage chieftains clad in skins. Its farm products, machinery, and war materials commanded high prices in Europe. All foreigners needed to do was

to order what they wanted, pay, and send their ships to pick up the goods. But here was the rub: Germany believed America's professed "neutrality" a fraud, designed to aid the Allies at its expense. When Berlin refused to halt the U-boat attacks, on April 6, 1917, ten days before Lenin's arrival in Petrograd, a joint session of Congress granted President Wilson's request for a declaration of war against Germany.

Overnight, public opinion did an about-face. Overcome with patriotic zeal, millions who had sung the hit "I Didn't Raise My Boy to Be a Soldier" changed their tune to "Over There":

> *Over there, over there,*
> *Send the word, send the word over*
> *   there,*
> *That the Yanks are coming, the Yanks*
> *   are coming. . . .*
> *And we won't come back till it's over*
> *   over there.*[16]

While the nation prepared to send soldiers overseas, it geared up to fight on the home front. As the French emperor Napoleon Bonaparte used to say, "An army marches on its stomach." Mass armies require masses of everything from beans to bayonets, boots to bombs. These are produced by civilians working in factories and mines and on farms. But Napoleon also said, "You can do anything with bayonets, except sit on them." By this he meant that governmental power, even in a dictatorship, has limits. To get the most out of people, they must believe in the nation's cause and want to do their utmost for it.

Getting them to believe was the job of propagandists. In America, the government sponsored a huge effort, employing every means of communication available at the time. Propagandists built their campaign to "sell" the war around two broad themes. The first theme appealed to idealism. Americans supposedly fought not for selfish ends, but for the highest ideals expressed in the slogans "The war to end all wars" and "The war to make the world safe for democracy." The second theme was hatred rooted in a basic human emotion: fear. Atrocities are inevitable in war; every side commits them, to a greater or lesser degree. Each side, too, exaggerates enemy atrocities or makes them up. The Germans told wild tales of sadistic French troops gouging out prisoners' eyes. London newspapers had front-page drawings of Germans shooting British nurses. Americans, too, portrayed the enemy as the embodiment of evil. Wherever you

turned, you saw strikingly colored posters depicting Germans as ugly, drooling, ravenous beasts.

The war to make the world safe for democracy tested American democracy—a test it often failed. Though millions supported the war effort with dignity and decency, hatred infected millions of others. Viewed in hindsight, much of this reaction was absurd, as in renaming sauerkraut "liberty cabbage" or hamburger "Salisbury steak." Colleges banned the teaching of German, "the language of beasts." "Hundred percent" Americans broke the

Bilingual edition of a Liberty Bond poster depicting Germans as ferocious beasts crucifying a captive Allied soldier. (1917)

windows of shops owned by those with German-sounding names. The Reverend Billy Sunday ignored the biblical command to love your enemy. The famous evangelist opened prayer meetings by damning Germany as "one of the most infamous, vile, greedy, avaricious, bloodthirsty, sensual and vicious nations . . . a great pack of wolfish Huns whose fangs drip with blood and gore!" God's people, the American people, he thundered, were in a holy war against the "devil's hordes," "the dirty Germans," "that bloodthirsty bunch of thugs."[17]

Meanwhile, on March 3, 1918, after intense negotiations, the Bolsheviks made peace with Germany, taking Russia out of the war. By train and truck, on bicycle and on foot, German troops streamed westward, toward the trenches in France. It was a race against time; they had to break through before America could fully join the fight. On March 21, the Germans launched a massive offensive aimed at encircling the French and British armies. Yet it was too little, too late. With 250,000 American "doughboys" landing in France each month, the Allies quickly replaced their losses, while German strength steadily ebbed. Outnumbered and outgunned, the invaders began evacuating sectors of the

Billy Sunday. (c. 1908)

front they'd held since the start of the war. The end came quickly. With his armies in retreat, Kaiser Wilhelm II fled to neutral Holland. Overnight, Germany became a republic. On November 11, 1918, the new government accepted Allied cease-fire terms. The war was over.[18]

THE GREAT RED SCARE

As the war reached its climax, Lenin set about spreading communism beyond Russia's borders. Acting on his orders, agents incited uprisings in defeated Germany and Hungary. "Do you think America is immune?" he asked an American journalist. This was no empty threat. By December 1918, his "Letter to American Workers" was circulating in the United States. In it, Lenin urged workers to rebel against their capitalist masters, a gang of "vultures," "scoundrels," "sharks," and "modern slave-owners," whose every dollar was "sullied with filth" and "stained with blood." And as in Russia, the Bolshevik leader said, these loathsome beings would never go away quietly, but would have to be killed in a "necessary and legitimate" reign of terror.[19]

Inspired by Lenin's appeal, radical members of the American Socialist Party broke away and formed two factions that eventually united to form the Communist Party of the United States of America (CPUSA). Crying "The people's hour has arrived," the Industrial Workers of the World (IWW), a trade union organization that recruited unskilled workers, joined the Party. A song captured their mood:

All hail to the Bolsheviks!
We will fight for our class and be free.
If you don't like the red flag of Russia,
If you don't like the spirit so true,

Then just be like the cur in the story
And lick the hand that's robbing you.[20]

At the same time, exaggerated reports of Soviet atrocities filled the American press. In grisly detail, they told of electrified guillotines that lopped off heads at assembly-line speeds of five hundred heads per hour and of how the Chekists declared women "national property," turning them into state-owned prostitutes. Yet the reality was awful enough. There already existed confirmed accounts of Red Guards tossing captives into furnaces, drowning them en masse in ice-filled rivers, and skinning them alive. Whether true or false, atrocity stories resonated with millions of Americans already inflamed by propaganda against the "Bloody German Beast."[21]

It was easy to shift the focus from the hate-Germany campaign to the hate-the-Bloody-Bolshevik-Beast theme. Early in 1919, a committee of the U.S. Senate issued a 1,200-page report, with photos, detailing real atrocities. One witness, a noted pre-1918 Russian reformer named Yekaterina Breshkovskaya, had narrowly escaped from the Cheka. "I have been a socialist for fifty years, and I wished to get my people free," she told the senators. "And the Bolsheviks are now saying, 'We must destroy, and destroy, and destroy.' Everywhere where the Bolsheviks are . . . they destroyed not only our factories and our mills, and not only our schools, but they destroyed, they killed, all the intelligent people, the best professors, the best professional men, the best men we had in Russia. We have no freedom in Russia."[22]

Lenin's "Letter to American Workers" (August 20, 1918), backing mass terror reports of Bolshevik atrocities and threats by Communist agitators, raised anxiety to a fever pitch. Maximilian Cohen, a founder of the CPUSA, took his cue from Lenin. Cohen, a dentist, told a New York State investigating committee in no uncertain terms: "Social revolution means the overthrow of the existing system. We all know enough to know that no ruling class will give up power without a fight. We tell you frankly that what we aim for is the overthrow of your government. That is the principle of all revolutionary organizations. We are carrying out revolutionary propaganda in this country, and we mean the overthrow of the United States government." Such statements became kindling for the Great Red Scare, an extension of wartime hate-Germany propaganda stoked by fear of those who would destroy "the American way of life."[23]

Nevertheless, the Party's bark was worse than its bite. Though its activists preached revolution, they lacked the means to turn words into deeds. America was not Russia. In 1919, the CPUSA had fewer than 10,000 members, hardly a serious threat to a nation of nearly 105 million spread over a vast continent, with a strong central government enjoying the loyalty of the overwhelming majority of its citizens. Though Communists used menacing words, they had no armed civilian units like the Petrograd soviets, no supporters in a defeated army, and no leaders of the caliber of Lenin and Trotsky; Joseph Stalin was practically unknown at this time, even among Bolsheviks. To understand why so many Americans panicked over the "Red Menace," we must look elsewhere.[24]

The nation's entry into the war created a severe labor shortage. While industry struggled to meet rising demands for military supplies by hiring women and African Americans who'd left the South in search of factory jobs, the shortage continued; there never seemed to be enough hands to do all that needed doing. This put union leaders in a strong position—but to show their patriotism, they took no-strike pledges in return for modest pay raises. Yet wars are expensive, and to pay for this one, the federal government raised taxes and borrowed from the public by selling Liberty Bonds. Despite these measures, it had to finance much of the war's cost by printing huge amounts of paper money. The result was inflation, in which rising prices on common items led to a fall in the dollar's buying power, wiping out any wage gains. Food prices soared, nearly doubling between 1917 and 1919, and clothing became expensive as the War Department bought trainloads of cloth for uniforms and leather for boots.

The war ended before plans could be made for shifting to a peacetime economy. Practically overnight, a worker shortage became a worker surplus as contracts for war materials were canceled and more than three million jobs vanished. At the same time, returning veterans, expecting to step into their old jobs, found themselves out in the cold. Meanwhile, peace released the unions from their no-strike pledges. Most of their leaders were practical men, not revolutionaries, who sought to protect those who still had jobs. Their demands seemed reasonable to them: wage increases to catch up with inflation, shorter hours, and collective bargaining, the right of a union to negotiate with employers on behalf of its members.

Business tycoons like Elbert H. Gary, for whom the city of Gary, Indiana, was named, would have none of this. Known as "Judge Gary" for his eight-year tenure as a county judge, he was chairman of the United States Steel Corporation, the industry's giant. In his steel mills, the typical workweek was sixty hours; some crews had to work eighteen-hour shifts for six days straight. In seeking absolute control of the workplace, Gary urged fellow industrialists to smash the unions. Encouraged by his tough stand, employers began firing union members and hiring goons to beat up union organizers. Paid snitches called "labor spies" roamed factories and stores, reporting anyone who dared speak of workers' rights. Offenders were fired on the spot.

These aggressive moves goaded unions into action. In 1919, more than 3,600 strikes involving 4 million workers, or a quarter of the labor force, swept the nation. The biggest, most bitter strikes made headlines. In Seattle, 60,000 workers from 110 unions, many wearing red bandannas, struck, paralyzing the city for a week. Another action shut down half the nation's steel industry for nearly four months, forcing factories that used steel to close their gates. The White House called the steel strike "a crime against civilization." In Gary, the U.S. Army took over and ruled by martial law, threatening to shoot anyone found on the streets after sundown. A strike by 349,000 coal miners crippled rail service and cut off the nation's main source of fuel.[25]

These strikes backfired on the unions. Operating individually or through their manufacturer and trade associations, employers followed two lines of attack. First, they used aggressive measures against the unions. Shotgun-toting guards, among them ex-soldiers hungry for a paycheck, escorted those willing to work across picket lines. If a strike seemed to be gaining too much support, management asked governors to use the state's National Guard to "restore order." Strikers and guardsmen often clashed. People died. It went without saying that corporations contributed generously to governors' political war chests.

Management's second line of attack targeted public opinion. Just as wartime propaganda aimed at demonizing Germany, in 1919 the same methods served in battling the unions. Though most Americans welcomed Czar Nicholas II's downfall as a victory for democracy, the Bolshevik Revolution was another matter. Bolshevik and German easily blended into

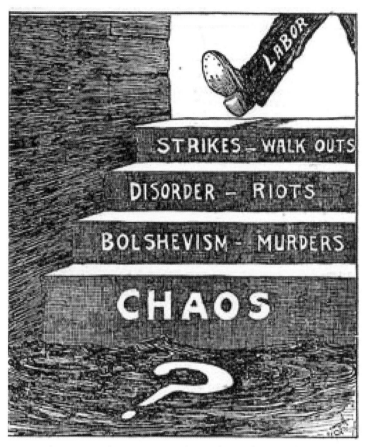

Anti-strike cartoon showing unions descending a slippery slope that ends in chaos. (1919)

each other; after all, Germany had sent Lenin back to Russia, freeing its troops to kill American boys in France. Management found it easy to blame Communists for the labor troubles. Its paid propagandists sought to create the impression that unions struck not over real grievances, but to incite revolution by promoting class hatred. All strikes, it was said, were "crimes against society," "conspiracies against the government," and "plots to establish communism." It followed that union members were not loyal Americans, but "agents" of a "demonic foreign conspiracy."[26]

In an age when radio, television, and the Internet did not exist, newspapers were the only source of current information. The Founders believed a republic could not survive without an informed public; hence, the U.S. Constitution guarantees freedom of the press. Yet journalists are human, with their own interests and biases. Sadly, the Great Red Scare saw some of America's foremost newspapers shirk their duty to inform truthfully. All too often, journalists slanted their stories to show organized labor in a bad light. For example, newspapers reprinted selections from radical speeches and publications to "prove" that unions were inspired by dangerous "foreign" ideas. Worse, journalists failed to check their facts and even deliberately lied. One humdinger of a newspaper lie had striking steelworkers spending their high wages on vacations in ritzy New York hotels![27]

Not to be outdone, the religious press featured anti-Communist and anti-union articles and sermons. Billy Sunday, true to form, ranted and raged. The popular preacher described the typical CPUSA member as "a guy with a face like a porcupine and a breath that would scare a polecat. If I had my way, I'd fill the jails so full of them that their feet would stick out the windows. . . . Let them rule? We'll swim our horses in blood up to the bridles first."[28]

The anti-Communist crusade spread beyond the business community. Thirty-two state legislatures passed laws against owning the red flag of communism and the black flag of anarchism. (Anarchists rejected all forms of government as oppressive, preferring to live in small self-governing voluntary communities.) Minnesota's law was typical, making it a crime "for any person to have in his possession, custody or control any red or black flag, or any picture or facsimile thereof, whether printed, painted, stamped, carved or engraved on any card, paper or insignia, with the intent to display the same in the state of Minnesota." Violators faced fines of up to $5,000 ($76,300 in today's dollars) and prison terms of five to ten years at hard labor.[29]

Vigilantes had a field day. As happened with anti-German hysteria, these self-appointed guardians of Americanism acted in grossly un-American ways. In Connecticut, a judge gave a man a six-month prison term for saying that Lenin was "one of the brainiest" political leaders in the world. In Indiana, a citizen shot a foreign-born man for shouting "To hell with the United States!" The jury took just two minutes to find the killer innocent. In Centralia, Washington, Wesley Everest, a member of the Industrial Workers of the World, was arrested for shooting up a patriotic meeting. As police officers looked on, a mob dragged Everest from his jail cell, drove a spike through his cheek, threw him off a bridge with a rope around his neck, and riddled his body with bullets.[30]

Two private organizations took violent action during the Great Red Scare. By far the largest and most important was the American Legion. Chartered by Congress in September 1919, the Legion focused on service to veterans and their families. Organized into thousands of local posts, the Legion's one million members were resentful of radicals and immigrants competing for scarce jobs. Many had personal grudges against Communists, having lost buddies to the Germans sent to the Western Front from Russia. "Leave the Reds to the Legion" became a popular slogan. In Detroit, a Legion post boasted of its "one thousand Bolshevik bouncers" bent on beating the daylights out of anyone who disrespected

Old Glory. In some places, club-toting Legionnaires ran suspected Communists out of town.[31]

The Ku Klux Klan (KKK) claimed to represent America's "best blood." A secret organization of violent racists, Klansmen wore white robes and masks as symbols of their "racial and moral purity." At nighttime ceremonies, they burned tall wooden crosses in recognition of what they defined as Christian (i.e., Protestant) principles and white supremacy. Founded after the Civil War, the KKK was strongest in the South, where it terrorized African Americans to keep them submissive to whites and away from communism. The KKK also denounced Catholics and Jews as "agents of Lenin." During the Great Red Scare, Klansmen attacked supposed Communist agitators. Whites were beaten up, and several Black men were killed by KKK-led mobs.[32]

BOARDING THE SOVIET ARK

On April 28, 1919, a clerk put a package on the desk of Seattle mayor Ole Hanson. Known as "the Savior of Seattle," he'd taken the lead in breaking the city's general strike two months earlier. Luckily, a secretary noticed that the package was leaking a foul-smelling fluid. When the police arrived, they found it contained a home-made bomb. The next day, a postman delivered a package to the Atlanta home of Thomas W. Hardwick. The former U.S. senator had enemies; he'd sponsored a law allowing for the deportation of foreign-born anarchists or those found in possession of anarchist writings. When Ethel Williams, his housekeeper, cut the string, the package exploded, blowing off both her hands and seriously injuring his wife, Maude. That these mail bombs were part of a wider plot became clear the following day, April 30. A vigilant clerk in the parcel division of New York City's main post office found sixteen identical packages lacking proper postage. These were addressed to top business leaders, among them oil tycoon John D. Rockefeller and banker J. P. Morgan. Upon examination, detectives found that each parcel contained a bomb. Postal inspectors discovered another dozen "infernal machines" before they reached their destinations. The bomb maker was never found.

Another would-be bomber was found in bits and pieces. Moments before midnight on June 2, 1919, an explosion on the front steps of Attorney General A. Mitchell Palmer's Washington home lit up the sky. Apparently, the bomb went off prematurely, scattering its carrier's remains across the neighborhood. Lumps of charred flesh dangled from tree branches, and bone fragments struck windowpanes like pebbles. Within the hour, bombs detonated in seven other cities: Boston; Cleveland; Newtonville, Massachusetts; New York City; Paterson, New Jersey; Philadelphia; and Pittsburgh.

Obviously, the culprits wished to terrorize Americans by showing they could strike distant places at once. Though their names have been lost to history, the Palmer house bomber carried leaflets that were signed "THE ANARCHIST FIGHTERS." Titled *Plain Words,* they announced: "The powers that be make no secret of their will to stop here in America the worldwide spread of revolution. Class war is on, and cannot cease but with the complete victory for the international proletariat. There will have to be bloodshed. There will have to be murder; we will kill, because it is necessary. There will have to be destruction; we will destroy to rid the world of your tyrannical institutions. We are ready to do anything and everything to suppress the capitalist class. Long live the social revolution! Down with tyranny!"[33]

The press jumped to conclusions. Although anarchists took credit for the bombings, the *Washington Post,* the capital's hometown paper, declared: "[This] first sample of Soviet government . . . ought to be highly satisfactory to the American champions of the Bolsheviki." That was absurd. Anarchists despised Bolsheviks as power-hungry tyrants; Bolsheviks loathed anarchists as hostile to all authority. It was no accident that the Cheka shot Russian anarchists in droves.[34]

Though Attorney General Palmer, a pious Quaker, was not a violent man, the near miss left him shaken and angry. The attack proved, at least to him, that the "Red Menace" was not a figment of feverish imaginations. Clearly, the bombings showed that a vast revolutionary conspiracy existed, resulting, he said, from "the real menace of evil thinking." The conspirators, he insisted, were homegrown extremists and the foreign-born, notably "a small clique of outcasts from the East Side of New York . . . the lowest of all types known to New York." The terms "outcasts" and "East Side" were none-too-subtle references to Jewish immigrants.[35]

In August 1919, Palmer formed a special unit within the Department of Justice. Called the General Intelligence Division, it was tasked with collecting information about revolutionary groups. The unit's

Attorney General A. Mitchell Palmer. (1919)

head was a twenty-four-year-old lawyer who'd never practiced law. Born in Washington, just blocks from the U.S. Capitol, J. Edgar Hoover had to go to work early to support his widowed mother. He attended George Washington University Law School at night, and during the day he worked as a file clerk in the Library of Congress. Before the invention of the computer, index cards were the only way to gather, update, and collate large amounts of information. The Library of Congress used card files to keep track of its millions of books, documents, and manuscripts. Upon joining the Department of Justice, Hoover applied the index-card method to police work. Each new fact about a person—height, weight, scars, birthmarks, addresses, friends, habits, memberships, jobs, fingerprints, photos, writings—was entered on an index card stored in an alphabetical file. A passionate fact collector, Hoover had within a few months created a card file with information on sixty thousand "dangerous radicals." He also became a self-taught "expert" on communism, reading whatever he could find on the subject. His conclusion: Communism was the embodiment of evil. It must be fought by every available means, legally when possible, illegally when necessary.[36]

Hoover's unit organized the Palmer Raids. On November 19, 1919, "G-men" (government men) backed by local police fanned out across eighteen cities, rounding up non-citizen radicals. On December 21, immigration officers hustled 249 of these aboard the *Buford,* a decrepit U.S. Army transport ship dubbed "the Soviet Ark." Its passengers, branded "undesirable aliens," were deported to the USSR not for committing any crime, but for their political beliefs. Among the deportees were two notorious anarchists. Emma "Red Emma"

Goldman and her companion, Alexander Berkman, had long criminal records, she for making speeches "menacing to the public order," he for attempting to murder a wealthy corporation head. Though an anarchist, Goldman had come to admire the Bolsheviks' determination to make a better world for ordinary people. As the Soviet Ark left the Ellis Island pier, escorted by a U.S. Navy destroyer, she cried out: "I do

Emma Goldman's deportation photo, taken at Ellis Island, New York. (1919)

not consider it punishment to be sent back to Soviet Russia. I consider it an honor to be chosen as the first political agitator to be deported from the United States."[37]

Despite the deportations, Palmer and Hoover still had much to do. In January 1920, they launched a second wave of raids specifically targeting non-citizen members of the CPUSA. Over the course of two days, G-men struck without warning in thirty-three cities and towns in twenty-three states. The lawmen, a report said, "entered bowling alleys, pool halls, cafés, club rooms, and even homes, and seized everyone in sight." They often trashed the place, breaking furniture, toppling file cabinets, and smashing pictures on the walls, Lenin's among them. In a few places, they found bomb-making materials, although some accused the raiders of planting these to frame the occupants. Of the roughly ten thousand people arrested, most were released within a few days; about five hundred were deported.[38]

While superpatriots hailed the attorney general as "Uncle Sam's Policeman," the Palmer Raids provoked a backlash. Not all Americans were hysterical; these feared G-men more than Bolsheviks or anarchists. For the raids involved massive violations of civil liberties, those individual rights pro-tected by law from unjust governmental in-terference. The violations were exposed by a group of eminent lawyers, among them Harvard Law School dean Roscoe Pound and professor Felix Frankfurter, a future Supreme Court justice. Their statement, titled *To the American People: Report upon the Illegal Practices of the United States Department of Justice,* appeared as a pamphlet in May 1920. In it, the authors accused the Justice Department of committing "continual illegal acts." Searches, seizures, and arrests without warrants! Prisoners held without charge and denied visits by family and friends and by lawyers! Prisoners threatened, beaten with blackjacks, placed in straitjackets, and left to wallow in their own filth! Prisoners brutalized into confessing to crimes they did not commit! The conclusion was damning:

Since these illegal acts have been committed by the highest legal powers in the United States, there is no final appeal from them except to the conscience and condemnation of the American people. Free men cannot be driven and repressed; they must be led. Free men respect justice and follow truth, but arbitrary power they will oppose until the end of time. There is no danger of revolution so great as that created by suppression, by ruthlessness, and by deliberate violation of the simple rules of American law and American decency.[39]

Inspired by this exposé, a group of civic-minded New Yorkers formed the American Civil Liberties Union (ACLU) to safeguard the liberties guaranteed by the Bill of Rights.

By the fall of 1920, Communist uprisings in Europe had been crushed by troops loyal to their governments. In America, on September 16, at precisely noon, as office workers took their lunch breaks, a powerful bomb exploded on Wall Street, the heart of New York's financial district, killing thirty-eight and maiming perhaps as many as three hundred others. The police suspected anarchists, but the culprits were never found, and for whatever reason, there were no more bombings. At the same time, labor peace returned as prices stabilized, consumer confidence rose, and businesses resumed hiring. During the November elections, presidential candidate Warren G. Harding called for "a return to normalcy," going back to the "simpler" time before the First World War. He also

signaled the end of the Great Red Scare, declaring, "Too much has been said about Bolshevism in America."[40]

A. Mitchell Palmer retired from government service and went into private law practice. J. Edgar Hoover stayed with the General Intelligence Division. In 1935, Congress renamed it the Federal Bureau of Investigation (FBI), with Hoover as its first director. He became a powerful figure in Washington, remaining at his post until his death in 1972.

For "Mr. Hoover," as staff called him, efficiency trumped civil liberties. Yet keeping his director's job trumped everything else, because, apparently, the man equated his personal goals with the nation's well-being. To achieve these, he did not hesitate to resort to blackmail. Over the years, Hoover amassed a secret "Official and Confidential" file kept in a locked cabinet in his private office in the J. Edgar Hoover FBI Building, named in his honor in 1972. The file held thick folders containing "dirt" collected by FBI agents, which he used to "convince" Washington bigwigs to see things his way. According to William Sullivan, a senior FBI official, "The moment [Hoover] would get information on a senator, he'd send one of the errand boys up and advise the senator that 'we're

Aftermath of the Wall Street bombing. (1920)

in the course of an investigation, and we by chance happened to come up with this data on your daughter. But we wanted you to know this. We realize you'd want to know it.' Well, Jesus, what does that tell the senator? From that time on, the senator's right in his pocket."[41]

During his tumultuous years as head of the FBI, Hoover oversaw cases in what historians call the Second Red Scare.

TRUE BELIEVERS:
A PARTY LIKE NONE OTHER

*Faith is a wondrous thing; it is not only capable of moving mountains,
but also of making you believe that a herring is a race horse.*
—Arthur Koestler, in *The God That Failed* (1949)

COMINTERN

Throughout American history, political parties have existed to win elections and organize government according to the ideas of their members and backers. Having won control of the government, however, a party does not expect to hold office forever. Regularly scheduled elections, mandated by law, guarantee that voters can turn it out of office if they please. Even when in control of the government, no party can do what it wishes all the time. Though in the minority, its opponents, also duly elected, have their own ideas. As a result, parties are forced to debate and compromise, giving something in order to get something else they value. Above all, they are pledged to uphold the rule of law as embodied in the U.S. Constitution, which gives government its legal basis while, at the same time, limiting its actions.

The Communist Party of the United States of America was not just another political party. From its beginning, the CPUSA was dedicated to serving the interests of a foreign power. It was bound to the USSR by the Communist International—Comintern for short. Founded by Lenin in March 1919, the Comintern was an arm of the Soviet government tasked with supervising the activities of foreign Communist parties. Dubbed "the General Staff of the World Revolution," it spelled out the Party line, which defined the tactics members had to follow and what all Communists were required to believe. But the line was not carved in stone; it was fluid, indeed instantly reversible, according to Moscow's needs at the moment. Yet one thing was constant: Moscow knew best—always. No CPUSA member, including the leadership, had the right to judge, debate, question, modify, or criticize the line. As a Comintern official put it, individual Communists must always "be ready to believe that black was white and white was black, if [Moscow] requires it."[1]

The Comintern kept a tight rein on its member parties. All their top officials had to be approved by Moscow, and could be removed on its orders. Each national party, in turn, had at least one representative stationed full time in the Soviet capital. When the Comintern held conferences, foreign delegates reported on local conditions and received orders from their superiors. To preserve secrecy, they traveled under assumed names, with stolen or forged passports. While in Moscow, they stayed in the Hotel de Luxe, a dingy, crowded, noisy place smelling of boiled cabbage. Foreign Communists who visited Moscow on official business or worked in the Comintern's various departments found themselves isolated. All lived under the watchful eye of the NKVD ("People's Commissariat for Internal Affairs," the secret police), successor to the Cheka. Peggy Dennis, the wife of Eugene Dennis, a Comintern agent and rising star in the CPUSA, called the hotel home for several years in the early 1930s. Early on, Peggy realized that "we were completely divorced from ordinary Soviet life. . . . We were living in Moscow, but were not part of it. . . . We never had direct contact and conversation with ordinary Soviet citizens." She knew better than to try to strike up conversations with ordinary Russians; unauthorized contacts with foreigners, however innocent, would get citizens into hot water. Informers, paid and unpaid, were everywhere; in Moscow, there was at least one for every six or seven families.[2]

Headquartered in New York City, the CPUSA was funded primarily by "Moscow gold." Practically from the moment the Bolsheviks seized power, they took possession of an enormous treasure. This included Russia's national gold reserves and valuables rifled from churches and bank vaults. In all, they had at their disposal an estimated five hundred tons of gold bullion, plus crates of jewelry studded with diamonds, pearls, emeralds, and sapphires. Some of this loot was smuggled into the United States by Soviet trade representatives and sailors from Soviet freighters; one sailor came ashore with a pouch of two hundred diamonds tucked under his shirt. CPUSA officials in New York then used underworld contacts to fence the valuables, turning them into dollars in return for paying a "service" charge. The dollars enabled the Party to buy a nine-story office building at 35 East 12th Street, fund daily operations, hire organizers, and support its propaganda activities. Additionally, in the late 1920s, the Comintern set up a secret plant in Germany to print counterfeit $100 bills. When these were smuggled into the United States, agents sold them at a discount to a gang led by Arnold "the Big Brain" Rothstein. This mob boss, a founding father of organized crime, also lent the Party nearly $2 million at 25 percent interest, the rate charged by loan sharks. No Communist, Rothstein cared only about how much he could make from the deal. In some years, Soviet agents handed CPUSA officials bags containing as much as $3 million in small bills. Moscow expected to get its money's worth. Its secret archives, opened after the fall of the USSR in 1991, bulged with detailed reports of every facet of CPUSA activities, including evaluations of its leaders, as well as orders sent to the New York headquarters and accounts of how they were carried out.[3]

THE PARTY GROWS

Though the CPUSA survived the Great Red Scare, the 1920s were not kind to revolutionaries. These were the "Roaring Twenties," remembered as a kind of American golden age. While there were plenty of people without jobs or with only low-wage jobs, on the whole these were years of prosperity. The outlines of the America we know today were already recognizable.

Industry boomed as mass-produced consumer goods—radios, washing machines, refrigerators, vacuum cleaners, electric toasters—became available at affordable prices. Inexpensive automobiles ($295 for a 1929 Ford Model T, nicknamed "Tin Lizzie") spurred road building and the growth of cities. With the economy booming and fortunes to be made, the New York Stock Exchange became a giant casino where speculators bought and sold shares, certain that prices would keep rising. Yet a brash nightclub owner named Texas Guinan wasn't so sure. As champagne corks popped and the band played hot jazz, she'd greet customers with a blast on

a police whistle and a shout-out: "Hello, suckers!"

On October 29, 1929—known as "Black Tuesday"—prices on the New York Stock Exchange took a nosedive and kept falling. Within days, investors lost $30 billion ($437 billion in today's dollars). The Wall Street "crash" signaled the onset of the Great Depression, the worst global economic crisis of modern times. In the United States, banks closed and depositors lost their savings, firms went bankrupt, employers laid off workers, and factories shut. Families evicted when they could not pay the rent or mortgage wound up in "Hoovervilles," clusters of shacks named

Headline printed in *Variety* after the crash of the stock market. (1929)

for President Herbert Hoover, who many blamed for the disaster. You could not have opened a newspaper without seeing articles about hungry children, broken homes, and adults at their wits' end. Near Wall Street, the nation's financial center, passersby saw "the Westside jungles" along the Hudson River, with their mounds of rubble resembling a battlefield. "Battered chimneys rise out of holes in the ground, where the unemployed have dug in for the winter. Shacks made of packing cases, old tin, dirty cement blocks, beams, tar paper, stand on some brick mounds, others are in the brick hollows." Places like this were home to hundreds of men, women, and children, who poked through garbage cans to get a bite to eat. Unemployment was no longer a temporary break between jobs; for millions, it became a way of life, lasting years and destroying hope and self-respect.[4]

New York governor Franklin D. Roosevelt defeated President Hoover in the election of 1932. Upon entering the White House, FDR asked Congress to appropriate billions of dollars for relief and recovery schemes. Known as the New Deal, this program was unique in American history. Never before had the federal government intruded so massively into the nation's economic life. To stimulate the economy, it created scores of agencies with names such as the Civilian Conservation Corps, the Farm Credit Administration, the National Recovery Administration, and the Civil Works Administration. These provided work on government projects, such as building dams, roads, schools, hospitals, and airports. Though the New Deal made many lives better, it failed to fully revive the economy. With businesspeople still uncertain about the future, they held back on investing in new plants and equipment, so jobless rates remained high.

The CPUSA appealed to thousands of Americans because the Depression had destroyed their belief in the ideas that governed their society, and they longed for a creed to believe in. Members wanted a world where man did not exploit man, a fairer community based on equality in which people valued and cared for one another. Like a religion that promised salvation, Marxism was a faith offering the answers they craved. Party member George Charney recalled: "I, too, was groping for a new spiritual center, for a new God to replace the Jehovah that had failed, for a new absolute, for a new faith. . . . Thus, it was not long after I joined the party that I came to accept each doctrine . . . as an 'article of faith,' never to be questioned." In a flash of insight, the world made sense, another convert said. "Everything happened so quick then. I *understood* everything. Everything! I knew it all at once. And all at once, I saw, and I could hardly believe this, *there was a way out for me.* I saw that being a worker was literally slavery, and that the slavery came from being like a dumb animal hitched forever to the machine, and this *idea* of us as a class relieved the slavery, gave you a way to fight, gave you a way to become a human being."[5]

The Party fostered a sense of belonging, of being part of a righteous cause greater than oneself. Members addressed one another as "comrade," a Party term for "brother," "sister," "friend," "colleague," or "companion." Having comrades helped affirm one's identity, giving meaning and purpose to life. Acting under the Party's direction, there seemed no limit to comrades' ability to change the world for the better. "Where I had been alone," recalled novelist Howard Fast, "I felt that I had now become part of an edifice dedicated singularly and irrevocably to the ending of all war, injustice, hunger and human suffering—and to the goal of the brotherhood of man." Surely this was something to work and sacrifice for.[6]

LIFE IN THE PARTY

CPUSA membership surged: 40,000 members in 1937; 55,000 in 1938; 70,000 in 1939. Joining was a big step, a commitment not to be taken lightly. In the mid-1930s, the procedure involved signing a registration form or swearing a loyalty oath before witnesses, as when new citizens swore allegiance to their adopted country. New members pledged: "I now take my place in the ranks of the Communist Party, the Party of the working class. . . . I pledge myself to rally the masses to defend the Soviet Union, the land of victorious Socialism. I pledge myself to remain at all times a vigilant and firm defender of the Leninist line of the Party, the only line that insures the triumph of Soviet Power in the United States."[7]

There was no vagueness here; these words meant exactly what they said. Benjamin Gitlow, twice a CPUSA vice-presidential candidate (1924, 1928), noted that members committed to a unique set of values: to begin with, though they lived in the United States, their loyalty lay elsewhere. He explained:

Communism was not just a political philosophy; it was a faith that was destined to convert the world into a Socialist paradise and solve all of man's pressing problems. Bolshevik Russia was our country from which we drew inspiration every moment of our conscious lives. Only good could come from Russia. . . . Soviet Russia was our fatherland, its Red Army our army, its red flag our flag. Patriots of Soviet Russia, we would not hesitate to commit any act of violence or treason against the country in which we lived, if ordered to do so by the Party, or if we believed that act would help Soviet Russia. . . . Above all, we enjoyed the idea that we were part of a state machine that ruled a mighty empire of millions of people. In fact, we became the most ardent agents of the Soviet government and were prepared to render any service it might require of us.[8]

Comrade Gitlow eventually grew disillusioned, broke with the Party, and became an anti-Communist. This was not unusual. The CPUSA had a constant turnover in membership; many quit or drifted away after just a few months or a year. Usually sensitive, intelligent people, they'd joined the Party because it seemed to champion social justice. Yet with an abrupt change

in the Moscow line, or as experience raised doubts about the Party's aims and methods, they left. Tragically, for some, leaving was not the end; the fact that they'd once been members would haunt them during the Second Red Scare of the 1940s and 1950s. Yet those who stuck with the Party through thick and thin were a different breed. It has been said that they wore "special glasses that allowed them to see only what Moscow saw and that rendered all else invisible." Among these "lifers" were the chosen few, who'd shown marked ability and risen through the ranks, earning Moscow's favor. People of this sort were tapped for the Party's inner circle of leaders.[9]

The CPUSA demanded total commitment. Unlike a "normal" American political party, it required all members to be active, devoting the bulk of their time and energy to its work. When you were in the Party, you had to be in all the way. Novelist Howard Fast did not exaggerate when he wrote: "Active involvement in the Communist Party commanded the whole life process. One ate and slept it." A Broadway actress known only as Dianne agreed. Diehard members' "identification with the Party," she recalled, "had become so complete, so absolute, they no longer knew the difference between their own selves and what I could now only call Party dogma."[10]

Rank-and-filers did all the routine tasks, the sheer grinding drudgery that kept the organization going. The comrade was supposed to begin each day by reading Communist literature, preferably the *Daily Worker,* an all-around newspaper with columns on sports, music, the arts, and fashion. Its lead articles and editorials, however, hammered away at issues of concern at the moment, but also fostered groupthink, a mentality that discourages individuality and the questioning of official "truths." Not only did the paper tell readers what and how to think about an issue, it gave them slogans and arguments to support the Party line. "More and more," an ex-member recalled, the Party exerted a "soul-destroying authority." Indeed, "our entire lives became enmeshed in the Party to the point where every judgment on every question ranging from high politics to family matters issued from this source." These matters included rules on making friends, dating, and finding a mate. Officials had no qualms about telling members to drop so-and-so as a friend, to not dress like that, and to stop reading an unapproved author's writings. Members were obliged to report others' lapses

to their superiors. Married men were expected to induce their wives to join the Party.[11]

Marriage was a serious undertaking; a Party member sought not only a mate, but a comrade. Take CPUSA activist and union organizer Albert Weisbord. In the 1920s, when he proposed to his future wife, Vera, he said: "You will go with me from one strike to another. . . . When we have the textile industry organized, we'll move on to steel, and so on, building the Party. You can never have children, not even a home. But you'll always be at my side, fighting with me, helping me."[12]

Some Communists used romantic relationships for political ends. Dorothy Healey, a California activist, began a two-year relationship with a seaman named Dutch not because she loved him, but out of cold calculation. "I stayed involved with Dutch for so long," she explained, "because I felt it was my Party duty to do it. We needed to have a seaman stay on the beach. And he was lonely and he was one of our best members and if that's what he wanted, and it's what he did want, then it was my Party duty to give him what he wanted." Years later, Healey told an interviewer that this was her "'Salvation Army' approach to love and marriage. You're bestowing yourself because that's what somebody else wants and what do you care? It shouldn't matter one way or another."[13]

Those who failed to bestow themselves, who were not in lockstep with Party dictates, might be subject to mock trials—in fact, struggle sessions meant to publicly humiliate and punish offenders. Verbally assaulted by friends-turned-persecutors, the defendant had to answer to charges of displaying "anti-leadership tendencies," "corrupting the Party with your ideas," and being "a petty bourgeois degenerate." The aim was to break the accused, make them confess their "errors," beg for forgiveness, and do penance in the form of carrying out a special assignment. If they refused, the penalty was expulsion. For the ardent Communist, expulsion felt like being cast into utter darkness. The sinner became a nonperson, one who had never existed. Former comrades, even close relatives, would have nothing to do with them. Communist neighbors brushed past them without saying a word, and Communist shopkeepers turned them away. Communist physicians and dentists refused to treat them. Communist nursery schools expelled their toddlers.

The members' real work began after leaving their day job, if they had one. Under orders from the leader of their district branch or section, they collected signatures on petitions, handed out leaflets on street corners, went to rallies, marched on picket lines, joined group discussions, carried banners at May Day parades reading "For a Soviet America," and attended

May Day parade in New York City where Communists carried posters of Lenin and Stalin. (1935)

endless fund-raisers, study groups, and lectures on the USSR, Marxist theory, and world politics. Sometimes an active member sat through six meetings a night, returning home bleary-eyed in the wee hours of the morning. The Party, too, had a network of schools that offered a wide range of courses—from homemaking and child care to history, politics, economics, and philosophy—from the Marxist point of view. The Jefferson School of Social Science (New York), the Tom Paine School of Social Science (Philadelphia), the John Adams School (Boston), and the People's Educational Center (Los Angeles) were the largest and busiest Party schools. Those able to scrape together $250 could broaden their horizons with a Party-sponsored weeklong tour of the USSR. All groups were led by trained Russian guides, who showed their charges only what they were meant to see.

Party talent scouts recruited the most promising students as activists. Experts taught them organizing skills and how to conduct meetings, vital for gaining influence in the trade unions. Elocutionists taught speakers the art of striking a pose, modulating their voices, presenting an argument, and sidestepping tricky questions. Should a critic claim, for example, that the USSR was not a democracy because it allowed only one political party, the speaker rattled off a pat reply, insisting that feuding economic interests dictated that capitalist countries have several political parties, while the USSR embodied a "*higher* stage of democracy." Having taken over the economy and abolished social classes, the Soviets allegedly made all citizens equal; voters agreed their leaders represented everyone's true interests. This explains why CPUSA official Gil Green could declare that the Soviet system, unlike America's, "is truly a government *of, by, and for the people.*" Activists were taught how to shut down discussion if persuasion failed. They would not engage with contrary facts and ideas, but turn the focus on personalities. The opponent would be accused of not being their own person, but a lackey and dupe of capitalist exploiters, and should therefore be ignored. Refusal to accept Communist claims at face value showed that the opponent was a fool at best and insincere at worst, because any "sympathetic," "caring" person readily accepted the "truths" of Marxist ideology. Finally, questioning of CPUSA motives was ridiculed as "red-baiting," branding the offender a foe of decency, social justice, and democracy.[14]

Speakers also became skilled at "Aesopian language," a code understood only by insiders. The term comes from the fables of the ancient Greek storyteller Aesop, in which animals teach moral lessons. Composed at a time when speaking one's mind could be fatal, fables such as "The Fox and the Crow" allowed citizens to use ambiguous terms to safely criticize rulers. The CPUSA employed this technique to suggest a benign meaning to the public at large, while reserving the true meaning for insiders. When, for example, Earl Browder, its general secretary from 1930 to 1945, said, "The Communist Party opposes the overthrow of American democracy," no sane comrade took him literally. For the comrade knew that capitalist-ruled America could become a democracy only after "the Revolution" brought the Party to power.[15]

Similarly, speakers insisted the Party championed "peace." On its face, the meaning is obvious: Peace is the absence of war. However, since Marxist ideology defined capitalism and communism as natural enemies, it followed that capitalist states would take every opportunity to destroy the USSR. Therefore, war was inevitable, and "true peace" possible only after the unification of the world under Communist rule. "Peace policy," as defined by the 1928 Comintern Congress, was "merely a more advantageous form of fighting capitalism." In effect, calls for peace were merely tactics in an ongoing war.[16]

STALINISTS

During the 1930s, hard-core CPUSA members grandly referred to themselves as "Stalinists." The man they idolized was born Joseph Vissarionovich Dzhugashvili in 1879. The son of a poor cobbler who beat him and his mother, he took the name Stalin, "Man of Steel," upon becoming a revolutionary in his teens. After Lenin's death in 1924, Stalin outwitted his rivals, taking over the Communist Party of the Soviet Union (CPSU), and with it the USSR. Five feet five inches tall, his face pitted by smallpox scars, Stalin had a shaggy mustache, yellowed teeth, and a withered left arm, the result of a childhood accident. Morbidly suspicious ("I trust no one, not even myself"), he was a very dangerous person. A Russian biographer, a retired Red Army general, captured the man's essence: "It was impossible to find and touch in him any chords of human feeling. . . . He despised pity, sympathy, mercy." Like his mentor, Lenin, "Stalin found no place for moral values in poli-

Joseph Stalin during the Great Terror. (1937)

tics." Nor was he capable of gratitude, even toward those who'd served him faithfully. "Do you know what gratitude is?" an adviser asked. The tyrant replied: "Oh yes, I know; I know very well: it is a sickness suffered by dogs."[17]

Murder came easily to Stalin; it was his way of resolving difficulties. "Death solves all problems," he'd say. "No man, no problem." Stalin applied this principle broadly. In the early 1930s, he ordered Russia's peasants to surrender their lands, which were to be combined into huge collective, or state-owned, farms. This, supposedly, would increase crop yields, producing a surplus to feed the cities and to sell overseas for cash to buy machinery and build factories. When the peasants resisted, Stalin sent bands of city activists to seize their houses, food stocks, seeds, farm tools, and animals at gunpoint. The result was a famine that claimed the lives of some 8.5 million people in Ukraine and in Kazakhstan in Central Asia, another wheat-growing region. Ukrainians still call it the Holodomor, or "extermination by hunger." The sight of dead peasants became commonplace; people became so inured that they walked by without seeming to notice. Local officials detailed hundreds of instances of destitute peasants eating corpses, even killing their own children for food. A doctor wrote to a friend that she was not yet a cannibal, but was "not sure that I shall not be one by the time my letter reaches you." It is a fact worth remembering that, while Adolf Hitler killed 1.5 million Jewish children during the Holocaust, Joseph Stalin may have been responsible for the deaths of an even larger number of Ukrainian children during the Holodomor.[18]

Stalin set out to crush any opposition

to his rule—real, possible, or imagined. In this, he was cold as ice and hard as steel. "We will destroy each and every enemy, even if he was an old Bolshevik; we will destroy all his kin, his family," he told a gathering of Communist Party officials. "We will mercilessly destroy anyone who, by his deeds or thoughts—yes, his thoughts—threatens the unity of the socialist state." Stalin went so far as to have most of his own relatives, including the families of both his late wives, shot because, he explained, they "knew too much."[19]

Stalin's campaign killed more Soviet Communists than any foreign enemy, including Adolf Hitler. The slaughter began with the Moscow Trials of 1936. Though these had all the appearances of trials—attorneys, prosecutors, judges, juries—in reality they were scripted performances in which the accused were forced to act out an elaborate charade. Top Party leaders, heads of government departments, and Lenin's old comrades stood accused as capitalist spies, traitors, and "enemies of the people," a catchall term that meant whatever Stalin wished. The worst charge, however, was "Trotskyism," loyalty to Leon Trotsky, whom Stalin had expelled from the USSR and would later have murdered, along with his two sons and dozens of distant relatives. Nearly all the defendants confessed after being brutalized by interrogators and were then shot in the head. Ironically, shooting was poetic justice, as some victims had been heartless killers themselves.

The Moscow Trials overlapped with the Great Terror of 1937–1938. The term was fitting, because it was a calculated policy of mass killing aimed at terrorizing the entire population so that none dared oppose his rule. During a period of about eighteen months, about 1.6 million people were arrested and 700,000 "enemies" shot, or about 1,300 shot each and every day. Fear enveloped society like a foul mist. Everyone was suspect, including stamp collectors, because they had contacts with, or at least knew about, foreign lands and might harbor "traitorous" thoughts. All members of a society of deaf-mutes were arrested for "conspiring" against Soviet power in sign language!

In the capital, the NKVD usually made arrests in the early morning, startling victims awake by pounding on their doors. Black Marias, vans with blackened windows, took them to one of several Moscow prisons. The Lubyanka, the most dreaded prison, was a massive yellow-brick building a few blocks from Red Square. "Shake someone awake at night," wrote one who knew, "and say the word 'Lubyanka' and he will stare at his feet, say goodbye to everybody, and break down and cry like a baby." To force prisoners to sign confessions, interrogators clubbed, whipped, or kept them awake until they felt they were going insane. Nearly everyone broke. Of the 1.5 million people arrested during the Great Terror, 681,692 were shot and went into the hundreds of unmarked mass graves that dotted the USSR. "Better too far than not far enough," NKVD chief Nikolai Yezhov warned his men. "[If] an extra thousand people will be shot, that is not such a big deal."[20]

Nearly all the rest wound up in the Gulag (an acronym of the Russian for Main Administration of Corrective Labor Camps). Novelist Aleksandr Solzhenitsyn compared the prison system to an archipelago, or chain of islands, of roughly 435 main camps and thousands of subcamps spread across the vast "ocean" of the USSR. The worst of these "islands" was Kolyma in eastern Siberia, bordering the Arctic Ocean, a camp system four times the size of France. No fewer than three million people perished in this frozen hellhole. In all the Gulag camps, slaves were not considered human beings. Termed "units of labor," they produced roughly a

Prisoners being exploited at a Soviet Gulag. (c. 1931)

Stalin's image was venerated by Communists around the world; this photo shows Chinese Communists celebrating his seventieth birthday in Beijing. (1949)

quarter of the nation's timber, coal, gold and other metals, and fish. There were also specialized camps for scientists and engineers; except for the armed guards and barbed wire, inmates had almost normal living conditions, because they worked on military and technical projects deemed useful to the state.[21]

Stalin ruled by propaganda as well as terror. On his orders, armies of writers and artists fashioned his "cult of personality." Wherever citizens turned, they saw the tyrant's image. While touring the USSR, American novelist John Steinbeck noted in his journal:

Nothing in the Soviet Union goes on outside the vision of the plaster, bronze, painted, or embroidered eye of Stalin. His portrait hangs not only in every museum, but in every room of every museum. His statue marches in front of all public buildings. His bust is in front of all airports, railroad stations, bus stations. . . . In parks he sits on a plaster bench, discussing problems with Lenin. His picture in needlework is undertaken by the students of schools. . . . And every house has at least one picture of him. He is everywhere, he sees everything. . . . At public celebrations the pictures of Stalin overgrow every bound of reason. They may be eight stories high and fifty feet wide. Every public building carries monster portraits of him.[22]

Though Soviet people rarely saw their ruler in the flesh or heard his voice over the radio, he was a constant presence, even in their most private and intimate moments. He seemed impossible to escape. A stressed-out woman wrote in her diary: "Stalin here, Stalin there, Stalin, Stalin everywhere. You can't go out to the kitchen, or sit on the toilet, or eat without Stalin following you. . . . He creeps into your guts and your very soul, creeps into your brain . . . gets into bed with you under the blanket, haunts your memories and your dreams." To be sure, the man inspired such fear that one woman had panic attacks when going to the toilet, because she might wipe herself with a bit of newspaper containing an article with his name. Even in the Gulag, inmates' barracks were adorned with posters showing his stern face and the slogan "Glory to Stalin, the Greatest Genius of Mankind."[23]

To drive home the message that Stalin was all-powerful, all-knowing, and all-wise, the country was filled with places named in his honor: countless streets, avenues, squares, parks, boulevards, power plants, and factories. Cities, too, bore his name, among them Stalingrad, Stalinbad, Stalinsk, Stalinir, Stalinkan, Staliniri, Stalinogorsk, and Stalino, to name just a few. Adolf Hitler was modest by comparison; no German city bore his name, though many a town had its Adolf Hitler Strasse ("street").

Hailed as "the Sun of the Universe," "the Great Driver of the Locomotive of History," and "the Father of the Peoples,"

Stalin was depicted as godlike. A hymn in his praise went like this:

O great Stalin, O leader of the peoples,
Thou who broughtest man to birth,
Thou who fructifiest the earth,
Thou who restorest the centuries,
Thou who makest bloom the spring,
Thou who makest vibrate the chords of
  music . . .
Thou, splendour of my spring, O thou,
Sun reflected by millions of hearts.

Other songs had the lines "Great Stalin, your hand guides us to ethereal heights" and "Stalin is our glory, our conscience, our word." The official term for the tyrant was "Beloved Father." At CPSU functions, the mention of his name was expected to trigger stormy applause. This was serious, and potentially lethal. After one event, an official was arrested and questioned for being the first to stop clapping after eleven minutes of nonstop applause. Satisfied by his answers, an investigator warned: "Don't ever be the first to stop applauding!"[24]

The CPUSA parroted every Soviet propaganda theme. General Secretary Earl Browder set the tone by hailing Stalin as "the greatest leader of democracy that mankind has ever produced, the greatest helper and guide of the common people of every land, the symbol of the united strength of the toiling masses in victory over their oppressors." Browder grandly called himself a "Stalinist"; nor was it accidental that the tyrant's framed photo gazed down from the wall behind his office desk. Browder and his minions ignored, excused, explained away, or brazenly lied about Stalin's atrocities. His genocide by starvation in Ukraine, the Party faithful insisted, was essential to boosting farm production to feed the growing industrial cities. If the peasants refused to do their duty, Browder implied, it was too bad; besides, they could not be allowed to stand in the way of achieving the Marxist paradise. The Moscow Trials and the Great Terror of the 1930s supposedly cleansed the USSR of "enemies of progress, of democracy, and of peace." According to Browder, those "murderous conspirators," "espionage rats," "vermin," "fascist spies and wreckers" deserved their fate—a bullet in the back of the head and an unmarked grave. What's more, they'd confessed their dirty deeds, declared Party official William Z. Foster, and had not been coerced in any way. "The confessions were voluntary and genuine." Those vile Trotskyites "confessed because . . . the proof of their guilt . . . was so overwhelming that it left no other alternative than confession."[25]

This was sheer claptrap. During the Great Terror, the vast majority of the accused were tortured into saying whatever their interrogators demanded; some of the signed confessions later found in Soviet-era archives were spattered with dried blood. To get them to confess, people were deprived of sleep or forced to stand, without moving a muscle, for days on end; when they collapsed, they were revived and the ordeal resumed. One man signed a confession because his young son was being beaten to a pulp before his eyes, another when interrogators dragged his teenage

Earl Browder.
(1939)

daughter into the room and proceeded to rape her. People will admit to anything under torture, as did the workers who admitted to building artificial volcanoes in order to blow up the entire USSR! The few who defied the torturers were simply shot and their families never told of their fate. In NKVD jargon, these murders were "wet jobs."

We may note that long ago the prophet Isaiah (5:20) warned about the world's Browders and Fosters: "Woe unto them that call evil good and good evil; that put darkness for light, and light for darkness; that put bitter for sweet, and sweet for bitter."

SPREADING THE MESSAGE

When the Bolsheviks seized power in 1917, the United States refused to recognize the Communist state as legitimate. As a result, neither country had an embassy or ambassador in the other's capital. This changed after Franklin Roosevelt became president. To help stimulate the economy, FDR sought overseas markets for American products. Stalin, in turn, wished to trade Russian products for American manufactured goods and machinery. So, in November 1933, representatives of both nations signed a treaty pledging to "forever remain normal and friendly" in their relations. At FDR's insistence, Moscow promised not to carry out propaganda in the United States. However, after diplomatic recognition—and with Moscow's backing—CPUSA propaganda grew by leaps and bounds.

Following the Soviet model, music played a key role in this effort. "Music," said Carl Sands, music critic of the *Daily Worker,* "is propaganda—always propaganda—and of the most powerful sort." Sands urged the development of Communist music as an essential "weapon in the class struggle." During the 1930s, the Workers Music League, a Communist group, published "revolutionary" songbooks and sheet music. A standard commonly used at rallies was "The Internationale," an anthem to worker solidarity dating from the 1880s:

Arise ye prisoners of starvation!
Arise ye wretched of the earth,
For justice thunders condemnation
A better world's in birth!
No more tradition's chains shall bind us,
Arise, ye slaves! no more in thrall!
The earth shall rise on new foundations
We have been naught, we shall be all.[26]

Many songs dealt with the difficulties faced by Depression-era labor unions.

"Which Side Are You On?" paid tribute to coal miners killed during a 1932 strike in Harlan County, Kentucky:

> *My daddy was a miner*
> *And I'm a miner's son*
> *And I'll stick with the union*
> *Till every battle's won.*[27]

Though music was important, the CPUSA relied most on the printed word. For the master of the Kremlin, it was the best way to spread the Communist message. Paper, Stalin observed, is shameless because "it will put up with anything that

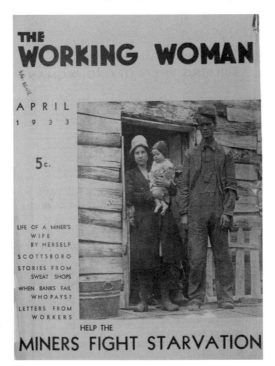

Cover of the *Working Woman,* April 1933 issue.

is written on it." Largely with Moscow's money, the Party funded a wide range of publications tailored to every age group, taste, and educational level. Besides the flagship *Daily Worker,* its presses turned out magazines like the *Communist,* aimed at intellectuals, and *Young Worker, Clarity, Young Comrade,* and *Champion of Youth,* aimed at grade schoolers and young adults. The *Working Woman* featured articles on subjects such as how to dress nicely but cheaply and which types of meals would nourish a family best. *New Masses* (after 1948, *Masses & Mainstream*) used the arts—fiction, poetry, drama, and film—to push the CPUSA line on current political and social issues. Each month the magazine had several bold, hard-hitting drawings and cartoons, some superb examples of these art forms, portraying bloated capitalists, hunger marchers' demand for "Work or Wages," and the plight of African Americans. *Soviet Russia Today* and *Soviet Russia Pictorial* were glossy photo magazines that showed the USSR as an ideal society, loyal to Stalin and striving to attain Marxist perfection.

A series titled the Little Lenin Library consisted of paperback reprints of the Bolshevik leader's major works. There was also the series International Pamphlets, scores

5ᶜ

LIFE and LABOR in the SOVIET UNION
by ROBERT W. DUNN and GEORGE WALLACE
INTERNATIONAL PAMPHLETS No. 52

Cover of International Pamphlet No. 52, touting the nobility of life and labor under Stalin. (1937)

of titles on subjects of interest to targeted audiences. Pamphlets were favored over hardcover books because, at sixteen to thirty-two pages, they were easily produced and sold for a nickel or a dime. Written in simple vocabulary, these explored what, to the Party, were the chief concerns of Depression-era readers. But whatever the subject, pamphlets followed a set pattern from the Marxist viewpoint. Each focused on a key topic—unemployment, working conditions, housing, health care, the role of women, abolition of child labor,

racial bias—explaining the situation and its causes and suggesting remedies. Finally, the pamphlet contrasted conditions in America to those in the USSR. Without fail, it concluded that everything was better under communism than in capitalist-dominated America.

Yet the ills in American society addressed in CPUSA pamphlets were genuine. It was right to point them out; today, we take for granted many of the reforms the Party demanded during the Depression era. Its pamphlets called for public housing to replace slums, and benefits for the jobless. "Our only means of livelihood are wages," stated one pamphlet, adding, "If capitalism cannot provide us jobs with wages, it must provide us wages without jobs. The capitalists must either give us *'Work or Wages.'*" Moreover, it called for a range of social benefits, including "old age pensions . . . and insurance against sickness and accidents . . . and maternity insurance for all working mothers," to be paid for by taxes on the wealthy. As for women, the Party adopted the stance: "No discrimination against married women workers. In other words, women must be paid the same for doing the same work as their menfolk."[28]

Words were backed by deeds. The

Party organized hunger marches to demonstrate the plight of the poor. During the International Unemployment Day protest on March 6, 1930, an estimated one million people across the country marched with signs reading "Fight for Work or Wages!" "Demand Full Wages for All Part Time Workers!" "Long Live the Unity of the Black and White Workers!" "Down with Imperialist War!" and, of course, "Defend the Soviet Union!" In New York, thousands jammed Union Square to hear CPUSA speakers call for "immediate relief for the jobless from the funds of the city treasury and from taxes on the wealthy exploiters." When a column of protesters set out for City Hall, policemen wielding nightsticks turned the square into a battlefield. In Oakland, the *Daily Worker* (January 22, 1932) reported: "A crowd of 1,000, mostly neighbors, fought fiercely against the brutal eviction of a widowed mother and her crippled daughter."[29]

Street demonstrations had a dual purpose: spreading the Party's message and serving as recruiting tools. Years later, a New York woman recalled what attracted her and how she became involved in the cause. "I met the Communists in the Workers Alliance. Whatever fault there was, cowardice was not one of them. They were dedicated. They were militant. They really cared. When I saw all this, I began to admire them. They respected me . . . [and so] I joined the Communist Party in March 1931."[30]

To stoke resentment of "capitalist oppression," the Party vilified President Roosevelt. Though born to wealth, FDR had always championed the underdog. Nevertheless, Communists charged the "imperialist," "warmonger," and "dictator" with wanting only "Hunger, Forced Labor, Terror and War" for American workers. That miserable wretch in the White House, according to a May Day 1933 leaflet, was "MOVING HEADLONG TOWARD FASCISM AND WAR."

The term "fascism" referred to a form of government based on unlimited state power. Under fascism, a political party and its leader crush all opposition and control the state, the media, the arts, the military, the police, and the courts. Where fascists differed from Communists was in their attitude toward the economy. Unlike the USSR, where the state owned the economy, fascist leaders Adolf Hitler in Germany and Benito Mussolini in Italy preferred to keep business in private hands, but direct it to serve the state's interests. Under fascism, according to one economist, businesspeople still earn profits but the government tells them "what and how to produce, at what prices and from whom to buy, at what prices and to whom to sell. It assigns every worker to his job and fixes his wages. . . . The government directs all production activities." Officially, Communists defined fascism as the most advanced, and thus the most warlike, stage of capitalism—hence the term "fascist warmonger." However, the CPUSA faithful played fast and loose with the term. By the 1930s, "fascism" and "fascist" had become all-purpose hate words for anything and anybody Communists disliked or disagreed with. One cartoon depicted a grinning FDR with his arms around Hitler and Mussolini while a Nazi cupid shoots a love dart at him.[31]

FDR was neither a fascist nor a warmonger. Throughout the 1920s and early 1930s, the U.S. Army was minuscule; with a top strength of 174,000, it ranked nineteenth in the world, behind the armies of tiny Belgium and economically underdeveloped Portugal. By contrast, in 1935, Stalin's Red Army had 1.3 million men and 10,000 tanks, the largest armored force on the planet. As for the New Deal, Communists branded it "the Raw Deal," "fascist economics," and "the Roosevelt New Deal of Hunger and Terror." FDR's efforts to

A cartoon of FDR cozying up to Hitler and Mussolini while a Nazi cupid shoots an arrow from a swastika bow. (c. 1940)

reform rather than abolish capitalism, they said, marked him as a phony, a stooge, and a vile puppet of Wall Street bankers. The president's jobs programs were allegedly intended "to militarize unemployed youth" by herding them into "forced labor camps under the direct supervision of the army." In reality, the camps of the Civilian

The Red Army in the 1930s was robust—the largest army on the planet at the time. (c. 1930)

Conservation Corps aimed at providing unemployed young men with pay, education, and wholesome surroundings in return for activities like replanting forests ruined by reckless lumber companies. Nevertheless, cartoonists portrayed FDR and his programs, such as the National Recovery Administration (NRA), decked with swastikas, the Nazi emblem symbolic of racism, oppression, and aggression.[32]

Party propaganda drew sharp contrasts between FDR's America and Stalin's USSR. After little more than a decade of Bolshevik rule, it was said, the country had leaped from the Dark Ages to the modern world. In doing so, it had become the "Workers' Paradise," literally "heaven brought to earth." Soviet workers, according to William Z. Foster, were the happiest and most productive in history, because they were free. "They own the country and everything in it. There is no exploiting class to rob them of the fruits of their toil," he asserted time and again. While industry under capitalism was a dog-eat-dog struggle, the comrades, echoing Moscow, declared Soviet workers had free health care, decent housing, vacations at Black Sea resorts, and old-age pensions. Best of all, though unemployment was rampant in Depression-era America, in the glorious "land of the worker," every Soviet citizen was guaranteed a job in a state-owned industry. These inducements were to have tragic results. Lured by the promise of steady work at decent wages, perhaps as many as ten thousand American workers and their families settled in the USSR. In doing so, they were required to hand over their U.S. passports, and not a few actually took Soviet citizenship. Trapped by Stalin's Great Terror of the 1930s, nearly all, including those who'd retained their American citizenship, were shot as spies or vanished into the Gulag.[33]

SOVIET REALITIES

An old proverb says, "If wishes were horses, beggars would ride." In other words, if wishing could change reality, the lowliest beggars would have anything their hearts desire. Likewise, much CPUSA propaganda was a pipe dream based on wishful thinking and outright falsehoods. Soviet reality was nothing like the way it was portrayed to rank-and-file Party members and to the American public. Emma Goldman and Alexander Berkman discovered this early on, to their dismay. The exiled anarchists had come to the USSR expecting to find a dynamic, open, thriving society. Sadly, by 1922, they could see only a hideous lie. "One by one the embers of hope have died out," Berkman wrote in despair. "Terror and despotism have crushed the life born in October. The slogans of the Revolution are foresworn, its ideals stifled in the blood of the people. . . . Dictatorship is trampling the masses underfoot. The Revolution is dead; its spirit cries in the wilderness. . . . The Bolshevik myth must be destroyed." In the couple's view, Soviet-style communism simply did not work—*could* not work—because it violated the innate human yearning for freedom and justice.[34]

What Berkman and Goldman found would have gladdened Judge Gary, who'd fought the labor unions during the Great Red Scare of 1919. Soviet workers were not free in any sense of the word. Their labor was state property. Their unions, as Lenin demanded, were "schools of communism," the state creating and using them for its own ends. There was no negotiation or bargaining between labor and management. Moscow bureaucrats set pay scales, hours, and working conditions. They ordered assembly-line speed-ups, forcing workers to move faster and produce more for the same wage. Often workers had to put in "voluntary" overtime at no extra pay. Strikes were banned,

and strikers jailed (or worse) as "deserters from the industrial front." Lateness and unauthorized absence were punishable by fines and jail terms; large factories had their own policemen and jail cells so managers could imprison anyone without trial. There was only one employer—the state—and no worker could refuse a job it offered, or quit without its written permission. Anyone who did so was fired and blacklisted from further employment, a virtual death sentence.[35]

The Soviet system was equal in name only. The powerful slogan "From each according to his ability, to each according to his need" was discarded the moment the Bolsheviks seized power. New slogans said: "From each according to his ability, to each according to his work" and "He who shall not work, shall not eat." Workers were paid according to their skills and duties. Thus, the skilled earned more than the unskilled, the office worker more than the coal miner, the engineer and chemist more than the mechanic, the factory manager more than the assembly-line worker, and so on through thirty-three pay grades.[36]

Different pay translated into different lifestyles. Lower-paid workers, the vast majority, had to cope with shortages of consumer goods. For them, Communist activist and journalist Peggy Dennis noted, "the search for food was a daily task." Even *babushkas,* elderly grannies, had to stand in line for hours, rain or shine, to buy a loaf of bread and a bit of sausage, which might sell out before they reached the counter. In the cities, the less skilled lived in apartments that had belonged to the middle and upper classes before the revolution. These were called "communal apartments." An entire family occupied a single room; large rooms were divided by sheets, with one family to a compartment. As many as seventeen families shared a toilet. And since toilet paper was often unobtainable, the inhabitants wiped themselves with newspaper, taking care not to soil Stalin's name or photo, which was an offense punishable by shooting. Stalin's image was supposed to be treated as sacred in the USSR. One dared not disfigure it, lay it facedown, or hang a picture above it. Any typesetter who broke Stalin's name at the end of a line had to explain why to the secret police.[37]

Under Stalin, highly skilled and productive workers enjoyed special privileges. They ate in segregated cafeterias, had better food, and vacationed at resorts along the Black Sea. Moreover, Communist Party chiefs, high-ranking military officers, and the *apparatchiki,* bureaucrats who ran the "apparatus" of the Party and state, were Russia's new aristocracy. A privileged class, as long as Stalin trusted them, they had their own apartments and *dachas,* country vacation homes; Stalin used three dachas, complete with gardens and swimming pools. Servants tended to their needs, maids cleaned their houses, and chauffeurs drove them around in imported American limousines, especially Packards, favored by Wall Street bankers. Nannies cared for their children, who attended exclusive CPSU schools. The best hospitals were reserved for the elite, who had access to medicines unobtainable by ordinary folk. Such people ate in restaurants that catered only to them and shopped for food, furniture, and household goods in stores open to them alone. They wore designer dresses from Paris and tailor-made suits from London's exclusive Savile Row. The Moscow store of the NKVD was known as "the best in the whole Soviet Union." Simply put, the "classless society" of Soviet and CPUSA propaganda did not exist, and never would.[38]

FELLOW TRAVELERS AND USEFUL IDIOTS

Certain comrades were trained to infiltrate an organization and "bore from within" until they took control. Here, too, Lenin offered guidance, especially in regard to the labor movement. Comrades must, he wrote, "resort to every kind of trick, cunning, illegal expedient, concealment, suppression of truth, so as to penetrate the trade unions, to stay in them, to conduct in them, at whatever cost, Communist work." The Depression had revived American unions as workers struggled to hold their own or better their conditions. Seeing an opportunity to gain influence, the CPUSA sent activists to join targeted unions. These were serious people who knew the issues and worked hard. Gradually rising through the ranks, they began to influence union policies and win elective office, all the while following Party directives. In time, they took over such unions as the International Longshore and Warehouse Union, which serviced the ports on the Pacific coast, and unions in the machine-tool and aircraft industries.[39]

Communists, too, formed their own organizations. Called "fronts," these masked Party control while it set the organizations' policies. Fronts had names that signaled virtue and idealism, such as the Labor Youth League, American Youth Congress, American Youth for Democracy, Congress of American Women, Emergency Civil Liberties Committee, and American Peace Crusade. Though worthy in themselves, the causes fronts championed were important only to the extent the Party could use them to further its aims. Accordingly, fronts roped in "fellow travelers," those who did not join the Communist Party but followed the current line as decreed by Moscow. Often people with good intentions and high ideals, these included writers, artists, actors, educators, social workers, scientists, and members of the clergy. Perhaps too busy or too gullible to look into an organization's nature and backing, fellow travelers spread Party propaganda and raised money for its use. Among themselves, however, the comrades scorned fronts as "innocents' clubs" and their members as "useful idiots," Lenin's term for naive Western sympathizers.

Whatever useful idiots might think, the CPUSA's goals were identical to Moscow's, as anyone who read its publications knew. William Z. Foster detailed them in a full-length book titled *Toward Soviet America.* In words echoing Lenin's and Stalin's, he left no doubt that the Party wished to tear down existing American society and remake it in the Soviet image. Upon seizing power, said Foster, it would unleash Bolshevik-style terror by "the armed Red Guard." As in the USSR, people and organizations would not be charged with specific crimes, the basis of all civilized law, but for who and what they were.

> Special courts to fight the counter-revolution will probably be necessary. The pest of lawyers will be abolished. The courts will be class-courts, definitely warring against the class enemies of the toilers. . . . Under the dictatorship of the proletariat all capitalist parties—Republican, Democratic, Progressive, Socialist, etc.—will be liquidated, the Communist party functioning alone as the Party of the masses. . . . There will be the immediate taking over by the State of all large factories, mines and power plants . . . the whole transport services of railroads, waterways, airways, electric car lines, bus lines, etc.; the entire communications organization, including telegraphs, telephones, post office, radio, etc. . . . All the land will . . . be nationalized, and all industry will be concentrated into the Socialist Soviet economy. . . . All houses and other buildings will be socialized. . . . The press, the motion picture, the radio, the theater, will be taken over by the government.[40]

USSR Communist propaganda poster. The caption reads "Emancipated woman—build socialism!" (1926)

WOMEN, CHILDREN, YOUTH

The CPUSA rightly pointed to certain advances in the USSR during the 1920s and 1930s. These, however, were not undertaken merely because they were right, but to achieve specific ideological, political, and economic goals. Take women. For centuries, most Russian women had suffered under what Lenin called the "barbarously unproductive, petty, nerve-wracking, stultifying and crushing drudgery" of housework and child care. The Bolshevik leader realized that if their first loyalty was to the family, women could not give themselves entirely to the state. Moreover, tying them down at home kept them out of the labor force, slowing the USSR's drive to become a world-class industrial power. So, to motivate the female workforce, factories gave new mothers time off to breastfeed their babies during the workday and provided nurseries, day-care centers, cafeterias, and laundries to lessen the burden of household chores. Divorce became easy, speedy, and inexpensive. Unwed mothers were no longer stigmatized. Traditionally male-only professions were thrown open to women. Every year, Soviet schools graduated thousands of female doctors, dentists, pharmacists, scientists, engineers, and technicians. Soviet women drove farm tractors; they even took combat roles in the Red Army, serving as military police, snipers, tank drivers, and fighter pilots. During World War II, the exploits of the Night Witches, an all-female fighter squadron, stunned German airmen. Women also did the most strenuous physical work: digging ditches, felling trees, paving roads, carrying sacks of coal, loading and unloading freight trains.[41]

Moscow believed in the power of education. "Give me just one generation of youth," said Lenin, "and I will transform the whole world." Adolf Hitler said much the same: "Who has the youth, has the future." Revolutionaries are human; they get old and tired, and they die. For their regimes to survive, they must plant their ideologies in young minds. Not that they valued the young as precious in themselves. They were, as a Soviet educator explained, "like soft wax," their minds easily molded by ideology. The formula was simple: Cut the young off from "bad" influences, control what they learned, suppress critical thinking, and channel their natural idealism into serving the Cause.[42]

Soviet schools had two objectives. To begin with, they acted as a ladder of social mobility, educating the poor for skilled jobs they could not have dreamed of in czarist times. However, in a nation where one in four was illiterate in 1917, the teaching of reading became a top priority. Thus, instruction was made compulsory; factory workers and farmers got time off during the workday to attend classes run by Communist instructors. Yet literacy was far more than a gateway to knowledge and skills. It was a way to get into people's heads, opening them to a ceaseless barrage of propaganda. Lenin explained: "An illiterate person stands outside politics and must, therefore, learn the alphabet. Without that there can be no politics."

Accordingly, in 1918, Lenin decreed, "The whole population . . . between the ages of eight and fifty who cannot read and write are obliged to do so." This was not a polite request, for anyone daring to shirk their duty "had criminal proceedings instituted against them," resulting in a prison term at hard labor.[43]

As for the young, Soviet schools educated them to believe, think, and act as Communists. Preschoolers played with toys designed to mold their thinking. Dolls depicted ugly czars, capitalists, and priests.

Factory workers and collective farmers were shown as handsome and beautiful, noble and loyal. Like their elders, children were expected to idolize Stalin. By the early 1930s, each classroom had its "Stalin corner," a sacred spot with his photo or plaster bust, framed quotations, and a vase of fresh flowers. Children learned that "Uncle Stalin," "the Great and Wise One," was also Grandfather Frost, the Russian Santa Claus, giver of toys and treats. Colorful posters showed a smiling Stalin surrounded by adoring children; captions

A propaganda poster featuring a painting of children encircling Stalin. The caption reads "Thank you, dear comrade Stalin, for our happy childhood!" (1936)

read "Thank You, Dear Comrade Stalin, for Our Happy Childhood!" and "Friend of the Little Children." Teachers ordered their classes to recite, with enthusiasm:

We have everything we need,
We live as a friendly family,
And our best reward is
That dear Stalin loves us.
Comrade Stalin, thank you,
That we live so well![44]

In 1936, a photo titled "Friend of the Little Children" was reproduced in the millions and displayed on billboards and in classrooms throughout the USSR. It showed a happy seven-year-old named Engelsina "Gelya" Markizova embracing a smiling Stalin, to whom she'd given a bouquet of flowers. The daughter of a minor official, a fervent Communist who named her after Friedrich Engels, Gelya adored "the Father of the Peoples." However, two years later, he had her father shot as a Japanese spy; her mother was later found dead under mysterious circumstances. As for Gelya herself, since "all-wise" Stalin could not be seen posing with the child of an "enemy of the people," and it was impossible to destroy all those photos, his henchmen changed her name instead of the photo. Now an orphan,

Stalin holding Gelya Markizova in the famous photo "Friend of the Little Children." Two years later, Stalin would have her father murdered and her mother exiled to Kazakhstan, where she mysteriously died. (1936)

she was lucky to be taken in by relatives in Moscow. This proved her salvation. Gelya went on to become a specialist in the study of China and India, marry, and have three children; she died in 2004.[45]

For countless families, the Soviet system broke the most basic of human bonds: those between parents and children. "Stalin's children" were taught that their loyalty was not to their families, but to the man in the Kremlin. If you overheard a parent make a "disloyal" remark, you must tell your teacher, who must tell the NKVD.

Historians have documented cases where a child's words led to a parent being executed or sent to the Gulag. Even if you denounced a parent, you might be deemed a "socially dangerous element" and a "social alien." If, for example, your father had been a priest or a civil servant before the revolution, you shared that "stain," regardless of your own beliefs. This barred you from universities, the professions, and training for skilled jobs. The stigma destroyed families. "I feel ashamed to call him my father. As an enemy of the people, he cannot be my father," a girl named Anna told her mother. "The Party of Lenin and Stalin will take the place of my father . . . they will care for me as a true daughter and . . . help me on my path through life." A boy named Vladimir railed against his mother: "Is it my fault that I was born the son of an enemy? I don't want you as my mother any more." Newspapers printed formal notices like this: "I, Nicholas Ivanov, renounce my father, an ex-priest, because for many years he deceived the people by telling them that God exists, and that is the reason I am severing my relations with him." Some changed their last names rather than bear the stigma of being related to a "class enemy."[46]

Many were legally defined as a "Member of the Family of an Enemy of the Revolution." Astonishingly, this category included small children, who were shipped to the Gulag with their mothers or born there if their mothers were pregnant when sent away. Because of Gulag officials, infants languished in prison-like barracks, ill fed, ill treated, and neglected. Many died, while survivors bore lifelong physical and emotional scars.

We get a good idea of what it was like from the CPSU member and author Eugenia Ginzburg. Arrested in 1937 as a "counterrevolutionary" and sentenced to eighteen years in the Kolyma camps, she never saw her husband, Pavel, or her son, Alexei, again. In her autobiography, *Within the Whirlwind,* Ginzburg described her life as a prisoner, albeit a lucky one, because she had a "soft" job in a child-care barrack, one among many in a self-contained world of woe. "The children's home," she wrote, "was also part of the camp compound. It had its own guardhouse, its own gates, its own huts and its own barbed wire." Ginzburg was shocked that, for lack of human contact, let alone love, "only certain of the four-year-olds could produce a few odd, unconnected words. Inarticulate howls, mimicry, and blows were the main means of communication. . . . In the infants' group they spend their whole time just lying in their cots. Nobody will pick them up, even if they cry their lungs out. It's not allowed, except to change wet diapers—when there are any dry ones available, of course." Eventually, Stalin's littlest victims wound up in state orphanages, dreadful places always short of the basic necessities—food, clothing, beds, washing facilities—whose directors often treated them with brutality. One former inmate told how the director would drag children out of their beds by the hair, bang their heads against the wall, and threaten them with his pistol. When they came of age, the most promising ones, boys and girls, were groomed for joining the secret police. Well might these children who never knew childhood sing their song of woe: "And now my soul is hardened."[47]

Soviet cities, too, had hordes of *besprizorniki,* or "neglected ones," bands of destitute waifs. Many had been orphaned during the Bolshevik Revolution and Russian Civil War. Many others were peasant children whose parents had died in Stalin's Holodomor or had been seized as "enemies of the people." Relatives, fearing to attract attention by sheltering such children, threw them out. These castaways, some as young as five, joined gangs, surviving by foraging in garbage cans, pickpocketing, and stealing whatever they could get

Homeless Russian boys. (c. 1942)

their hands on. To stay warm at night, they might sleep in trash bins, public lavatories, and even in holes dug in the ground. The engineer Victor Kravchenko saw them during his inspection tours. "As we drew into a station beyond Kharkov, I was in the dining car. I was startled by several little faces peering at me through the window, with sad, hungry, envious eyes. These were *besprizorniki,* homeless little girls and boys in motley rags. They were staring at one of their 'socialist uncles' at lordly ease under the dictatorship of the proletariat." Though efforts were made to round up and place at least some in "homes," where boys received military training prior to being taken into the Red Army, the vast majority remained on the streets. That didn't suit Comrade Stalin. In 1935, "the Friend of the Little Children" signed a decree titled "On Measures of Struggle with Crime Among Minors," extending all criminal penalties, including death by shooting, down to the age of twelve. Former NKVD general Alexander Orlov recalled, "Stalin issued orders to shoot secretly these children who were plundering and stealing food from railway cars in transit." Many, too, wound up in the Gulag, where they were thrown together with adult criminals. In his *History of the Gulag,* Russian historian Oleg Khlevniuk tells how the hardened brutes mistreated these youngsters, often abusing them sexually.[48]

Though CPUSA members may not have known about the children of the Gulag, they admired and imitated Soviet educational methods. To be sure, ardent Communists copied the Russian fad of giving youngsters exotic "Red" first names. Twin boys might be called Marx and Engels; Vladin stood for Vladimir Lenin, and Lesta for Lenin and Stalin. Girls could start out in life as Stalina, Ninel (Lenin spelled backward), Proletaria, and Octobrina (October Revolution).

Party members valued simply written books, such as *Teachings of Marx for Girls and Boys,* that explained the world in Marxist terms. Many books were English translations of Soviet works issued by International Publishers, the Party's New York publishing house. During the 1930s, Soviet children's books were things of beauty, illustrated by first-rate artists. Picture books for pre-readers introduced the alphabet with lines such as "K is for Kremlin, where our Stalin lives." A biography titled *Our Lenin* taught children to revere the Bolshevik leader and despise capitalists, portrayed as horned devils with big bellies and puffy faces. The verses of Ned Donn's 1934 "Pioneer Mother Goose" demolished the Capitalist Pig in all his forms:

> *This bloated Pig masters Wall Street,*
> *This little Pig owns your home;*
> *This war-crazed Pig had your brother*
>   *killed,*
> *And this greedy Pig shouts "More!"*
> *This Pig in Congress shouts "War, War!"*
> *All the day long.*
>
> *These Pigs we'll send to market—*
> *And will they squeal? You bet!*
> *Down with Capitalism!*
> *Long live the Soviet!*[49]

The CPUSA formed youth organizations modeled on those in the USSR. These aimed at capturing the young for communism, thereby setting the stage for the future overthrow of capitalism. Naturally, they glorified Joseph Stalin. A writer for a Party magazine needed capital letters to drive home the message: "EVERY ONE OF COMRADE STALIN'S UTTERANCES IS A MIGHTY SEARCHLIGHT LIGHTING UP THE PATH OF THE REVOLUTIONARY YOUTH MOVEMENT, AND FILLS THE HEARTS OF THE YOUTH WITH FAITH IN THE VICTORY OF THE WORKING CLASS."[50]

As in the Soviet Union, the Young Pioneers (YP) enrolled boys and girls eight to fifteen years of age. At gatherings, they gave the YP salute, raising their open hands at right angles to their bodies while reciting the motto "Always ready!" Despite its similarity to "Be prepared," the motto of the Boy Scouts of America, the organizations had nothing in common. A pamphlet titled *Who Are the Young Pioneers?* explained why workers' children should avoid the Boy Scouts like the plague: "The Boy Scouts teach you to use your knowledge for the boss class. They teach you to be 'patriotic.' . . . The 'patriotism' of the Boy Scouts and the bosses means defend-

Anti–Boy Scout cartoon inside *Young Pioneer.* (1929)

ing the government and property of rich and corrupt millionaires and their politicians." YP meetings often began with the chant "Smash the Boy Scouts."[51]

Young Pioneers were encouraged to think of themselves as a chosen generation, destined to do great things for the working class. Growing up in Communist families and steeped in the Party's ideology, they were set in their beliefs by the time they entered their teens. Peggy Dennis, who joined at the age of thirteen, recalled that she and her friends were "confident that we alone were tapped by history to fulfill its mission for humanity's liberation from exploitation and oppression. We alone had the answer as to how this could be done, and because there was only one socialist state to emulate, the Soviet Union was our blueprint."[52]

These youngsters were, in effect, Soviet patriots living in an alien land. In school, they defiantly refused to salute the Stars and Stripes or recite the "bosses' pledge" of allegiance. YP members did not celebrate July 4, Independence Day; their holiday was May 1, traditionally a day for honoring workers. One year, the cover of *Young Comrade,* the official YP magazine, had a picture of a boy waving a red flag outside a schoolhouse, captioned: "Out of School on May Day!" "Remember, comrades," fourteen-year-old Jesse Taft urged her classmates, "the only cause we have is Soviet Russia." The USSR was their true homeland, others said, "our Soviet Fatherland," and so "the only flag the Pioneers salute is the Red flag." As in the USSR, Young Pioneers denounced the clergy of all religions as "Dope Peddlers" who "poisoned" minds with superstition. Religion, according to *Young Comrade,* "is only another tool of the bosses to keep the workers and the workers' children obedient slaves. For the priests and rabbis tell the workers that they must not worry about bad conditions on earth—the worse their conditions are, the better they'll have it after they die!" YP members left no doubt that they were Soviet patriots. A YP leaflet declared: "DEFEND THE SO-VIET UNION, THE ONLY WORKERS' FATHERLAND!"[53]

Adult leaders devised activities to occupy Young Pioneers' spare time. Clubs met in homes, basements, and Party-run schools. There were also a bevy of "people's" choirs, glee clubs, dramatic societies, dance troupes, art programs, and hobby groups. Weather permitting, youngsters went on hikes "in the country," a treat for city kids. In summertime, children attended camps with names like Camp Robin Hood and Camp Woodland, basically Soviet colonies on American soil. There campers were placed in groups named Marx, Lenin, Stalin, Red Sparks, Red Builders, and the like. Each day began with raising the red hammer-and-sickle Soviet flag and reciting the YP pledge, a takeoff on the Pledge of Allegiance: "I pledge allegiance to the workers'

Children in the Young Pioneers were encouraged to denounce religious practices in schools. (1930)

C'MON, HELP ME SHOVE HIM OFF!

RELIGIOUS DOPE IN SCHOOLS

red flag and to the cause for which it stands, one aim throughout our lives, freedom for the working class." During the day, campers hiked, swam, did arts and crafts, played sports, and took classes "to teach the children the condition of the workers and their children." At assemblies, they sang songs from the *Pioneer Song Book,* such as:

With ordered step, the red flag unfurled,
We'll make a new and better world.

In New York State alone, in 1930, summer camps served fifteen thousand children from CPUSA and fellow-traveler families.[54]

YP training aimed at fostering activism. During strikes, local groups collected money for the striking union's welfare fund and handed out leaflets supporting its demands. To encourage those on the picket lines, they organized strikers' children. Comrades led them in union songs and chants of "Come on! We'll fight with you!" Some carried signs scorning scabs, those willing to take strikers' jobs because they could not find work otherwise. Signs read "We Don't Want Our Fathers to Be Scabs!"[55]

Upon turning sixteen, Young Pioneers became eligible for the Young Communist League (YCL). Modeled on the Komsomol (the USSR's All-Union Leninist Communist League of Youth), this organization groomed young adults for membership in the CPUSA. Founded in 1922, the YCL established units in several colleges with histories of political activism. Among these were New York's City, Hunter, and Brooklyn Colleges, Temple University in Philadelphia, and the University of Chicago. The YCL offered members friendship, entertainment, recreation, and "a life with a purpose." That purpose involved infiltrating non-Communist campus groups, spreading Marxist ideology, and participating in anti-capitalist demonstrations. All YCL members, however, understood that their ultimate goal was revolution. The YCL program clearly stated: "The aim of the YCL is the attainment of the Communist Society. This can only be done through the complete forcible overthrow of the capitalist state and the establishment of the dictatorship of the proletariat."[56]

Essential to reaching that goal was the CPUSA's efforts to turn Black citizens into Reds.

BLACK COMRADES AWAKEN!

Black comrades awaken!
Come, steel your dark shoulders!
. . . Our foe we meet face to face.
—"Hunger March," Communist song (c. 1930)

A JIM CROW WORLD

In the Depression era, African Americans made up nearly 10 percent of the total U.S. population of 123 million. Though countless Americans suffered during the economic collapse, for most Black people misery was nothing new. Even in the best of times, they did not fully share in the nation's prosperity. Anti-Black racism was even more pervasive then. Among its most insidious practices—some of which will be detailed in this chapter—were lynching, rape, slurs, and fake convictions.

While the Civil War had ended slavery six decades earlier, formerly enslaved people and their kin still bore heavy burdens. Soon after enslaved people gained legal freedom,

Southern legislatures passed hundreds of Jim Crow laws. The laws took their name from an 1840s minstrel-show clown played by a white man made up in black-face who danced to the banjo tune "Jump Jim Crow!" Bigots used the Jim Crow figure, a deliberate insult, to represent the entire Black community.

A Black Alabamian described life as he knew it: "Every chance is used to keep the black man in his 'place.' Let a Negro raise his voice. Let him resent a kick in the shins, let a black man stand up straight—he'll be kept put. Get a rope, hang him, burn him, get a gang and beat him to a raw steak in a pool of blood!" Such outrages were possible because racism was woven into the American mind-set, particularly in the South. That form of racism considered one skin color naturally "inferior" or "superior." According to its perverse logic, because whites were biologically "superior" beings, they deserved to be treated as the lords of creation, God's chosen race.[1]

In the South, Jim Crow seeped into nearly every aspect of the African American's daily life. He saw that Black doctors and midwives only delivered Black babies. Black teachers could only teach Black children in all-Black schools. If found guilty of a crime, invariably by all-white juries in courts presided over by white judges, Black people served time in segregated prison blocks. Public toilets, water fountains, park benches, restaurants, and movie houses—all had "White Only" and "Colored Only" signs. (In Philadelphia, near Independence Hall, there was a "colored" fountain.) In public transportation, Black people had to sit in the back of buses and streetcars, surrendering their seat if a white person asked. Black barbers cut only Black men's hair, and Black beauticians only made up Black women. While African Americans had the right to vote, Southern legislators devised ways to keep them from the polls. A "poll tax" as low as two dollars was still too high for a person barely eking out a living as a tenant farmer. Some states required first-time voters to pass a literacy test. This involved reading a passage and explaining it to an election official, who had the power to disqualify whomever he pleased, including a Black minister or schoolteacher. Absurdly, illiterate whites were exempt if their fathers or grandfathers had voted in 1867.

Lynching, or killing an alleged criminal without any pretense of a trial, enforced Jim Crow. Lynching was premeditated murder meant to exact control by instilling fear. A mob, often led by hooded

Ku Klux Klansmen, would seize a person accused of a crime or of breaking an unwritten rule of white society. Such rules included trying to register to vote, arguing with a white person, or acting "uppity"—a racist term for being cocky, impolite, cross, outspoken.

The worst offense was sexual. In slavery times, Southern white men were horrified at the idea of "savage" Black men "violating" their mothers, sisters, wives, and daughters. Not only did they think this dishonored white manhood, they thought it "polluted" the blood of infants conceived during such "unnatural unions." That fear carried into the twentieth century. As Ellison "Cotton Ed" Smith, a Democratic senator from South Carolina, put it, the threat of lynching was necessary "to protect the fair womanhood of the South from beasts." Yet the rape charge was bogus, a lie concocted to justify social and economic oppression. Geneticists have found that, on average, African Americans are about 17 percent white, suggesting that white men raped their maternal ancestors. Visitors to the South often commented on the large number of light-skinned African Americans with Caucasian features.[2]

Lynching was no secret; whites often learned the time and place of an impend-

Announcement of a Mississippi lynching in a New Orleans newspaper. (1919)

ing lynching from newspaper ads. Parents brought their children to the ghastly spectacle as if to a county fair. Vendors sold ice cream, popcorn, and wish-you-were-here picture postcards of past "lynching-bees." With police officers looking on, doing nothing, a mob would break into a local jail to seize its victim. Torture preceded murder; the defenseless person (occasionally a woman, even a pregnant one) was beaten, whipped, and blinded. Then he or she would be hanged or burned alive.

On February 2, 1893, the *New York Sun* reported a lynching in Paris, Texas. Henry Smith, an unemployed Black man, had been arrested on suspicion of murdering a four-year-old white girl. On lynching day, a crowd of ten thousand gathered, many having come on reduced-fare excursion trains. As the crowd watched, a visiting New Yorker cried, "For God's sake, send the children home." Irate townsmen shouted him down, saying, "No, no, let them learn a lesson." Meanwhile, the bound victim, protesting his innocence, was dragged onto a platform with the word "Justice" painted in large white letters across a beam, stripped, and chained to a wooden post. A small charcoal brazier near the post held red-hot pokers. What happened next was a scene reminiscent of the execution of religious heretics during the Middle Ages:

Smith was placed upon a scaffold, six feet square and ten feet high, securely bound, within the view of all beholders. Here the victim was tortured for fifty minutes by red-hot iron brands thrust against his quivering body. Commencing at the feet, the brands were placed against him inch by inch until they were thrust against the face. Then . . . kerosene was poured upon him, cottonseed hulls placed beneath him and set on fire. . . . It was horrible—the man dying by slow torture in the midst of smoke from his own burning flesh. Every groan . . . every contortion of his body was cheered by the thickly packed crowd.

Henry Smith being publicly lynched on a platform with the word "Justice" inscribed. (1893)

Afterward, men sifted the ashes for unburned body parts; one souvenir hunter made a watch charm from Smith's kneecap. From 1882 to 1968, 4,743 people were lynched in the United States; 3,446 of them were African Americans.[3]

Racism infected the rest of the nation as well. In the industrial cities of the North, whites-only unions excluded African Americans, leaving most to find work in the hardest, dirtiest, lowest-paid occupations. Popular culture, in turn, reeked of racial prejudice. On stage, screen, and radio, African Americans were portrayed as clowns, cutthroats, or simpletons. Russian-born Al Jolson, the toast of the Broadway stage, sang jazz and the blues in blackface, hence his nickname "the King of Blackface." In Hollywood films, a critic observed, "the Negro gets special Jim Crow treatment." In *For Massa's Sake* (1911), a slave tries to pay off his white master's gambling debts by secretly offering himself for sale. *The Battle* (1911) romanticized the "sweet slavery days" and the "happy, carefree state" of plantation life. *The Birth of a Nation,* a 1915 film produced by D. W. Griffith, celebrated the "Knights" of the Ku Klux Klan as defenders of white men's honor and white women's virtue. President Woodrow Wilson, an

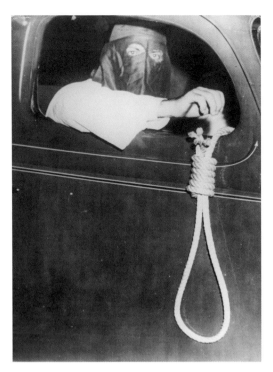

Ku Klux Klan member with noose. (c. 1939)

avowed racist, admired the film, the first ever shown in the White House, saying it was "like writing history with lightning." The white narrator of the documentary *Africa Speaks!* (1930) deplored the native African, claiming: "He is tired. L-a-z-y tired." A weekly radio program, *Amos 'n' Andy,* portrayed Black people as innately ignorant and childlike, shiftless and cunning. The hit series was created, written, and acted by two white men who played the different characters and spoke in their version of "Black" dialect.[4]

There was a whole genre of songs demeaning African Americans. Examples abound. One tune may be regarded as the lyrical representation of Jim Crowism. The 1931 song "That's Why Darkies Were Born" was made popular by Kate Smith, later famous as "the First Lady of Radio" for her rendition of the national anthem at sports events. This racist song, heard by a radio audience of millions, depicted Black people as created by God to be beasts of burden for their "betters." Here is a small excerpt:

> Someone had to pick the cotton,
> Someone had to pick the corn . . .
> That's why darkies were born.[5]

FISHERS IN TROUBLED WATERS

Marxism rejects racism. Social conditions, it holds, result not from inborn traits such as skin color, but from the capitalist system. For Communists, then, the approach to what they called the "Negro question" was never about whether humans are genetically superior or inferior, but how the "haves" used racial bigotry to justify their greed and oppressive methods. It followed that if racism was a myth, Jim Crow had to be rooted out. It also followed, in Moscow's view, that African Americans' genuine grievances could be used to vilify the leading capitalist nation in world opinion. As early as 1920, Lenin called upon the comrades to ignite a revolution among "the Negroes of America." Accordingly, the Comintern formed a Negro Department, which ordered the CPUSA to take up "Negro work."[6]

The Party made a determined effort to recruit Black people from North America and the islands of the Caribbean. Promising young men and women were invited to visit—all expenses paid—study, and take jobs in the USSR. During the 1930s, when perhaps two thousand Black people were in the country, many had satisfying experiences. Agricultural researcher Homer Smith was amazed to find "the complete absence of any racial prejudice or discrimination. As a matter of fact, a Negro in Russia had no reason at all to think of color." Well, not quite. Everyday Russians were often fascinated by dark skin; children rubbed Smith's arms to see if the color came off. While vacationing on the Black Sea coast, CPUSA official Harry Haywood heard passersby remark, "How beautifully sunburnt he is." At get-togethers, blond, blue-eyed women were known to ditch their dates to dance with a *negritianskii tovarisch* (Negro comrade). Dozens of Russian women married Black men. A select group of Black men and women enrolled in the International Lenin School, an elite academy in Moscow. It offered regular academic subjects, but also required courses for revolutionaries. A course on conspiracy, for example, dealt with the techniques of civil warfare, weapons use, codes, sabotage, and "agitprop"—agitation and propaganda.[7]

In a more peaceful vein, the Comintern invited Black artists and intellectuals to visit the USSR, hoping they would praise the "workers' paradise" in their creations. Paul Robeson, a celebrated singer

Paul Robeson.
(1942)

and actor, was astounded by the absence of racial prejudice. The son of a runaway slave, Robeson "felt like a human being for the first time since I grew up. Here I am not a Negro but a human being. Before I came I could hardly believe that such a thing could be. . . . Here, for the first time in my life, I walk in full human dignity." The performer imagined Stalin's Russia as a corner of heaven brought to earth. "This is home to me," he said during a 1934 visit, the first of several. "I was not prepared for the happiness I see on every face in Moscow." Yet Robeson had only a partial view. He hobnobbed with the Soviet cultural elite: artists, writers, filmmakers, performers. He never mentioned visiting communal apartments or seeing street children and trainloads of slaves leaving Moscow for the Gulag. Instead, he defended Stalin's show trials as legitimate self-defense measures. "From what I have already seen of the workings of the Soviet Government," he told a *Daily Worker* reporter, "I can only say that anybody who lifts his hand against it ought to be shot! It is the government's duty to put down any opposition to this really free society with a firm hand. . . . It is obvious that there is no terror here, that all the masses of every race are contented and support their government." Over the years, he would deny, ignore, excuse, or shrug off all manner of Stalinist atrocities. Robeson died in 1976, at the age of seventy-seven. In May 1998, on the centennial of his birth, CPUSA leader Gus Hall announced, with pride, that Robeson had been a longtime member. By then, a Russian climbing club had named a peak, Mount Robeson, in his honor.[8]

Langston Hughes was one of the most important writers and thinkers of the Harlem Renaissance, that explosion of African American creativity in the Harlem neighborhood of New York City during the 1920s. Dubbed "the Poet Laureate of Black America," Hughes was enthralled by the USSR. In 1932, when his train stopped at passport control on the Finnish-Soviet border, he saw Black and white passengers fall to their knees and kiss the ground. During his travels, Hughes was so moved by his reception that he wrote a poem cycle glorifying the Bolshevik Revolution. "Good Morning Revolution" began:

Good-morning, Revolution:
You're the very best friend
*   I ever had.*
We gonna pal around together from
*   now on. . . .*
Let's go, Revolution!

Lenin became Hughes's hero, his tomb in Red Square a shrine, as we learn from "Ballads of Lenin":

Comrade Lenin of Russia,
Alive in a marble tomb,
Move over, Comrade Lenin,
And make me room. . . .
Comrade Lenin of Russia
Speaks from the marble tomb:
On guard with the workers forever—
The world is our room!

Though Hughes never joined the Party, he hoped to see an American replica of the USSR. His "One More 'S' in the U.S.A." appeared in the *Daily Worker*:

Put one more s in the U.S.A.
To make it Soviet.
One more s in the U.S.A.
Oh, we'll live to see it yet.
When the land belongs to the farmers
And the factories to the working men—
The U.S.A. when we take control
Will be the U.S.S.A. then.[9]

Yet it was not all sweetness and light. Despite official policy, more than a few Black people encountered racial prejudice as foul as anything they'd ever experienced.

Part of the problem was language. Students found certain entries in Russian-English dictionaries deeply offensive. For example, among the English variants given for the Russian word *negr* (Negro) were "nigger" and "darky"; the word "pickaninny," a vile slur in America, was the accepted term for a Black child. Students also resented that authors of Russian textbooks portrayed Black people "as talk[ing] with their hands and bodies." When walking down the street, Russians might jeer at those with dark skin and "ask them to say a few words in 'Negro.'" One African student, a merchant seaman who'd seen the world, was appalled. "I've come up against greater [racism] here," he wrote, "than in capitalist countries. . . . No one spat on me there the way they . . . [do] here in Moscow." In a railway station, he was startled when a man came up to him and growled, "What's this? A monkey?" While riding a streetcar, Robert Robinson, a toolmaker employed in a tractor plant, struggled to keep his composure when a woman fell to her knees before him, crossed herself, and exclaimed: "My God, there's a devil there." Despite the fine talk about brotherhood, Robinson noted, "the Soviets tried to use me for their propaganda. They tried to get me to denounce capitalism on broadcasts to the West, but I refused."[10]

Back in the States, neither major political party defended the rights of African Americans. The business-friendly Republicans, heirs to Abraham Lincoln's anti-slavery legacy, ignored Black concerns. The Democrats were of two minds. By and large, Northern Democrats paid lip service to grievances of the Black community, but did little to remedy them. Southern Democrats were the party of Jim Crow. Mississippi senator Theodore Bilbo was notorious. A rabid racist, Bilbo titled a book he'd written *Take Your Choice: Separation or Mongrelization,* a coarse term for "breeding" "superior" with "inferior" humans. The senator was especially resentful of Langston Hughes, who'd urged that schoolbooks be rewritten to stress that skin color had nothing to do with a person's ability or character. If that were done, Bilbo bristled, "the road would then be clear for the immediate and speedy mongrelization of both the white and the Negro races."[11]

The CPUSA was the only political party to actively oppose Jim Crow. For many rank-and-filers, this was a matter of personal morality, a felt duty to one's fellow man. Racism, to them, was simply wrong, and they needed no directives from Moscow or New York to tell them so. Thus, if the electricity was turned off for failure to pay the bill, a Communist might take it upon himself to turn it back on with a jumper cable. If a family was evicted from their apartment, comrades might ask the landlord, politely, to let them go back. If he refused, a penny postcard might land in his mailbox, saying: "The workers are watching you." Translation: Do the right thing, or else. In Harlem and on Chicago's South Side, Party members organized eviction protests, rent strikes, and sit-ins.[12]

Party higher-ups had a broader agenda. In 1928, the Comintern adopted a plan to dismantle the United States. On the basis of census maps, a select committee ruled that African Americans were a majority in the "Black Belt," roughly 150 counties stretching from Virginia to Louisiana. Black people in these counties were defined by the Comintern as an "oppressed nation," and therefore entitled to "national self-determination"—the right to have their own country and choose its form of government. The idea was for the CPUSA to agitate among Black people living in the South, turning them into "the greatest and most effective forces for the revolutionary overturn of the United States." When the time came, rebels would forcibly detach the Black Belt from the United States, setting up a Black republic. According to

POPULATION PER SQUARE MILE, BY COUNTIES: 1920.

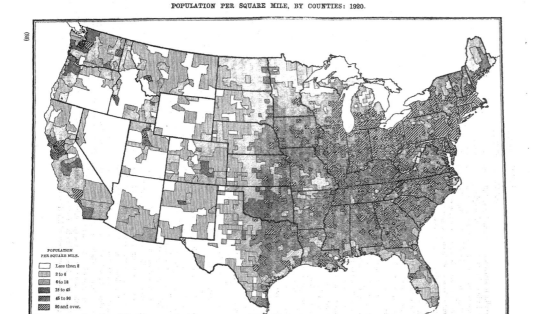

The Comintern used official United States census maps, such as this one from 1920, to create plans to agitate in the South and eventually overthrow the U.S. government.

the League of Struggle for Negro Rights, a Communist front, the rebels, led by Party activists, would seize all land belonging to the big (white) landlords and destroy every vestige of Jim Crow. Then they would form a grand alliance of Black and white "toilers" in the cities of the industrial North, overthrow capitalism, and reunite the nation as a Soviet republic under the dictatorship of the proletariat.[13]

The policy makers misjudged African Americans. Though oppressed, they'd fought valiantly in every one of the nation's wars since the Revolution; it was a way of asserting their rights as Americans. The overwhelming majority had no wish to create a breakaway nation; they simply wanted the same rights of every American to social, legal, economic, and political equality. Besides, any attempt to form a separate nation was doomed to end in tragedy. Louis Rosser, an African American and a former Party member, understood this perfectly. "If the Negro would rebel in the South," he told a congressional committee, "the rest of the country would shoot them down like a bunch of dogs." Sadly, Rosser observed, that seemed a price the Communist leaders were willing to pay to disrupt America.[14]

Meanwhile, the CPUSA sought to ingratiate itself with Black Northerners. In 1930, it banned "white chauvinism," jargon for attitudes and acts of prejudice against African Americans. Certain expressions became taboo, banned on pain of expulsion from the Party. Members were forbidden to use terms like "Negro girl" or "black as night," since both implied racial biases. To eliminate social barriers, white female Party members were asked to date Black men. According to ex-Communist

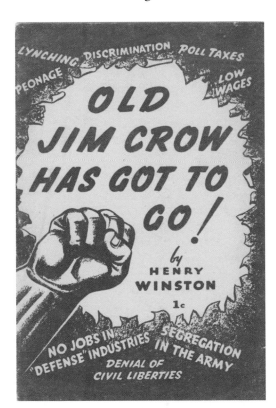

Pamphlet issued by the CPUSA advocating the end of segregation, discrimination, and lynching. (1941)

Sylvia Crouch, "White girls were instructed to have close relations with Negro boys." Party officials ordered white male members to take dancing lessons to make them feel more comfortable with Black women. To set an example, the Party staged show trials for the crime of white chauvinism. In Detroit, a man was convicted of forbidding his daughter to date an African American. Before going to trial, another man pleaded guilty to avoid expulsion. The CPUSA, he explained, meant everything to him; it was his whole life: "I would prefer to have my body riddled with bullets than to be expelled from the Communist Party."[15]

The most sensational white-chauvinism trial involved August Yokinen, a recent immigrant from Finland. Yokinen worked as a caretaker at the Finnish Workers' Club, a Communist front. Located on West 126th Street in Harlem, the club had meeting rooms, a steam bath, and a poolroom and held weekly dances in the gym. In January 1931, three Black men dropped in during a dance. The moment they appeared, the band stopped playing and couples hastily left the dance floor. Several Finnish men made it clear that they were not welcome, and they left rather than make a scene. Harlem was outraged. When word

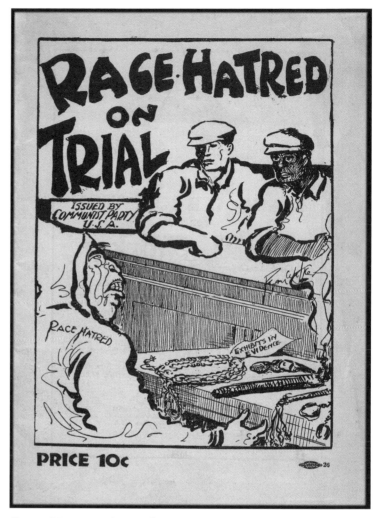

Cover of *Race Hatred on Trial,* a Communist propaganda pamphlet featuring August Yokinen's trial. (1931)

of the incident reached Party headquarters downtown, officials were sent to investigate. Yes, Yokinen admitted, he'd done nothing to make the visitors feel welcome; in fact, he resented their presence and was appalled at the idea of sitting naked in a steam bath with sweaty Black men!

A *Daily Worker* headline, "Close Ranks Against Chauvinist Influences," spelled trouble for Yokinen. On Sunday afternoon, March 1, more than two thousand Black and white "toilers," including women with babies in their arms, packed into the New Harlem Casino at 116th Street and Lenox Avenue, a main thoroughfare. A huge wall banner read "Race Inferiority Is a White Ruling Class Lie! Smash the Jim Crow Laws and Practices!" The "Workers' Court" did not try Yokinen for anything he'd done, but for "failing to jump at the throats of those who would eject the Negro comrades."

The mixed-race jury found Yokinen guilty and recommended his expulsion from the Party. For him, as for others tried for similar offenses, this was the worst possible verdict. However, the jury asked for mercy. If Yokinen apologized and mended his ways, the judge ruled, he could rejoin after six months. The trial ended with the audience giving a hearty rendition of "The Internationale," clenched fists raised in the Party salute. Reports of the trial in the mainstream and African American press showed readers that Communists would not tolerate Jim Crow. What's more, the duty of every Communist was to "jump at the throat of any person who . . . persecutes a Negro."[16]

But did they mean it? The test came soon enough. Just three weeks after the Yokinen trial, one of twentieth-century America's most dramatic battles for racial justice began in Alabama.

THE SCOTTSBORO BOYS

It was called "hoboing." Unlike a tramp, who works only when driven by an empty belly, a hobo is an unemployed person who travels seeking work. In Depression-era America, thousands left their impoverished families to fend for themselves, hitchhiking or hiding in railroad boxcars. Going wherever the train took them, they got off when it stopped at a likely place, then sought odd jobs to earn enough to keep them going a while longer. Government estimates had two hundred thousand people under the age of twenty-one riding the rails in the early 1930s. They all led rough, dangerous lives.[17]

On March 25, 1931, two groups of Black and white youths hopped aboard a freight train heading south from Tennessee through Alabama. Racial taunts led to a fight that ended with the Black teens throwing the white youths off the slow-moving train. The seven whites, bruised and bloody, stumbled along the tracks until they came to the village of Stevenson,

Many people resorted to hitchhiking or traveling illegally in railroad boxcars during the Depression era. This was known as hoboing. (Date unknown)

where they told their story to the station-master. Irate, he phoned Painted Rock, the next station down the line. The Painted Rock sheriff formed a posse, which arrived in time to signal the engineer of the approaching train to stop. As it screeched to a halt, gun-toting deputies climbed aboard. They soon found nine Black youths in the boxcars. The lawmen roped them together, hustled them onto a flatbed truck, and took them to jail in Scottsboro, the county seat of Jackson County. The youngsters were Olen Montgomery, seventeen; Clarence Norris, nineteen; Haywood Patterson, eighteen; Ozie Powell, sixteen; Willie Roberson, nineteen; Charlie Weems, nineteen;

Eugene Williams, thirteen; Roy Wright, thirteen, and his brother Andy, nineteen. All products of an educational system that shortchanged African Americans, most were unable to sign their names. Within days, the nation would know them as "the Scottsboro Boys."

Ordinarily, they would have spent a few days behind bars for illegally riding a freight train. But it soon became clear that this was no ordinary case. As the youths were being rounded up, deputies found two white women in a boxcar. Victoria Price, twenty-one, and Ruby Bates, seventeen, wore men's caps and overalls and spat snuff juice "with wonderful aim." Both were victims of their time and station in life. Hailing from Huntsville, Alabama, they lived with their single mothers in shacks on muddy, garbage-strewn streets. Like their mothers, they worked in the cotton mills when there was work, for wages barely enough to keep body and soul together. Journalist Mary Heaton Vorse described their situation. "What," she asked, "did Huntsville or Alabama or the United States offer a girl for virtue and probity and industry? A mean shack, many children for whom there would not be enough food or clothing or the smaller decencies of life, for whom at best there would be long hours in the mill—and, as now, not even certainty of work." For women like these, hoboing and prostitution offered temporary relief from a brutal existence. But they, too, had broken the law by riding the freight train. So, when questioned, they changed the subject. They said they'd been gang-raped by "them colored boys" bound for the Scottsboro jail. That changed everything.[18]

A town of two thousand inhabitants, Scottsboro lay amid rolling hills and well-tended farms. Townspeople did not rush about like city folks, and they welcomed strangers with traditional Southern hospitality. But whenever the word "rape" was heard, it set white hearts pounding and minds reeling. On the day of the arrests, rumors shot through the community like bolts of lightning. Those "horrible black brutes," townspeople said, had chewed off one of the women's breasts!

Hollace Ransdall, an investigator for the American Civil Liberties Union, arrived within days of the arrests. Her report is a brilliant overview of the mood and mind-set of a "typical" Southern town during the Jim Crow era:

It is hard to conceive that anything but kindly feelings and gentle manners toward all mankind can stir the hearts of the citizens of Scottsboro. It came as a shock, therefore, to see those pleasant faces stiffen, those laughing mouths grow narrow and sinister, those soft eyes become cold and hard. . . . Suddenly those kindly-looking mouths were saying the most frightful things. To see people who ordinarily would be gentle and compassionate at the thought of a child—a white one—in the least trouble, who would wince at the sight of a suffering dog—to see those men and women transformed by blind, unreasoning antipathy so that their lips parted and their eyes glowed with lust for the blood of black children, was a sight to make one untouched by the spell of violent prejudice shrink. . . . They said that all Negroes were brutes and had to be held down by stern repressive measures or the number of rapes on white women would be larger than it is. . . . They could not conceive that two white girls riding with a crowd of Negroes could possibly have escaped raping. A Negro will always, in their opinion, rape a white woman if he gets the chance.

Therefore, there is no question that they raped them. . . . The thing that stands out above everything else in their mind is that the black race must be kept down; as they put it, "The Nigger must be kept in his place." Repression, terror, and torture are the means that will do it.[19]

The Jackson County grand jury charged the Scottsboro Boys with "forcefully ravaging and debasing Victoria Price and Ruby Bates," rape being a capital offense in the state of Alabama. This was Jim Crow law; the death penalty was never imposed on white men who raped Black women. The first trial began on April 6, just twelve days after the arrests. The atmosphere was tense, as before a lynching. A crowd of locals and farmers numbering in the thousands, many with pistols in their waistbands, gathered outside the courthouse. To keep order, a detachment of 120 Alabama National Guardsmen protected the building with rifles and machine guns.[20]

The outcome was a foregone conclusion; everyone expected the trial to end with a lynching—a *legal lynching,* murder under the guise of capital punishment. The accused knew this from the moment they set foot in the courtroom. "The courtroom," noted Haywood Patterson, "was one big smiling white face." Judge Alfred E. Hawkins had already made up his mind, declaring a jury trial a waste of time and money. Nor were the court-appointed white defense lawyers at the top of their game. Sixty-nine-year-old Milo C. Moody hadn't tried a case in years; besides, his memory was failing, a sign of advancing senility. So Stephen R. Roddy led the defense. A real estate attorney, Roddy knew little about criminal law and too much about whiskey. When "stewed," a court officer recalled, "he could scarcely walk straight." Worse, at no time before the trial did he interview his clients. He first spoke to them in the courtroom, only minutes before the judge entered.[21]

To save time, the authorities decided to try the youths in groups of three and four, rather than individually. Victoria Price and Ruby Bates were the prosecution's main witnesses. Both testified that the accused raped them repeatedly and brutally. However, two doctors had examined them as soon as they'd arrived in Scottsboro. Under questioning, both testified that neither woman had shown signs of rough treatment—blood, bruises, lacerations—or the mental trauma usual in rape victims.

Their findings suggested that the women were lying. Nevertheless, the jurors ignored the doctors' testimony. Like Judge Hawkins, they'd made up their minds before hearing any evidence. After two hours of deliberation, the verdict on the first group came down: guilty as charged. Judge Hawkins's sentence: death by electrocution. Only Roy Wright was spared, because he testified that he saw the other defendants rape the women; he later admitted that he'd done so after being threatened and beaten by the police. When the jury failed to agree on Wright's punishment, the judge sentenced him to life in prison. Moments after the jury announced its verdict, the courtroom and the crowds outside erupted with cheers. The other trials ended with convictions three days later, on April 9. There, too, the sentences were death.[22]

RED LEGAL EAGLES

The sentence, so cruel and unjust, struck sparks of anger and resistance. Langston Hughes spoke for the Black community in "Scottsboro Limited," a poem published in October 1931. The first two verses throb with indignation:

> *That Justice is a blind goddess*
> *Is a thing to which we black are wise.*

Cover of *Scottsboro Limited* by Langston Hughes. (1932)

> *Her bandage hides two festering sores*
> *That once perhaps were eyes.*

> *Scottsboro's just a little place:*
> *No shame is writ across its face—*
> *Its court too weak to stand against a*
> *   mob,*
> *Its people's heart, too small to hold a*
> *   sob.*[23]

Yet the Alabama authorities were wrong to think they could get away with a legal lynching. Back in New York, CPUSA leaders sympathized with the boys' plight, but also saw it as an opportunity. By handling the case in a "politically correct" fashion, as Lenin defined the term, they thought they might achieve several goals. A vigorous defense would enable the Party to set up front groups, attracting civil rights–minded whites and their dollars. Equally important, the Party stood to reap a propaganda bonanza, advertising its dedication to racial justice while shaming America in the eyes of the world. Finally, it aimed to discredit mainline Black civil rights groups, clearing the way for deeper inroads into African American communities.

The International Labor Defense (ILD), the Party's legal arm, was composed of scores of lawyers scattered across the nation. The organization's aims were at once political and legal. "The task of the ILD," said William L. Patterson, an African American who served as the CPUSA's national secretary in the 1930s, "is to destroy the illusions of a democracy and justice [in the United States]." To that end, the ILD took up worthy causes desperately in need of a champion. It provided legal aid and bail for those unable to afford either. It exposed harsh conditions at a time when physical abuse was considered routine and

acceptable in the nation's jails and prisons. Inmates' families received small gifts of cash, clothing, and food. Every June, the Prisoners Relief Department held its Summer Milk Fund Drive for inmates' children.[24]

ILD publications described how to use the American legal system against itself. These always started from the premise that nothing about the police and courts was legitimate, but merely a device to ensnare innocent workers and deprive them of their rights. "It is absolutely essential," said a five-cent pamphlet titled *Under Arrest! Workers' Self-Defense in the Courts*, "to remember that the policeman . . . arresting you is a servant of the boss class. He is your enemy." The accused must recognize that the legal system existed to enforce "boss law, boss justice, boss ideas of right and wrong." Thus, for the ILD, a courtroom was as much a working-class battleground as a picket line. When arrested, the accused must say nothing, admit nothing, sign nothing, and, above all, never reveal a comrade's name. During trial, one must take the offensive, "make capitalism the defendant, and yourself the prosecutor, in the name of millions of toilers." As for ILD lawyers, their chief aim in court was to attack any aspect of capitalism they could,

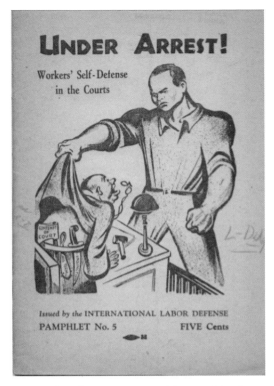

Cover of *Under Arrest!*, a pamphlet issued by the International Labor Defense. (1933)

but without using Communist jargon, a sure turnoff for jurors.[25]

The ILD set out to save the Scottsboro Boys. Its lawyers' first move was to win a stay of execution, pending the outcome of an appeal to the United States Supreme Court. After hearing the evidence, in 1932, the justices overturned the convictions because the boys' court-appointed lawyers had not properly represented them in a death-penalty case. They would have to stand trial again. With the stakes so high, the ILD decided it needed a legal star to head the defense team. It chose one of the nation's leading criminal defense attorneys. No Communist, Samuel S. Leibowitz was a staunch civil libertarian. When a Black Party member convinced him of the boys' innocence, the New Yorker agreed to serve without fee. Unlike the ILD, however, Leibowitz refused to use the case to score political points. For him, saving the Scottsboro Boys was a matter of justice, pure and simple.

The second round of trials began in March 1933, in Decatur, Alabama, fifty miles west of Scottsboro. Decatur was a Ku Klux Klan stronghold; as a reminder of the Civil War, a statue of a Confederate soldier stood in the square facing the courthouse, rifle in hand. Racism was so ingrained in the Decatur community that a physician, otherwise a kindly, decent person, was at a loss to understand its dreadful hold on him. He could only say: "It's just in my blood. I can't explain it. That's the way it is."[26]

Sam Leibowitz took the offensive the moment the trial of Haywood Patterson began. Noting the all-white jury, he declared that a jury without Black members hearing a case involving Black defendants was inherently biased. "We don't consider

Lawyer Samuel Leibowitz surrounded by the Scottsboro Boys and their jailers. (1932)

niggers fit for jury service," a court officer exploded. "No nice, respectable, decent nigger would want to be on a jury," noted a Decatur shopkeeper, with all the assurance of an ignoramus. Others used more menacing language. Leibowitz and several members of his team were Jewish. Their presence touched a nerve of anti-Semitism—Jew-hatred—present throughout American society at this time. Outraged townspeople cursed all ILD lawyers as "Russian Jews," "Jews from New York," and "nigger lovers who ought to be hung." Clearly, Decatur was a dangerous place for Yankee lawyers. When leaving the courthouse one afternoon, Leibowitz's co-counsel, Joseph Brodsky, heard a muttered threat: "Get that Jew lawyer from

New York." Hurriedly, he and a friend sped off in their car, a battered vehicle that had seen better days. As they bounced along dusty back roads, Brodsky glanced in the rearview mirror. Stunned, he saw a row of cars following them. Those cars, it turned out, were full of armed Black men—"a security escort to see us safely on our way!"[27]

James Horton, the presiding judge, denied Leibowitz's motion to integrate the jury; such a thing was simply not done in Alabama. Nevertheless, the attorney had an ace up his sleeve: a surprise witness destined to become the heroine of this squalid affair. Ruby Bates had a troubled conscience. After the 1931 trials, she vanished. Nobody in the South knew what had become of her. Actually, she'd hitchhiked to New York with a girlfriend, where she found work with "a Jewish lady." One day, she heard about the Reverend Harry Emerson Fosdick. Ruby visited the prominent minister and told him that there had been no rape and she didn't want innocents killed on account of her lies. Fosdick urged her to return to Alabama and tell the truth, whatever the cost. "Sure, I know I took a chance of going to prison for perjury for lying the first time. But, Mister, I feel better right here," Ruby told a reporter, pointing to her heart. Black people, she continued, "are human. They get treated worse than us poor whites. Yes, sir. I finally saw what I had done did, so I told the whole truth."[28]

When Ruby took the witness stand, she was not wearing overalls. She wore a gray suit, a gray hat, high heels, and silk stockings and carried a purse. Under Leibowitz's questioning, Ruby admitted that she and Victoria Price had lied. They'd cooked up the rape story because they feared arrest for vagrancy and crossing state lines for the purpose of prostitution. Under cross-examination by Wade Wright, a prosecutor, Ruby admitted that her clothes had been paid for by the ILD. At that, Wright had a meltdown. Turning to the jury, he roared: "Show them, show them that Alabama justice cannot be bought and sold with Jew money from New York." The audience responded with amens and yeses. Leibowitz leaped to his feet, demanding a mistrial. Judge Horton refused. And since the jurors had already made up their minds, no evidence, however true, could sway them. After just five minutes, they found Patterson guilty and recommended the death penalty.[29]

Leibowitz was stunned by the verdict, comparing it to "the act of spitting on the tomb of Abraham Lincoln." Upon returning to New York, he vowed to defend his clients "until hell freezes over." At rallies, he told enthusiastic audiences that he'd fight until Alabama finally gave up. "It'll be a merry-go-round," he said, "and if some Ku Kluxer doesn't put a bullet through my head, I'll go right on until they let the passengers off." Leibowitz's determination won people's hearts. "I love him more than life itself," said Haywood Patterson.[30]

Despite the jury's verdict, Ruby Bates's testimony troubled Judge Horton. An honorable man, he set aside the conviction, because Victoria Price now seemed so unreliable. In a third set of trials, in 1934, the Scottsboro Boys were again found guilty and sentenced to death.

CPUSA vs. NAACP

Meanwhile, the CPUSA hoped to use the Scottsboro case to boost its influence. But for that to happen, it had to discredit the National Association for the Advancement of Colored People (NAACP), viewed as its chief rival for influence in Black communities across the nation. Founded in 1909, the NAACP had fought many court battles to defend or secure civil rights for Black people. Long before the CPUSA latched onto the lynching issue, it struggled to raise the nation's awareness of this outrage.

Upon learning of a lynching, the NAACP issued press releases demanding that Congress pass a national anti-lynching law and flew a flag from a window of its New York headquarters. The message: "A Man Was Lynched Yesterday."

Made up of educated, middle-class Black and white people, the NAACP was hesitant at first about coming to the Scottsboro Boys' defense. Its leaders felt they might be guilty after all, so getting involved would damage the organization's credibility. Instead, they preferred to rely on "influential and just-minded whites" to

Flag hanging from the NAACP New York headquarters, with the message "A man was lynched yesterday." The NAACP would fly this upon learning of a lynching, along with demanding anti-lynching laws. (c. 1938)

do right by the accused rapists in Alabama. W. E. B. DuBois, the eminent Black historian and a founder of the NAACP, asked African Americans to have faith in the "fairness and justice" of Southern courts, trusting in the goodwill of "intelligent whites." However, after the first round of trials, the NAACP reversed course. "The public interest," said Walter White, a top executive, "is so deep that we cannot afford not to be in the case." That was exactly what Communists did not want.[31]

To discredit the NAACP, ILD propaganda attacked it as capitalists' "Negro hirelings and professional bootlickers." NAACP membership, it charged, consisted of "Negro misleaders," "agents of the ruling class in the ranks of the Afro-American people," "tools of the capitalists," and "Judases who would sell their brothers' flesh for thirty pieces of silver." *Labor Defender*, the ILD's monthly magazine, ran articles branding the civil rights group as race traitors. One notably vicious piece by Harry Haywood was titled "NAACP—Assistant Hangman." The author declared that the NAACP aimed to "defend the lynchers, and their system, and not the intended victims of the lynching." Elsewhere, Haywood denounced "Negro reformist lackeys" and "their cringing servility to the white ruling class." CPUSA activists, specially trained for their role, went so far as to disrupt NAACP meetings. They would scatter through the audience and, at their leader's signal, shout in unison for the right to speak. When allowed to speak, they'd launch into an anti-capitalist, anti-NAACP tirade. If denied the microphone, they yelled, cursed, pushed, and shoved to create chaos. The Communist press ridiculed the Black churches as well, particularly their "jackass Uncle Tom preachers." Finally, ILD lawyers approached the Scottsboro Boys' parents with offers of financial aid and promises of mass actions on their behalf. Early in 1932, the NAACP withdrew from the case.[32]

MASS ACTIONS

Since the CPUSA had no faith in the American judicial system, it backed ILD efforts by mass actions. Some African Americans, however, saw this as a cynical ploy to advance the Party's political agenda. Journalist George S. Schuyler thought Communists wished "to make political capital out of the race problem." Even worse was the stunning admission a Party official made to him: "We don't give a damn about the Scottsboro Boys. If they burn, it doesn't make any difference. We are only interested in one thing, how we can use the Scottsboro case to bring the Communist movement to the people and win them over to Communism."[33]

CPUSA strategists, writers, and speakers appealed to the widest audiences. In the North, organizers created fronts with names like the Scottsboro Defense Committee and Justice for the Scottsboro Boys. Party presses churned out pamphlets, posters, and leaflets denouncing the trials as part of a capitalist plot to "enslave" white workers. During demonstrations, marchers carried placards calling for working-class solidarity: "Negro and White, Unite & Fight." Speakers at rallies thundered: "So long as the Negro is used by the boss class as the lowest sort of beast of burden—to work for the lowest sort of wage—that's how long the wages of white workers will stay down. White and black toilers must fight together—shoulder to shoulder—without the color line."[34]

The Party sent organizers into Dixie. Besides drumming up support for the Scottsboro Boys, they helped unionize hundreds of thousands of sharecroppers, mostly Black families living in near bondage. A landowner would supply a poor family with a few acres of land, a shack (no toilet or running water), seeds, and other necessities, including food and cash advances, their cost deducted from the cropper's portion when the harvest was sold. More often than not, the family wound up owing money, forcing it to keep working for the landlord to discharge the debt, a goal rarely achieved.

Efforts at unionization triggered landlord violence. Several Party organizers were murdered, their killers miraculously leaving no clue for lawmen to follow. Some organizers simply vanished, literally swallowed by the earth. In the summer of 1931, sharecroppers met in a Camp Hill, Alabama, church to discuss the Scottsboro Boys as well as union affairs. When the local sheriff learned of the meeting, his deputies ended it with shotgun blasts, killing several men. Other participants were arrested, and some lynched. The Ku Klux Klan may have been behind this reign of terror, but we cannot be sure about its role. What is certain is that the KKK tacked up handbills across Alabama: "Negroes Beware. Do Not Attend Communist Meetings. The Ku Klux Klan Is Watching You." Brave souls posted their own handbills: "KKK! The Workers Are Watching You!"[35]

ILD efforts to save the Scottsboro Boys became the talk of the nation. In the spring of 1933, it planned the first big march for African American rights ever held in Washington. On May 8, five thousand people, both Black and white, but overwhelmingly Black, streamed into the capital by train, bus, and automobile. Their slogans—"Equal Rights for Negroes" and "The Scottsboro Boys Must Not Die"— were aimed at defeating Jim Crow in education, jobs, and voting and at making lynching a federal crime. The marchers dressed for the occasion, men in suits, ties, and hats, women in neat dresses and hats. They wore their Sunday best to signify self-respect, but also to show they were serious people. Ruby Bates marched with the lead group. By then, she'd joined the ILD and was a member in good standing. A crowd-pleaser at rallies, Ruby combined Communist themes with personal apologies. "I was excited and frightened by the ruling class of white people of Scottsboro and other towns," she'd explain, adding that the ruling class would have had her lynched had she not told the rape story.[36]

The marchers' organizing committee asked to meet with President Roosevelt, but he refused. And when the White House was flooded with mail urging him to act

Protesters in front of the White House demanding the freedom of the Scottsboro Boys. (1933)

on behalf of the Scottsboro Boys, he kept silent. Among those letters was one from a teenager: "Pres. Roosevelt . . . can you for God's sake save those poor Scottsboro colored boys from death. Why should they die? Help us please for Christ's sake. I am a Southern colored girl in New York." No reply came from the White House. Ever the cautious politician, FDR claimed he needed Southern support in Congress to pass vital New Deal legislation, so dared not speak out on such a divisive matter. Though privately opposed to lynching, FDR would not endorse a federal law against what he termed a form of "collective murder." Nor did he ever comment on the Scottsboro case for the record, a stunning lack of moral leadership.[37]

The ILD enlisted the Scottsboro Boys' mothers in their defense. To publicize the case, and also to grab headlines, it featured the women at rallies and meetings of front groups across the country. Shy at first, the mothers gained confidence with each event. Like her companions, Janie Patterson bridled at the notion that Communists were using her son Haywood for their own ends. "I haven't got no schooling, but I have five senses and I know that Negroes can't win by themselves," she'd say. "I don't care whether they are Reds, Greens or Blues. They are the only ones who put up a fight to save these boys and I am with them to the end."[38]

African American audiences could express the same idea in song. A favorite included these lines:

Close your fists and raise them high,
Labor defense is our battle cry.

"The Scottsboro Song" changed a traditional gospel song, "Give Me That Old-Time Religion," into a fight song about the verdict:

It's good for the big fat bosses,
For workers double-crossers,
For low-down slaves and hosses,
But it ain't good enough for me.[39]

As the ILD intensified its campaign at home, foreign Communists, directed by the Comintern, joined the struggle. The Scottsboro case was widely covered in the world press, sparking resentment by ordinary non-political people. To show their outrage, crowds demonstrated outside American embassies and consulates. However, when Communists stepped in, they subtly shifted the focus. Rather than attack Jim Crow, the real culprit, they used the boys' plight to rail against "capitalist America" in general. The NAACP's Walter White resented their use "all over the world of the Scottsboro case to vilify American democracy and to create distrust of it, especially among the dark-skinned peoples of Asia, Africa and Latin America."[40]

Europe, however, was the Communists' main focus. In 1932, ILD staffers took Ada Wright, the mother of Roy and Andy Wright, on a European tour. "Mother" Wright was only a generation away from slavery; her grandmother had been sold for $300 and whipped on the auction block. After the Civil War, her mother picked cotton from sunup to sundown for twenty-five cents a day. During visits to sixteen countries, Ada Wright told her life story and described her sons' ordeal in terms ordinary people could relate to. The tone of her voice and her manner conveyed the same message: This woman was honest and decent. Her words went to listeners' hearts. Whenever she addressed an audience, tears flowed and cries for justice filled the air.[41]

Moscow rolled out the red carpet for Mother Wright. The CPUSA had already laid the groundwork by demonizing its American rival. A group of "American Negro Cotton Specialists" working in

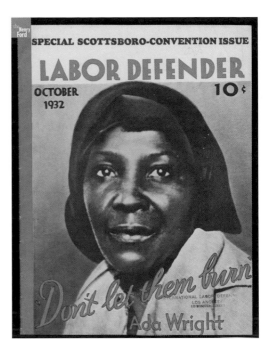

Ada Wright, mother of accused Roy and Andy Wright, on the cover of *Labor Defender.* (1932)

the USSR wrote: "We condemn the role played by the leaders of the NAACP in the Scottsboro case. The Negro reformists are the most dangerous element of the Negro masses." Joseph Stalin's government followed up by naming a collective farm Scottsboro. Dmitri Moor, Russia's leading propaganda artist, created a poster that read "Freedom to the Prisoners of Scottsboro!" and showed a hideous Uncle Sam holding an electric chair while soldiers corral Jim Crow's chained victims. Articles in *Pravda* (*Truth*), the official Soviet Communist Party newspaper, declared the youths staunch "revolutionary fighters." Demonstrations and parades, thousands strong, filled Red Square. Placards and banners read "Down with U.S. Imperialism!" and "The Soviet Union—Friend of the Oppressed Blacks."[42]

Ironically, Adolf Hitler's takeover of Germany on January 30, 1933, set the wheels of Alabama justice turning in the right direction. Once in power, the Nazi leader began rebuilding the German military, crippled by the treaty ending World War I. At the same time, he destroyed the German Communist Party, branding it a "Jewish conspiracy" based in Moscow. By 1935, he'd adopted an aggressive anti-Soviet foreign policy. In response to this looming threat, Stalin changed the Party line. To protect the USSR, the Comintern ordered member parties to form a popular front, alliances with liberal groups to press their governments to take pro-Soviet positions. Like it or not, they must bury their differences with those they'd been attacking as "capitalist lackeys." In the United States, the ILD and the NAACP had to join forces on behalf of the Scottsboro Boys.

They did, and though court battles continued, many Alabamians had by then grown weary of the case and the shame it brought to their state. Officials hinted that they would settle for something less than the death penalty after all. In later trials, prosecutors asked for life sentences instead of the electric chair. In 1937, Alabama released four of its prisoners—the two youngest and the two most sickly—while four others were eventually paroled. Haywood Patterson escaped from prison, killed a man in a barroom brawl, and died in a Michigan jail. By then, Ruby Bates had moved to Washington State, where she married. She returned to Alabama in the 1960s and died in 1976, at the age of sixty-three. Victoria Price married, but never escaped from poverty. She died in 1983, at the age of seventy-three, without apologizing for attempting to frame the Scottsboro Boys. Sam Leibowitz returned to New York, where he became a criminal court judge. A supporter of the death penalty, he thought it a deterrent to violent criminals. He died in 1978, at the age of eighty-four. In 2013, after eighty-two years, Alabama governor Robert Bentley granted pardons to Weems, Andy Wright, and Patterson, the only ones who had neither their convictions overturned or received a pardon.

No love was lost between the CPUSA and the NAACP. Like so many others,

NAACP leader Roy Wilkins never forgave the CPUSA for hijacking the Scottsboro case and its efforts to discredit the Black community's foremost civil rights organization. In 1949, when the Party asked for its cooperation in another case, Wilkins wrote: "We remember that in the Scottsboro case the NAACP was subjected to the most unprincipled vilification. We remember the campaign of slander in the *Daily Worker.* We remember the leaflets and the speeches and the whole unspeakable machinery that was turned loose upon all those who did not embrace the 'unity' policy as announced by the Communists. We want none of that unity today." Herbert Hill, the NAACP's director of labor relations, agreed. However fair-minded individual comrades might be, Hill noted, Party leaders always obeyed Moscow's commands. Therefore, the "American Communist Party's interest in the Negro can be neither genuine nor sincere. Quite the contrary. . . . Whenever the interests of Negroes come into conflict with the political interest of Russia, the Communists abandon Negroes like rats a sinking ship."[43]

No new revelations have changed Hill's judgment. Bottom line: The Party was cynical in the way it used the Scottsboro case to promote class warfare. We should also remember that important historical events are never one-sided; they arise from multiple motives and have ambiguous results. Here Sam Leibowitz deserves the final word. "I am no Communist," he said, "but had it not been for the International Labor Defense, these nine Negro boys would be in their coffins"—for a crime they did not commit. Justice can indeed have strange bedfellows.[44]

THE PARTY AND STALIN'S WAR

Marxist-Leninist ideology influenced Stalin, because his illusions arose from it. The most important one was the belief . . . that capitalists would never be able to cooperate with one another for very long. Their inherent greediness . . . would sooner or later prevail, leaving communists with the need only for patience as they awaited their adversaries' self-destruction.
—John Lewis Gaddis, *The Cold War: A New History* (2005)

THE ROAD TO WAR, AGAIN

Adolf Hitler had big plans. In his writings and speeches dating from the early 1920s, the Nazi Führer (leader) claimed that the German "master race" was destined to conquer the world, and that his Third Reich—Third German Empire—would last a thousand years. To achieve that goal, Hitler believed he had to seize land and natural resources to fuel his war machine. Rejecting Germany's strategy in World War I, he did not want to rely on essential supplies brought by ships across oceans patrolled by hostile navies. Everything he needed was available in virtually unlimited quantities in the USSR, a nation whose people he despised as "subhumans" destined for slavery and eventual extermination under Nazi rule.

To strike Russia, Hitler's forces would have to cross Poland, a natural corridor for armies moving from west to east. Invading Poland, however, would plunge Germany into a two-front war, the same problem that beset it during World War I. The USSR could not tolerate German forces in Poland, poised to strike whenever Hitler gave the order. Worse, Germany would have to fight not only the USSR, but Great Britain and France, which had defense treaties with Poland. The only thing to do, the Führer decided, was to get Stalin to allow him to have his way in Poland. With Poland conquered, Hitler could turn his armies against the Western Allies, defeat them, and then crush the USSR at his leisure. This should be easy, he reckoned, because Stalin had killed thousands of Red Army officers during the Great Terror on suspicion of being German and Japanese

spies and, most importantly, of being disloyal to him.

Stalin seemed like the last person to help the Nazis. The leader of world communism detested fascism as embodied in Hitler and the Italian dictator Benito Mussolini. Nevertheless, Stalin decided to help the Nazis for two reasons. The immediate reason was to gain Hitler's permission for the USSR to grab eastern Poland, thereby thickening its western border defenses. Stalin's second reason was more sinister. On August 19, 1939, he told his inner circle: "Comrades! It is in the interest of the USSR, the workers' homeland, that a war breaks out between the Reich and the capitalist Anglo-French bloc. Everything should be done so that it drags out as long as possible with the goal of weakening both sides." After they'd bled themselves white, Stalin planned to unleash the Red Army, the largest on earth, to overrun the whole of Western Europe.[1]

On August 23, German diplomats arrived in the Soviet capital. As they stepped from their plane, they saw the swastika flag fluttering over the Moscow airport's main terminal while a Red Army band struck up a Nazi marching tune. Hours later, in Stalin's Kremlin office, they agreed to the Hitler-Stalin Non-Aggression Pact. In it,

Diplomats signing the German-Soviet Boundary and Friendship Treaty as Stalin (second from right) smiles and Lenin's portrait hangs above. (1939)

each party pledged not to attack the other and to stay neutral if the other fought a third power. Stalin smiled as diplomats from each country signed the document while a portrait of Lenin looked on. Then he ordered champagne and toasted Hitler: "I know how much the German nation loves its Führer, and should therefore like to drink to his health." Later that evening, Stalin said something almost unimaginable for a Soviet leader: "And if in the coming period Germany should be forced to its knees, I would come to her aid with

a hundred Red [Army] divisions!" Hitler was elated. When the call from the German negotiators came from Moscow, he pounded the wall with his fists, shouting, "Now I have the world in my pocket!" Deliberately, cunningly, Stalin had given Hitler the go-ahead to start World War II. As time would tell, it was the worst decision Stalin ever made, one that would cost the lives of 27 million Soviet citizens.[2]

The Hitler-Stalin Pact brought an abrupt reversal of the Moscow line. Since the early 1920s, Communist propaganda had damned fascism as a tool of beastly capitalism. In the USSR, every newspaper and newsreel featured accounts of "Hitlerite" brutality. Cartoons depicted the Nazi leader as a crazed monster drooling bloody saliva. Schoolchildren played a Soviet version of cowboys and Indians, with the Soviet good guys battling evil fascists. Now Russians risked their lives if overheard saying a harsh word about fascism, Hitler, or Germany. Publications critical of Germany vanished from newsstands, and anti-German films from the silver screen. A Russian observer noted that "everything German was in vogue." Schools had lectures on German culture, and museums held exhibitions of German art, complete with flattering, larger-than-life statues of the Führer. Eager to show his goodwill, Stalin handed over to the Gestapo, Hitler's secret police, nearly a thousand Communist Germans and other Europeans who'd fled to the USSR. All vanished, never to be seen again.[3]

Rather than describe the Hitler-Stalin Pact as the gangsters' deal it was, the CPUSA leadership supported Moscow's every claim. In the days before Hitler invaded Poland, the CPUSA's general secretary, Earl Browder, praised the pact as "a wonderful contribution to peace." Thanks to Stalin, that sly genius, Hitler had agreed not to attack the USSR or to join any alliance aimed against it! When Hitler at-

tacked Poland on September 1, the Party cheered for the "heroic Poles." But when Britain and France declared war on Germany two days later, the Party press slimed Poland as a nest of fascist brutes and the Allies as vile imperialists bent on destroying their "Socialist Motherland." To make sure New York understood the new line, Browder received a directive from Moscow ordering the Party to drop all hostile references to fascism and to brand the war as imperialistic aggression. The directive came by way of a secret shortwave radio transmitter kept in Party headquarters. On September 17, as the Red Army stormed into eastern Poland, Party leaders shame-

Cover of the *Daily Worker* framing the signing of the German-Soviet treaty as an act of peace. (1939)

lessly echoed Stalin's lie. "It was not Germany who attacked France and England," declared William Z. Foster, following Moscow's directive, "but France and England who attacked Germany, assuming responsibility for the present war." Anyone who dared question this rubbish was shamed as a "capitalist stooge" and expelled from the Party.[4]

Hitler's forces waged *Blitzkrieg,* "lightning war," attacking, surrounding, and destroying Poland's poorly armed troops. By the time the Red Army struck, Poland's defenders were already defeated; it merely gave the country the death blow. Upon Poland's surrender on September 27, the partners held joint celebrations. Grinning officers shook hands, exchanged salutes, toasted each other's leader, and held victory parades. The Kremlin sent congratulations to Berlin: "The friendship of the German and Soviet Russian people is cemented in blood . . . and has every reason to be lasting." Germany took all of western Poland, while the USSR seized a large chunk of eastern Poland. By a secret agreement with Hitler, the Red Army marched into the small nations bordering the Baltic Sea: Estonia, Latvia, Lithuania. "The Soviet Union is now the strongest force for peace in the world" became the CPUSA's slogan

of the day. Party propaganda demanded a "people's peace"—that is, one that would secure Stalin's aggressions without involving the USSR in a world war.[5]

On Moscow's orders, Comintern member parties justified the rape of Poland as part of Stalin's grand humanitarian strategy. The Soviet invasion, the CPUSA insisted, saved millions of Christian Poles from Nazi rule and kept untold numbers of Polish Jews out of Hitler's clutches. Not only had the Soviets rescued Jews in their zone of occupation, they sheltered Jewish refugees fleeing Nazi persecution! A CPUSA pamphlet boasted, "Jews throughout the world rejoice at the fact that the overwhelming majority of the Jews of Europe now reside in the Soviet Union" and *"no longer know anti-Semitism, thanks to the Soviet Union."* Forged letters from grateful Polish Jews appeared in New York's Jewish Communist press. Jews in the "liberated" areas told of their joy and relief at the arrival of Soviet troops. One letter read: "Our brothers in the land of the Soviets, the sons of the greatest man in the world, Joseph Stalin, have brought us happiness and freedom." Another declared: "Long live comrade and friend, comrade and educator, Comrade Stalin," savior of the Jews. Any Jewish American who criticized Stalin's actions was accused of trying "to whip up an anti-Soviet lynch-spirit."[6]

It was not so simple. Many Jewish Americans were immigrants or children of immigrants who'd fled czarist oppression. Anti-Semitism was a fact of life in the old country. Under Czar Nicholas II, more than 140 anti-Semitic laws, covering more than a thousand pages of small print, were on the books. However, Lenin had always denounced Jew-hatred as a ruse to distract workers from their real enemies, the capitalists. *Pravda* declared: "To be against the Jews is to be for the Tsar!" So when the Bolsheviks took power, one of their first acts was to make anti-Semitic propaganda and violence a crime. At the same time, they opposed Judaism, as they did all religions, closing religious schools, synagogues, seminaries, and publishing houses.[7]

The CPUSA's claims to stand for social justice attracted Jews to the Party, chiefly those in New York's immigrant neighborhoods. Small wonder that Stalin's cozying up to Hitler came as a shock. When the Hitler-Stalin Pact was announced, some Jewish comrades explained it away, as per the Party line. Countless other Jews, Party members and ordinary folk, felt betrayed. For them, Hitler was the essence of evil; everything about him was *dreck*— crap, filth, muck. The *Forward,* the largest Yiddish-language newspaper, was appalled that "all of us who put our trust in Stalin were exposed naked in front of the world as a pack of idiots." In August 1939, hundreds of Jews tore up their Party membership cards in disgust. Irate men and women raided newsstands, tossing copies of the *Daily Worker* into the gutter, mocking passing Communists with shouts of *"Heil Hitler!"* Party members speaking on the street feared for their safety.[8]

When Poland fell, the Party's claims that Jews greeted the Red Army with "hearts filled with happiness" and "dancing and celebrating" were treated with the scorn they deserved. Like the Nazis, the Soviets began to "decapitate" Poland— that is, to murder anyone who might lead resistance to the occupier. In the fall and winter of 1939, they shot thousands of Polish army officers, landowners, Catholic priests, government officials, civic leaders, teachers, and journalists. The Soviets also deported 1.25 million Polish Catholics to the Gulag in foul cattle cars. As for Jews, the Germans ordered them confined in ghettos, the first step toward extermination. It is true that tens of thousands fled to Soviet-occupied territory. But Stalin, morbidly suspicious, ordered them treated as likely spies. The NKVD rounded up tens of thousands of Polish Jews and shipped them to labor camps in Siberia. For those left behind, conditions became so bad that crowds waited at border crossings for permission to return to German-occupied territory, even bribing guards to let them through. A German officer could scarcely believe his eyes. "Jews," he bawled, "where are you going? Don't you know that we will kill you?" Yet CPUSA boss Earl Browder said, to his everlasting shame, that Jews had nothing to gain from an Allied victory over Nazi racism.[9]

With his eastern border secure, Hitler moved the bulk of his forces westward, a replay of 1918, when Russia's leaving the war allowed the Germans to shift masses of troops to the Western Front. In the spring of 1940, they seized Norway and Denmark, overran the Low Countries—Holland, Belgium, and Luxembourg—and invaded France. The French and their British allies fought courageously, but they were no match for Hitler's battle-hardened army. As in Poland, fast-moving tank columns supported by swarms of dive-bombers burst through or slipped around the defenders' positions.

Nazi Germany had an ally who gave it critical aid without firing a shot. The French Communist Party (PCF, for its French initials) was slavishly obedient to Moscow. On Stalin's orders, it betrayed its compatriots. PCF members of the National Assembly, France's legislature, demanded that the government sue for peace on Hitler's terms. When officials banned its publications, the PCF printed its defeatist propaganda on German presses. Communist leaflets and speakers urged French fighting men to desert and defense workers to lay down their tools "for peace." The propaganda campaign succeeded, as Communist railwaymen refused to move troops and supplies to the front. When American journalist William L. Shirer crossed the war zone on his way from Berlin to Paris, both German and French officers told him what had happened. "Among large masses of troops," Shirer wrote, "Communist propaganda had won the day. And its message was 'Don't fight.'" And many didn't. When France capitulated in June, Stalin congratulated Hitler on his brilliant victory. As Nazi tanks rolled into Paris, fueled largely by Soviet-supplied gasoline, PCF members greeted them with raised fists, the Communist salute, and cries of "Comrade!" In its July 13 edition, *L'Humanité,* the PCF newspaper, had banner headlines urging "Franco-German Friendship," noting that "friendly conversations between Parisian workers and German soldiers increase by leaps and bounds." Indeed, PCF posters appeared in the Paris *métro* (subway) urging the French not to engage in "terrorist acts" against the Nazi occupiers. However, when some Communists struck back, they did so as individuals, and in open defiance of official PCF orders. There are also indications that PCF loyalists cooperated with the Gestapo in uncovering secret resistance groups. Only when Hitler invaded the Soviet Union in June 1941 did French Communists officially join in *La Résistance*.[10]

The Battle of France ended and the Battle of Britain began. The Luftwaffe (Germany's air force) bombed British cities, particularly London, the capital. As in World War I, German submarines sank British merchantmen, so many that it seemed the island nation might be starved into submission. Stalin showed himself a loyal partner, aiding Hitler in important ways. Advance Soviet weather reports gave the Luftwaffe precise information about conditions over British targets. The "friend of peace" allowed the German navy to build Basis Nord (Base North) on its Arctic coast to service and supply Nazi warships. The icebreaker *Stalin* cleared a path through the Bering Strait into the Pacific Ocean, allowing Hitler's raiders to attack British freighters. Soviet agents bought Asian rubber and sent it to Germany via the Trans-Siberian Railway. Each week, several hundred-car trains delivered thousands of tons of Soviet grain, oil, cotton, and other raw materials to Germany in exchange for machinery and samples of certain weapons. Benito Mussolini joked that Stalin was so generous "he's already become a secret fascist. He helps us and weakens the antifascist forces like no one else could." Hitler agreed: "A hell of a fellow! Stalin is indispensable," he chuckled.[11]

PEACE OFFENSIVE

President Roosevelt saw Britain as the last hope of democracy in Europe. If the island nation went down, he feared, the Nazis, allied to the USSR and Japan, would be free to gang up on the United States. With the danger of war growing, FDR urged the nation to prepare for the worst. To aid Britain, in September 1940 he gave the Royal Navy fifty aged World War I destroyers to protect supply convoys from German U-boats. To build up his nation's military, FDR convinced Congress to approve of "selective service," a euphemism for the draft. To equip the growing armies, the White House ordered a massive overhaul of American industry. Though America was still at peace, its factories began to convert to producing war materials. Government contracts pumped massive amounts of money into the economy, creating jobs and finally ending the Great Depression. In January 1941, at FDR's request, Congress approved the Lend-Lease Act, which established a program to send the British whatever they needed to stay in the fight. Stalin, however, had other ideas. To keep the British-German war going as fiercely as possible, Moscow ordered the CPUSA to oppose lend-lease, the draft, and rearmament. The Party, in turn, launched a propaganda blitz on the theme of "peace," code for halting American aid to Britain.

Party presses worked overtime, churning out propaganda based on the Moscow line. Earl Browder wrote *Socialism, War and America;* William Z. Foster penned *The War Crisis: Questions and Answers* and *Roosevelt Heads for War.* John Henry Williams's *A Negro Looks at War* argued that Black people had no stake in "the present imperialist war." Every dollar spent on defense, speakers barked, was a dollar stolen from America's needy. In a reverse of the World War I slogan, marchers chanted,

Cover of *The War Crisis: Questions and Answers* by William Z. Foster, which proclaimed that going to war favored American capitalists and was harmful to working-class interests. (1940)

"The Yanks are not coming!" as well as "Keep America out of the imperialist war," and "Support the peace policy of the Soviet Union." Stalin, that wise "champion of peace," was the Party's hero. "Long live

THE YANKS ARE NOT COMING

NEWSTAND
5th & BROADWAY

WAR

Published by
KEEP AMERICA OUT OF WAR COMMITTEE
District Council No. 2, Maritime Federation of the Pacific
Price 3c

Communist pamphlets, such as this one, discouraged citizens from supporting America's entry into World War II. (1940)

the Great Stalin!" crowds cried. "Long live our leader! Long life to the protector of the socialist fatherland! Down with Roosevelt's war program!"[12]

Famed CPUSA activist Elizabeth Gurley Flynn attacked defense preparations in the name of motherly love. Her pamphlet *I Didn't Raise My Boy to Be a Soldier— for Wall Street* tugged at the heartstrings. "Who wants to be a Gold Star Mother?"—the mother of a fallen soldier—Flynn asked.

Do you want it to be *your son*? Or your husband? American women, the time to say *No* is now. Before it is too late. Is there one among you who craves to be a "Gold Star Mother"? Can a gilded pin mend a broken heart? Who wants a medal for a dead son? . . . This war is to make the world safe for the handful of billionaire families that rule the capitalist countries. The capitalists everywhere hate the Soviet Union because that country and its institutions belong to the workers, the plain people. The best insurance to keep off the toboggan slide into war is an ultimatum to our government: *"Stay neutral, not a dollar for war."* Starve the war; feed America first! . . . Only by stopping the war today can we say the dead of yesterday did not die altogether in vain. We didn't raise our boys to be soldiers of Wall Street![13]

The Party subjected FDR to a level of abuse seldom used against a modern president. Its publications went overboard, branding him a "fascist dictator," a cruel, calculating blood brother to Hitler and Mussolini. At a Lenin memorial rally in New York's Madison Square Garden, Earl Browder tore into the man in the White House for adopting the "Hitlerian tactic" of gradually leading the nation into war on Britain's behalf. Official Party statements accused "warmonger" FDR of having "studied well the Hitlerian art" of propaganda and of being "a willing servant" of imperialism. The vilest charge, however, related to Jews' supposed debt of gratitude to Stalin for invading Poland. Whereas Stalin "saved" Jews, Browder charged, Roosevelt led "all the forces of anti-Semitism and reaction in the country." This was ridiculous. Those who knew the president swore he did not have an anti-Semitic bone in his body. When accused of being Jewish himself, FDR snapped, "I wish I was." In private, however, he said there were too many Jews in America, and these congregated in cities, which fostered anti-Semitism. In other words, Jew-hatred was partially the Jews' own fault![14]

Communist-led "peace" fronts began to sprout like mushrooms after the rain. There was the American Peace Mobilization, Hollywood Peace Forum, Peace Committee of the Medical Professions, Mother's Day Peace Council, Brooklyn Community Peace Council, and Massachusetts Peace Council, to name a few of the scores that opposed aid to beleaguered Britain. As often happened, many of their members were what the Party called "useful idiots," sincere folks who genuinely despised war and wanted to keep America out of this one. Others, however, obediently followed the Moscow line. A dazzling example was Theodore Dreiser, author of the acclaimed novel *An American Tragedy* and vice-chairman of the American Peace Mobilization. A dyed-in-the-wool Communist, Dreiser condemned every British man, woman, and child to Hitler's mercies. "The British people," he declared, "should be allowed to be engulfed by Hitler because they were a cruel people who hunted foxes. The wealthy class in England is splashing around in a stagnant, reeking pool of blood profits." Dreiser ignored the fact that Nazis hunted not foxes, but Jews and democrats to the death.[15]

As they had done in France, Communists set out to sabotage America's military buildup. Activists handed out leaflets at draft centers, urging men to resist the capitalists' war. Communist union officials would seize on a legitimate demand, such as higher overtime pay, and use it to

Cover of *Can the People Win Peace?*, written by the American Peace Mobilization, one of the Communist fronts seemingly advocating for peace but actually serving the Soviet Union's interests. (1940)

incite a strike. Even if management offered a compromise, union officials demanded more—anything to keep workers on the picket lines. The vast majority of strikers were patriotic Americans unaware that they were being manipulated at the behest of a foreign power. Nonetheless, the strikes did serious damage and indirectly cost lives.

For the first six months of 1941, roughly 2.5 million work hours were lost in key sectors of the defense industries.

Vultee Aircraft in Downey, California, had to close for a month. A strike crippled the Allis-Chalmers plant in Milwaukee, a prime manufacturer of machinery, stalling work on vessels desperately needed for British anti-submarine operations. The Die-Casters Union shut the Cleveland plant of the Aluminum Company of America, delaying production of castings for airplane parts. The most serious walkout involved eleven thousand workers at North American Aviation's plant in Inglewood, California. This strike tied up 20 percent of American warplane production and was so dangerous that on June 9, 1941, FDR ordered the army into action. Twenty-five hundred soldiers broke up the picket lines, reopened the plant, and protected anyone willing to work. The *Daily Worker* was outraged, declaring, "The use of troops against strikers is bringing a military dictatorship to our very doorsteps." William Z. Foster lambasted FDR for practicing the same "Hitlerite terrorism that Wall Street capitalists have in mind for the working class." In an article titled "Bayoneting Labor," the magazine *New Masses* (June 17, 1941) howled, "The President has declared war on labor. . . . The President moves swiftly toward fascism." Five days later, the world turned upside down.[16]

On June 22, Hitler's armies invaded the USSR. Stalin was stunned. When a Red Army general asked permission to return fire, Stalin replied: "Permission not granted. This is a German provocation. Do not open fire or the situation will escalate." Despite contrary evidence from Soviet military intelligence, the dictator had convinced himself that while Hitler truly wanted peace, rogue Nazi generals aimed to provoke a war. When the blow fell, Stalin wasted precious hours, refusing to allow Soviet forces to defend themselves. In the months following the invasion, the Nazi blitzkrieg rolled ahead, destroying entire Soviet armies and taking millions of prisoners, most of whom would be deliberately starved to death in hellish prison camps. Stalin held their lives cheaply; he declared soldiers who surrendered to be traitors and deprived their families of government benefits, in effect a death sentence for many. After the war, the dictator had nearly two million returned prisoners shipped to the Gulag as "traitors to the Socialist Motherland."[17]

"OUR GREAT SOVIET ALLY"

Hitler's "betrayal" stunned Communists and fellow travelers. Hollywood screenwriter and Broadway playwright Lillian Hellman, elegant in a tailored white suit, blurted out, "The Motherland has been attacked!" Magically, the "peace" fronts pulled up stakes or changed their names to patriotic ones; thus, the American Peace Mobilization became the American People's Mobilization. For weeks, picketers had marched around the White House with signs reading "Mothers' Crusade" and "I Didn't Raise My Boy to Die for Britain." When word of the invasion came, they quietly left. Folk singer Woody Guthrie, a Communist who wrote articles for the *Daily Worker,* had opposed every one of FDR's defense measures. By June 23, he'd changed his tune. Guthrie sang "Round and Round Hitler's Grave":

Folk singer Woody Guthrie posing with his fascist-killing guitar. (c. 1945)

I wish I had a rope to tie
Around old Hitler's neck.[18]

The CPUSA's new slogan was "All Out for the People's War Effort," because the "dirty imperialist war" had become "the People's War." Its propaganda transformed FDR from fascist tool to freedom fighter. It praised him for extending lend-lease aid, once cursed as a ploy to save the corrupt British Empire, to the USSR. What rank-and-file Party members did not know was that American seamen were forbidden to say that the cargo they risked their lives to deliver was unloaded by Gulag slaves, and some of the food they brought fattened guards in Siberian camps. Yet the massive aid was hardly enough to suit America's Soviet patriots. The CPUSA frantically called for a U.S. declaration of war against Germany. No longer was "draft" a dirty word; the comrades demanded that compulsory military training be made part of everyday life. All Americans, speakers cried, must join the "battle of production." To keep the supplies flowing, FDR was urged to ban strikes as unpatriotic. Communists, allegedly the workers' friends, denounced union leaders who threatened strikes as "agents of Hitler," "defeatist," and "pro-Nazi," declaring that they belonged in jail

or in front of firing squads. If necessary, Communists said, they would deal with strikers in their own way, implying the use of goon squads. Party boss Earl Browder crowed with pride in being called a strike-breaker. It would be the "greatest honor," he boasted during a coal miners' strike, "to be a breaker of this movement."[19]

The CPUSA was just as ready to sacrifice African American interests to Soviet needs. When the Hitler-Stalin Pact was still in effect and the U.S. military buildup was getting into full swing, the Party insisted that Black people had no stake in the "imperialist war" raging in Europe. Its speakers and publications urged Black men to evade the draft and "skip the next war." Party agitators called upon Black merchant seamen to jump ship in neutral ports rather than risk their lives bringing aid to Britain.[20]

By June 24, however, the Party had gone silent about Jim Crow. NAACP executive director Roy Wilkins had distrusted its motives since the Scottsboro case; its current stance confirmed his view. Wilkins recalled: "As soon as Russia was attacked by Germany, they dropped the Negro question and concentrated on support of the war in order to help the Soviet Union. During the war years [the Party] sounded very much

like the worst of the Negro-hating south-
erners." Wilkins was right; Communists
expected Black people to knuckle under to
white supremacy for the sake of the "higher"
objective of defending the USSR. The *Daily
Worker* did not mince words: "Hitler is the
main enemy," it said in an editorial. "The
foes of Negro rights in this country should
be considered as secondary." By this line of
reasoning, Ku Klux Klan terrorism was also
secondary, a minor irritation—nothing to
get riled up about![21]

Meanwhile, several African American
newspapers promoted the "Double V."
The capital letter *V* held special signifi-
cance at this time; Prime Minister Winston
Churchill flashed the sign with his fingers
to show that Britain could take whatever
Hitler dished out. For Black people, the
Double V, or Double Victory, campaign
meant victory over Jim Crow at home and
fascism abroad. Communists, however,
gave Double V supporters the same treatment as the NAACP during the Scottsboro
trials. Demanding civil rights in wartime,
they charged, was "endangering the unity
of the American people" and "sabotaging
the war effort." In this regard, A. Philip
Randolph, head of the all-Black Brotherhood of Sleeping Car Porters, came under
ferocious attack. When the civil rights hero

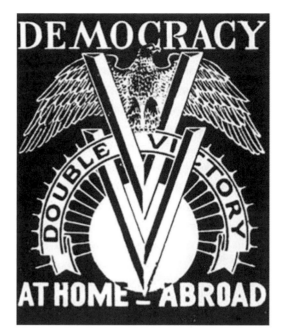

The Double V logo, used to symbolize victory at
home against Jim Crow and overseas against the
Nazis. (Date unknown)

announced support for Double V, the *Daily
Worker* smeared him as "a fascist helping
defeatism" and a traitor who "guaranteed
the triumph of fascism." That was absurd.
Worried about Hitler's growing aggressive-
ness, in 1941 he'd helped found the Union
for Democratic Action, a group that called
for American aid to the foes of fascism.
With regard to the Party's concern for Black
workers, Randolph thought it "a sometime
thing" that vanished when it came to serving the Kremlin's interests.[22]

On December 7, 1941, planes from
Japanese carriers bombed the American

naval base at Pearl Harbor in the Hawaiian Islands; the next day, Congress declared war on the Japanese Empire. Hitler declared war on the United States on December 11.

Just as the CPUSA sidetracked the fight against Jim Crow to aid the Soviets, after Pearl Harbor it edged away from its anti-racism policy. A year earlier, Charles R. Drew, an African American surgeon and medical researcher, devised the method still in use today for preserving blood. Though blood transfusions saved lives, the CPUSA went along with the Red Cross decision to segregate donations because the blood of Black donors allegedly "polluted" white recipients. This outraged African Americans, among them Richard Wright. The grandson of slaves, Wright was a longtime CPUSA member and the foremost Black novelist of his generation. Party critics had already charged that *Native Son* (1940), his novel about a Black youth living in poverty in Depression-era Chicago, called undue attention to racism during the time of the Hitler-Stalin Pact. The Party's stance on blood segregation was the last straw. In November 1944, Wright wrote to a fellow traveler:

There are 13,000,000 black people in the United States who practically have no voice in the government that governs them; who must fight in the United States Army under Jim Crow conditions of racial humiliation; who literally have the blood, which they so generously offer out of their veins to wounded soldiers, segregated in blood (plasma) banks of the American Red Cross, as though their blood were the blood of subhumans. . . . Can you know this and hesitate to speak out or act? . . . If you reject my plea, then, pray, tell me, how you will finally determine when to express yourself?

Wright was so appalled that he left the Party because, he said, of its dishonesty, bigotry, and intolerance of others' ideas. In return, its spokesmen branded the novelist "a petty bourgeois degenerate" and a "bastard intellectual" who spread corruption.[23]

As if blood segregation were not bad enough, Communists came down in favor of a shameful injustice by the White House. In the months after Pearl Harbor, panic gripped the West Coast, especially California, home to large numbers of Japanese Americans. As bigoted white Californians put it, "A Jap is a Jap." In other words, all persons of Japanese heritage, including

American citizens, were the same as those who'd attacked the United States. To make matters worse, rumors spread that a Japanese fleet was on its way at full speed and Japanese Americans would help the invaders when they arrived. FDR, who should have known better, caved to the hysteria. In February 1942, he signed Executive Order 9066. With a stroke of the presidential pen, 120,000 men, women, and children of Japanese ancestry were forced from their homes and put into remote camps guarded by military police. Communists applauded the outrage as "a necessary war measure," declaring that "the question of the time of their release is a matter for the federal authorities to decide." Veteran Communist union organizer Karl Yoneda claimed that all people of Japanese ancestry "are grateful to our government for the way this grave question of evacuation is being handled." Yoneda, too, called for suspending all members of Japanese origin and their non-Japanese spouses from the Party to promote "national unity." CPUSA chief Earl Browder agreed, saying racially based expulsions were right and proper during this time of crisis.[24]

Countless Americans were uneasy about fighting one mass murderer with the help of another. For them, Stalinist Russia was a land of injustice. The main difference between Stalin and Hitler, jokers said, was the size of their mustaches; otherwise, they were the same—cold-blooded monsters. FDR, however, believed the alliance served American interests. Though the USSR was taking dreadful losses, its forces rallied after the initial surprise and began inflicting equally dreadful losses on the invaders; indeed, over 90 percent of German casualties, killed and wounded, occurred on the Eastern Front. Yet Russians did not fight for love of Soviet power. As Stalin admitted to an American diplomat, the people fought as they always had, "for their homeland, not for us," meaning the Communists. Still, FDR understood the arithmetic of war. By his reckoning, every German soldier put out of action by the Red Army was one less German liable to harm an American soldier. For the president, the old proverb "The enemy of my enemy is my friend" was true as ever. So, personal feelings aside, he had to preserve Allied unity at all costs.[25]

To win over public opinion, the White House tasked the government's propaganda agency, the Office of War Information (OWI), with organizing a campaign to whitewash Communist rule in the USSR. The result was a deluge of Soviet propaganda by Americans for Americans. Major sectors of the press and media went overboard, abandoning serious reporting to burnish Stalin's image. Mass-circulation magazines put the dictator's picture on their front covers. *Time* featured "Uncle Joe" on its cover three times; its January 4, 1943, issue named Stalin "Man of the Year." Sentimental make-believe, wishful thinking, and plain rubbish were sold to readers as truth. For example, the December 1943 issue of *Collier's* magazine noted, without a shred of proof, that the USSR was evolving "toward something resembling

This man is your FRIEND

Russian

He fights for FREEDOM

U.S. propaganda poster showing a Soviet soldier as a friend, not an enemy. (1942)

our own and Great Britain's democracy." *Life* glorified all things Soviet. The nation's leading photo magazine praised Lenin as "a normal, well-balanced man who was dedicated to rescuing 140,000,000 people from a brutal and incompetent tyranny"— that is, czarist rule. In what we may call the Americanization of the Russian image, the magazine described Russians as "one hell of a people" who "look like Americans, dress like Americans, and think like Americans." Its ultimate bit of nonsense was the portrayal of Stalin's secret police, the NKVD, as "national police similar to the FBI," whose job was "tracking traitors." And if Soviet leaders tell us anything, *Life* added, "we can afford to take their word for it." Not to be outdone, the sober *New York Times* (April 2, 1944) declared, "Marxian thinking in Soviet Russia is out. The capitalist system, better described as the competitive system, is back." At the same time, the Daughters of the American Revolution applauded Stalin as a gentleman and a scholar. "Stalin," one of its members insisted, "is a university graduate and a man of great studies. He is a man who, when he sees a great mistake, admits it and corrects it." She neglected to say that he "corrected" mistakes with sham trials, torture, slavery, and bullets.[26]

Russian-themed films from major Hollywood studios usually followed guidelines set by the OWI; indeed, some scripts were sent to the Soviet embassy in Washington for comment and approval by its "technical consultants." America was a nation of moviegoers; some commentators said it was "movie-crazy." During World War II, more than half the population saw at least one film a month, while over a third took in one picture a week. Since an average feature film reached more people than any single copy of a printed work—book, newspaper, or magazine—it was bound to influence viewers' attitudes. This even showed up in clothing choices. In 1934, to cite a famous example, undershirt manufacturers complained about falling sales because heartthrob Clark Gable revealed himself as a nonuser in *It Happened One Night,* a romantic comedy about a spoiled heiress and a cynical newspaper reporter.[27]

Russian-themed films aimed at changing the popular image of Stalinist Russia as a tyranny that partnered with Hitler until the very moment he attacked. Releases such as *Moscow Strikes Back, The Boy from Stalingrad,* and *The Battle of Russia* depicted ordinary citizens as selfless patriots devoted to their leaders. In *Days of Glory,* guerrilla fighters appeared as heroic

Scene from *Song of Russia,* one of many American Russia-themed films released during the war. (1944)

defenders of democracy worldwide. Other films focused on Nazi brutality. *The North Star,* for example, featured a sadistic German doctor who forces village children to give blood for wounded German soldiers; I was seven when I saw it with my mother in 1943, and she had an awful time calming me down. *Mission to Moscow,* based on the book of the same title by former ambassador Joseph E. Davies, was made at FDR's personal request. For anyone who knew anything about recent history, this film was a shabby apology for Stalin's crimes. Stalin, played by Academy Award winner Walter Huston, is seen as a kindly, cuddly leader who loves children—no mention of Gelya Markizova here. While justifying the Moscow Trials as necessary for unmasking traitors, the film showed how much the Russian people revered Stalin and lived happily under his wise rule. Davies had allowed himself to be so taken in by the Russians that he told a Chicago audience, "The word of honor of the Soviet Government is as safe as the Bible."[28]

Victor Kravchenko, a Soviet engineer assigned to the lend-lease program, knew better. During his travels in the United States, he recalled that such over-the-top praise made him cringe with embarrassment. "A thousand times I had to listen in frustrated silence while the Soviet dictatorship was being given full credit for the achievements of the Russian people. . . . Stalin's grip on the American mind, I realized with a shock, was almost as firm as his grip on the Russian mind." How, the engineer wondered, could Americans be so gullible? In 1944, Kravchenko abandoned his post. When Moscow branded

him a traitor and demanded his return, the United States gave him asylum. In 1946, he published *I Chose Freedom*, a scathing exposé of the Stalinist regime.[29]

Meanwhile, the tide of war had turned against Germany and Japan. Both nations lacked the manpower, raw materials, and industrial capacity of the United States, which produced more weapons than all the warring powers combined. In Europe, the Red Army, bolstered by massive American aid, halted the German drive and by 1943 was advancing along a thousand-mile front. In 1944, American, British, and Canadian forces mounted the largest seaborne invasion in history. On June 6, they crossed the English Channel in 6,900 ships and landed in Normandy on the French coast. Hitler's worst nightmare became a reality. Caught between enemies closing in from east and west, his forces steadily gave ground. By the spring of 1945, the Red Army was nearing Berlin. On April 30, as Soviet shells burst above, the Führer blew his brains out in his underground shelter. On May 7, the German high command surrendered unconditionally, ending the European phase of World War II.

In the Pacific, the United States soon replaced its Pearl Harbor losses. Gradually, its combined navy, marine, and army

American troops marching up Omaha Beach in Normandy. (1944)

forces captured strategic Japanese-held islands. Each capture brought fleets of American bombers closer to the Japanese home islands. Massive air raids devastated Japanese cities, while U.S. submarines sank nearly every freighter and oil tanker flying the Rising Sun flag. Though the noose steadily tightened, the militarists running Japan's government refused to yield. Pentagon analysts estimated that an invasion of Japan would cost one million American casualties, killed and wounded, and likely four times as many Japanese lives.

That the invasion never happened was due to the Manhattan Project, a secret program to build a radically new weapon. The United States and Britain had developed the atomic bomb for use against Germany, but the war in Europe ended before it was ready. Just three months after the German surrender, atomic bombs destroyed Hiroshima (August 6) and Nagasaki (August 9). Within seconds, the temperature in these cities rose to 5,400 degrees Fahrenheit, melting ceramic tiles and turning human beings into tiny black blobs. A fifth-grade boy gave his impressions of the aftermath in Hiroshima:

The flames blaze up here and there from the collapsed houses as though to illuminate the darkness. The child

The mushroom cloud erupting over Nagasaki after the drop of the atomic bomb. (1945)

ping, rushing around as though he has gone mad and calling the names of his wife and child—ah—my hair seems to stand on end just to remember. This is the way war really looks.[30]

On September 2, Japan surrendered, ending World War II.

Victory found America the richest, most powerful country in history. By late 1945, it held one-half of the world's industry and two-thirds of its gold reserves. Though vast swaths of Europe and Asia lay in ruins, the American mainland had suffered no enemy damage. The man in the street expected his country, guarded by two oceans and a monopoly on atomic bombs, to dominate world affairs for generations to come. Equally optimistic, Washington dismantled the massive war machine, slashed military spending, and returned factories to civilian production. The armed services shrank from 12.2 million at war's end to 1.5 million in 1947. Hundreds of warships and thousands of planes were mothballed, and the Office of Strategic Services, the nation's wartime spy agency, shut down. Few expected any trouble with the USSR. Pro-Soviet propaganda had apparently done its job. A poll taken in August 1945 showed that a majority of Americans trusted the So-

making a suffering, groaning sound, his burned face swollen up balloon-like and jerking as he wanders among the fires. The old man, the skin of his face and body peeling off like a potato skin, mumbling prayers while he flees with faltering steps. Another man pressing with both hands the wound from which blood is steadily drip-

viets and expected good relations with them after the war. Around this time, General Dwight D. Eisenhower, the supreme commander of Allied forces in Western Europe, told a congressional committee: "Nothing guides Russian policy so much as a desire for friendship with the United States." The future thirty-fourth president was wrong. Dead wrong.[31]

DAWN OF THE COLD WAR

Late in the summer of 1945, Victor Abakumov, who would soon become Soviet minister of state security, met with his staff. Though the European conflict had just ended, Stalin's chief spy hunter was mentally fighting the next war. The democracies: What naive fools they are! What sentimental hogwash they spout! "The British and Americans . . . dream of lasting peace and building a democratic world for all men. . . . All their slobber plays into our hands, and we shall thank them for this, in the next world, with coals of fire. . . . We shall disrupt them and corrupt them from within. . . . The whole 'free western' world will burst apart like a fat squashed toad. Our aim justifies all this. Our aim is a grand one, the destruction of the old, vile world." This was not the ravings of a lunatic. Abakumov was a hard-boiled thug

with much blood on his hands. Yet he knew his master's mind, and likely heard similar words from him.[32]

Stalin had not changed. Regardless of what American magazines and films said, he still despised the capitalist democracies. He'd never courted them as allies; Hitler's double cross had driven them together, but only in a marriage of convenience. Like Lenin, he did not believe lasting peace was possible. Stalin's mentor had written, "As long as capitalism and socialism exist, we cannot live in peace: in the end, one or the other will triumph—a funeral dirge will be sung either over the Soviet Republic or over world capitalism." The tyrant echoed Lenin in the closing days of the European war. Stalin's inner circle understood that he wished to avoid another war only until the USSR had the advantage. During a Kremlin banquet, a high official in the Yugoslav Communist Party was amazed to see Stalin spring from his chair, hitch up his pants, and cry, "The war shall soon be over. We shall recover in fifteen or twenty years, and then we'll have another go at it." Sergo Beria, an aide, recalled that Stalin assumed the democracies were enemies. "During all the sittings of his government," Beria noted, "he said that the Third World War would take place, and that this war would take place during his life." Unlike the Americans, Stalin did not demobilize his forces after victory, but kept the ten-million-man Red Army intact and supplied at the expense of the civilian population.[33]

Stalin began a clampdown at home, in effect a continuation of the Great Terror and the Moscow Trials of the 1930s. Composer Dmitri Shostakovich, who'd miraculously survived despite Stalin's denunciations of some of his best musical works, saw the effects. "Stalin hated the Allies and feared them," he noted. "Almost immediately after the war he dealt cruelly with his citizens who had had relations with the Allies. . . . This was a tragedy for thousands upon thousands. A man received a letter from America and was shot. And the naive former Allies kept sending letters. And every letter was a death sentence." Indeed, Stalin had the Soviet criminal code updated, making it a crime, punishable by twenty-five years at "corrective labor," to "praise American technology" and to "praise American democracy."[34]

Stalin's immediate concern, however, was security. In 1944 and 1945, his forces had driven the Germans from Soviet soil and the lands they'd occupied in Central and Eastern Europe. Though he signed agreements to hold free elections, Stalin had no intention of living up to his promises. Wherever his forces went—Estonia, Latvia, Lithuania, Poland, Hungary, Romania, Bulgaria, Albania—he ordered "satellites" or "people's democracies" set up. He did so for two reasons. First, and most important at the moment, he wanted to protect his country's western borders; twice in the twentieth century, German armies had swept over them like locusts. Second, he meant to use the captive nations as advance bases for launching the next war.

Though homegrown Communists held every public office in the satellites, they were puppets; Soviet civilian "advisers," secret policemen, and troops were actually in charge. And they ruled with iron fists. Anyone believed to be anti-Soviet was arrested, sent to the Gulag, or murdered outright. Patriotic groups that had fought Nazi occupiers were crushed, sometimes in pitched battles, as in Poland; the NKVD used former Nazi concentration camps to house its Polish captives. When schools reopened, the first thing students noticed was Stalin's grim portrait staring at them from their classroom walls. Germany was a special case. There, the victors carved the defeated nation into four occupation zones: American, British, French, and Soviet. Berlin lay 110 miles inside the Soviet zone, and was in turn divided into four sectors. On February 9, 1946, Stalin gave a speech in which he blamed the democracies for starting the war! This revising of history made a deep impression in the West. Widely covered in the press, the speech raised grave doubts about Soviet intentions.[35]

The reaction came quickly. During the war, Winston Churchill had praised Soviet leaders as people who only "wish to live in honorable friendship with the Western democracies." Now the blinders were off. On March 5, the former prime minister spoke at Westminster College in Fulton, Missouri. While praising the USSR for its role in defeating Nazi Germany, Churchill warned about the looming threat. It was at that point that he used the term "iron curtain" to describe what he saw unfolding in Europe. "From Stettin in the Baltic to Trieste in the Adriatic, an iron curtain has descended across the Continent. Behind that line lie all the capitals of the ancient states of Central and Eastern Europe. . . . This is certainly not the liberated Europe we fought to build up. Nor is it one which contains the essentials of permanent peace, [but of] a growing challenge and peril to Christian civilization."[36]

Churchill's speech signaled the start of the Cold War. Until it ended with the collapse of the USSR in 1991, the Cold War involved every means of struggle— ideas, diplomacy, propaganda, economic pressure, espionage—short of "hot war," a direct military conflict between the USSR and its satellites and the United States and its allies. Both sides realized that an armed clash, especially after the USSR gained its own atomic bomb in 1949, would bring about MAD (mutually assured destruction), the end of human life on earth. Yet the Cold War was not bloodless; indeed, it claimed millions of lives in nearly every part of the globe. Each side fought through "proxies," nations or armed groups instigated by, or acting for, superpowers that kept out of the fighting themselves. In America, the Cold War sparked the Second Red Scare, a panicked fear of Communists that gripped the nation from 1946 through the 1950s and whose effects are felt to the present day.

NIGHTMARE YEARS

As I struggled through my first years back home . . . I began to wonder
if my beloved country was turning into a lunatic bin. I had lived
through the nightmare years of Nazi Germany. Were there
to be nightmare years at home?
—William L. Shirer, American journalist (1990)

THE CRISIS BUILDS

When Franklin Roosevelt died on April 12, 1945, he was succeeded by his vice president,
Harry S. Truman. The new man in the White House was no fan of dictators. The day
after Hitler attacked the USSR, Truman, then a Democratic senator from Missouri, saw
little to choose from. "If we see that Germany is winning," he growled, "we ought to help
Russia, and if Russia is winning, we ought to help Germany, and that way let them kill
as many as possible." Truman was being facetious. Though he despised both sides, Hitler
posed the greater threat, so he supported aid to the Soviets.[1]

President Harry S. Truman. (c. 1945)

As World War II drew to its close, Truman became incensed at Moscow's behavior. On April 23, just days after FDR's funeral, Soviet foreign minister V. M. Molotov visited the Oval Office. The meeting did not go well. Despite his bland appearance, Truman, a World War I combat veteran, was a feisty fellow. The moment Molotov sat down, the president let go, charging the Soviets with breaking solemn agreements, particularly to hold free elections in Poland. Molotov, stunned at the dressing-down, blurted out that no one had ever talked to him that way. Truman shot back, "Carry out your agreements, and you won't get talked to like that." The foreign minister stormed out of the room.[2]

His Kremlin master kept up the pressure. In Greece, Stalin's agents supplied rebels with advice and weapons, while moving to increase Communist influence in Turkey. As a result, 1947 became a pivotal year in the emerging Cold War. On March 12, Truman declared that the United States would provide political, military, and economic aid to all free peoples resisting "armed minorities or outside pressures." Christened "the Truman Doctrine," the president's declaration broke with American tradition. Ever since George Washington in his Farewell Address (1796) called for America to trade with foreign countries but have as little political connection with them as possible, the nation had avoided "entangling alliances." The Truman Doctrine, however, put the United States on record as ready to intervene in distant conflicts to check Soviet expansion. For starters, Congress voted $400 million in aid to Greece and Turkey.[3]

This was just a down payment. During the winter of 1946–47, morbid graffiti appeared on Berlin walls: "Blessed Are the Dead, for Their Hands Do Not Freeze."

This expressed the prevailing mood, for postwar Europe had scarcely begun to recover from the war. Winston Churchill described the Continent as "a rubble heap, a charnel house, a breeding ground for pestilence and hate." Not to be outdone, the *New York Times* dubbed Europe "the New Dark Continent," a place "which no American could hope to understand."[4]

But George C. Marshall understood. A brilliant military strategist, he'd overseen all American operations in Europe and the Pacific. After victory, the general showed equal skill as a statesman. Appointed secretary of state by President Truman in 1947, Marshall took charge of the nation's foreign affairs. Communism, he knew, thrived on misery; he remembered how the CPUSA had grown during the Great Depression. So, in June 1947, the secretary proposed what became known as the Marshall Plan, basically a $17 billion ($193 billion in today's money) donation to kick-start Europe's economy. Though Western governments grasped the offer as a lifeline, Moscow denounced it as "dollar imperialism," an American plot to seize control of Western Europe while undermining the "people's democracies" of Eastern Europe. Stalin forbade Soviet satellites from accepting American aid.

Protesters in East Berlin rallying against the Marshall Plan. (1950)

Meanwhile, Truman realized that disbanding the Office of Strategic Services had been a mistake, all but paralyzing the nation's ability to gather information on developments overseas. To remedy the error, Truman signed the National Security Act of 1947, creating the Central Intelligence Agency (CIA). Operating with a large but secret budget, the CIA collects and analyzes information on foreign economic, military, political, and scientific developments as they relate to American national security. The CIA has also carried out secret "black" operations—kidnapping, assassinating, and bribing foreign politicians and overthrowing "unfriendly" governments. As a top CIA official put it, "We're not in the Boy Scouts."[5]

The Cold War nearly turned hot in 1948. February saw Communists overthrow the elected government of Czechoslovakia (today's Czech Republic and Slovakia). In June, the Western powers merged their zones and invited them to create West Germany, the common English name for the Federal Republic of Germany. Stalin retaliated by threatening West Berlin. All food, medicine, and fuel for the city's two million people came on roads, trains, and canals connecting it to West Germany. On June 24, Stalin ordered these closed "for repairs," hoping the threat of starvation would force the Allies to abandon the city. President Truman, however, feared that if Stalin's "Berlin Blockade" succeeded, Communist parties throughout Western Europe would be emboldened to seize power. "The Russians," he declared, "have no right to get us out by either direct or indirect pressure. . . . We stay in Berlin, period."[6]

What to do? A number of generals wanted to push supply convoys spearheaded by tanks across the Soviet zone to relieve the city. That, of course, ran the risk of killing Soviet soldiers and prompting Stalin to escalate the crisis. Truman had a better idea. Nothing prevented the Allies from using the air corridors over the Soviet zone; these remained open by treaty, despite the land blockade. To make sure Stalin understood he'd better not have any transports shot down, the president sent two squadrons of B-29 Superfortress bombers to Britain—the same kind of planes that had dropped atomic bombs on Japan.

Dubbed "Operation Vittles," the relief effort soon became known simply as "the Berlin Airlift." Each day, weather permitting, upward of 350 American and British planes landed at West Berlin's three airports, as often as one every three minutes. The Soviets were astonished at the scale and efficiency of this "air bridge." To a Red Army officer, it seemed that the pilots deliberately flew their planes low to impress his troops. "One would appear overhead, another would disappear over the horizon, and a third emerge, one after another without interruption, like a conveyor belt," he reported. The airlift put the ball in Stalin's court: clearly, if he really wanted to starve West Berlin, he would have to use force. The dictator backed down; the USSR was not ready for another war just yet. On May 12, 1949, Stalin lifted the blockade. During the course of its 324 days, planes had delivered 2.5 million tons of supplies to the city. Toward the end,

American pilots became so confident that they launched "Operation Little Vittles," dropping bags of candy on miniature parachutes to Berlin's children.[7]

The Berlin crisis convinced Western leaders of the need to present a unified front to Moscow. On April 4, 1949, a month before Stalin's backdown over Berlin, the United States took the lead in creating the North Atlantic Treaty Organization (NATO). Under the treaty's Article 5, twelve nations pledged "that an armed attack against one or more [members] in Europe or North America shall be considered as an attack on them all." This groundbreaking treaty ensured that American combat forces would remain in West Germany, "the tip of the spear" in the Cold War, as long as necessary. They are still there. Communists, however, claimed that NATO was a nefarious scheme to rearm Germany in preparation for an all-out attack on the "peace-loving" Soviet Union.[8]

THE SECOND RED SCARE

The Cold War did more than change Americans' attitudes toward foreign affairs; it had a deep and lasting effect on life in the States. During the late 1940s, information from defectors revealed the existence of Soviet spy rings in the United States, a subject explored in the next chapter. For now, it is enough to note that the scores of federal agencies created during the Great Depression and World War II offered opportunities for Communists and fellow travelers to infiltrate the government. By 1947, the public had become so alarmed that the president felt he had to act to soothe it, but also to avoid criticism from his Republican rivals. On March 21, nine days after announcing the Truman Doctrine, he issued Executive Order 9835, which authorized the creation of the Federal Employee Loyalty Program to investigate and dismiss any of the over three million federal employees suspected as "security risks" or of "disloyalty."[9]

Investigations were initiated by the

West Berlin children waving at a Berlin Airlift plane. (1947)

FBI. Ever since the Great Red Scare of 1919, Director J. Edgar Hoover had seen communism as the worst threat facing America, worse even than Nazi Germany. Hoover's hatred ran deep, and he used strong language to denounce that "cowardly, slithering mass of humanity," that toxic "'ism' scum . . . seeking to engulf America." The director ordered his agents to comb through the personnel file of every federal employee and job applicant. If anything seemed amiss, the bureau began a "full field investigation." This was FBI-speak for an in-depth probe of the individual's habits, activities, beliefs, likes, dislikes, writings, and memberships. At the same time, other agents interviewed people from his current and past relationships: friends, neighbors, teachers, colleagues, and acquaintances. Nothing was too trivial to ask about. Has the person ever acted oddly, murmured against the government, or praised the USSR? Tell us what books, newspapers, and magazines the person reads. What are the person's favorite radio programs? Does the person have a drinking problem? Is the person trustworthy? Every scrap of information was written down, assembled into a report, and turned over to one of the hundreds of "loyalty boards" scattered across the coun-

FBI director J. Edgar Hoover. (c. 1940)

try. After studying the report, board members decided whether to drop the matter or hold a formal hearing.[10]

These hearings were meant to inspire fear in their targets. Due process, the government's duty to respect all rights guaranteed by the Constitution, took a backseat. Under the American system, the accused is entitled to know the charges against him, see the prosecution's evidence, confront accusers, and have an attorney question them under oath. These rights were largely ignored in loyalty hearings. The names of informants were not revealed, and they were not required to testify. The bureau prized secrecy; if informants had to testify, an official admitted, its sources would dry up, and "the FBI would have to go out of business." This meant that anyone could cook up a story, ruin another's life, and not be held accountable. What's more, the FBI wished to hide its own shady activities. During the Second Red Scare, the thirst for information led it to carry out all sorts of "black" operations: tapping telephone lines without a warrant, illegally opening mail, and making "surreptitious entries"—a refined term for burglaries.[11]

Under due process, a person is, above all, assumed to be innocent until proven guilty. Loyalty hearings assumed the very opposite. As a member of a Coast Guard panel said, "The presumption of innocence does not apply to these proceedings." Questioners sought to embarrass and entrap suspects. They might ask: "You have been accused of sympathetically associating with members of an organization known to be subversive. What say you?" What *could* you say? The question was so vague that it was impossible to know whom it referred to, which organization, when, or where. Other questions had nothing to do with political beliefs or disloyal activities, but with lifestyle choices. "Do you go to church? How often?" a person might be asked, or "What do you think of sex before marriage?" Racism, too, reared its ugly head. African Americans started with two strikes against them. Some were asked, "Have you ever had dinner with a mixed group?" or "Have you ever danced with a white girl?" These were trick questions. Since the CPUSA vocally opposed Jim Crow, a positive answer indicated "subversive" inclinations.[12]

To avoid answering, the accused might "take the Fifth." The Fifth Amendment is part of the Bill of Rights, the first ten amendments to the Constitution, which include such basics as freedom of speech, assembly, and worship. It states that the accused cannot be forced "to be a witness against himself." In old-time Europe, efforts to force self-incrimination were legal. The Spanish Inquisition, for example, tortured suspected heretics into confessing their sins and implicating others; then they were burned at the stake. In England, those accused of certain crimes were "pressed"—as they lay spread-eagled on a flat surface, heavy stones were gradually placed on their chests until they confessed or died when their ribs collapsed. The Founders intended the Fifth Amendment as a safeguard against such practices. To take the Fifth, one simply said, "I refuse to answer on the grounds that it may tend to incriminate me." Yet this protection could also become a trap. As Supreme Court justice Hugo Black put it, "If there is nothing to conceal, then why conceal it?" Loyalty boards assumed that anyone who took the Fifth had something to hide and must be a security risk. Such people were branded "Fifth Amendment Communists."[13]

Loyalty boards were also suspicious of women "of a certain type." The expansion of government acted as a magnet, drawing women, largely single, to Washington. Most worked as file clerks, stenographers, typists, and telephone operators. Professional women, all college graduates, held positions as lawyers, administrators, and social scientists. During the Second Red Scare, many anti-Communists imagined a connection between femininity and loyalty. Plain-looking, opinionated women supposedly had the telltale traits of Communist women! Yet a capable, attractive woman might be deemed more dangerous. Communists were said to use them as femmes fatales, seductresses loyal to no man, but to the Party alone. Though there might be no evidence against either type of woman, their loyalty was questioned, and they were thus barred from government service.[14]

The best estimate is that 2,700 federal employees were fired between 1947 and 1956 as a result of Truman's program, and another 12,000 resigned under pressure. Though loyalty boards might violate civil liberties, administration officials defended their actions as necessary. "Civil rights," one declared, "have to be subordinated to the right of the nation to defend itself against Russia, which is the enemy of all civil rights and all the freedoms." Another explained, in harsher terms: "The issue—Freedom versus Communism—is a life-and-death matter. To my mind it is the struggle of the ages. This fact arouses justifiable concern about Communism in our own Government." We hear in these statements echoes, albeit unintentional, of Lenin's notion that the end justifies the means—that all is permitted to the "righteous" in what they define as a "just" cause. The nation's Founders would have been appalled at this, for they designed the Constitution to safeguard the rule of law against attacks in the name of "necessity."[15]

The frenzy spread beyond the federal government. In the private sector, leading civil rights groups became loyalty-conscious. Still smarting over the CPUSA's role in the Scottsboro case, the NAACP rid itself of suspected fellow travelers.

Leaders of the American Civil Liberties Union told the FBI about the politics of its members and refused to take on cases involving accused Communists. Newspapers touted their loyalty in various ways. The *New York Times* refused to carry ads from alleged Communist front groups. Not to be outdone, the *New York Herald Tribune* ran chilling exposés of "the Red Underground." *Look,* a mass-circulation magazine, published a how-to guide titled "How to Spot a Communist." This urged loyal Americans to be on the lookout for such traits as "declaring that capitalism and democracy are 'decadent' because some injustices exist under those systems."[16]

Local governments hired full-time snoops, preferably retired FBI agents, to check the loyalty of their employees. City councils passed "anti-Red" ordinances making it illegal for known CPUSA members to live in their communities. Violating an ordinance brought stiff penalties. In Osceola County, Florida, police arrested Alexander W. Trainor, an ex-Communist and activist in the defense of the Scottsboro Boys. A court sentenced Trainor to four years in prison for continuing to live in the county. Certain communities—how many is unclear—required residents to sign loyalty oaths when applying for hunting and fishing licenses. Elsewhere, graduating high school students had to sign loyalty oaths to receive their diplomas, as did tenants in public housing projects when they paid their monthly rent.[17]

Educators came under intense scrutiny. Here, however, the authorities claimed they were only taking the CPUSA at its word. For example, a lead article in the *Communist,* the Party's official magazine, clearly gave the official view of the role of American public education and of the Communist teacher. "The function of the bourgeois school can," it said, "be expressed simply as being the *training of efficient and docile* wage earners. . . . [Therefore] the Party must take careful steps to see that all teacher comrades are given thorough education in teaching Marxism-Leninism. Only when teachers have really mastered Marxism-Leninism, will they be able skillfully to inject it into their teaching at the least risk of exposure and at the same time to conduct struggles around the schools in a truly Bolshevik manner." That there were CPUSA members teaching in the nation's public schools is certain. That they corrupted young minds "in a truly Bolshevik manner" is something else entirely. Various aspects of history, political science, and economics do lend themselves to Marxist interpretations. But it is hard to see how anyone could inject Marxism into mathematics, geometry, geology, astronomy, chemistry, and physics.[18]

While the Second Red Scare affected public school teachers nationwide, it hit hardest in large urban centers. New York set the pattern. In 1949, the state legislature passed the Feinberg Law, which barred from the classroom anyone who'd ever called for the overthrow of the government. This law further ordered that a security officer, who would submit a yearly report on the politics of every administrator, teacher, school nurse, crossing guard, lunchroom worker, and janitor, be placed in every school district. Any current CPUSA member or former member was to be dismissed and deprived of all benefits, including whatever retirement pension had been earned over years of otherwise faultless service. In 1952, the U.S. Supreme Court upheld the Feinberg Law in a 6–3 decision that affirmed the state's right "to protect the immature minds of children in public schools from subversive propaganda" by those "to whom they look for guidance, authority and leadership."[19]

New York City's public school system, the nation's largest, underwent a full-blown purge. In 1949 and 1950 alone, more than three hundred teachers were fired and another two hundred resigned rather than submit to a hearing. As with Truman's loyalty boards, hearings could be brutal affairs. On the basis of a rumor or an anonymous tip, security officers and school administrators grilled the suspect. "We hear that you read the *Daily Worker*. Do you?" "You've been seen in the company of a known Communist. Is that so?" "Your name has been found on a petition sponsored by a Communist front group. Are you a Communist? If not, why did you sign?" The questions came nonstop, like verbal battering rams. The only way out was to confess to one's "errors" and show remorse by giving the names of other "Communists." I like to think that Mr. M., my ninth-grade homeroom teacher, kept mum. A former combat infantryman, he walked with a limp from a steel splinter in his leg, a souvenir of the Italian campaign of 1943. A gentle, soft-spoken man, he never talked politics; his eyes blazed and his face hardened only when he recalled seeing the aftermath of a Nazi atrocity in some caves outside Rome. Without saying goodbye, he vanished from school; we were told that he had "loyalty issues." But at least Mr. M. lived; we learned that he'd gone into another line of work.

Russian-born Minnie Gutride died. A middle-aged widow, childless and alone, she taught in P.S. 21, an elementary school on Staten Island. In December 1948, just before the Christmas recess, the principal and inquisitors from the board of education called her into the teachers' room. Without further ado, they bombarded her with questions about her political beliefs and attendance at "certain Communist meetings" in 1940 and 1941. When she asked to see a lawyer, which is every citizen's right, they threatened to charge her with "conduct unbecoming a teacher." The frightened woman may have been a Communist or a fellow traveler, or not; nobody really knew. Anyhow, that night she turned on the gas jets on the stove and fell asleep forever. When neighbors found her body, they also found a stack of toys she'd planned to give to the children in her class. No one could think of any harm she'd ever done to another person. "She was a sensitive and unassuming teacher who for seventeen years taught children with love, sympathy and quiet effectiveness," colleagues wrote. "No complaint has ever been made against her in all these years."[20]

For good measure, boards of education rid libraries of books they thought likely to "subvert the American way of life." What follows is a small sample of titles that appeared on various lists of banned books. *The Tales of Robin Hood* was deemed subversive because its hero, a medieval outlaw who fought Bad King John, stole from the rich and gave to the poor. Henry David Thoreau's essay "Civil Disobedience," published in 1849, criticized slavery, arguing that when a government is unjust, a just person must disobey its laws. John Steinbeck's Pulitzer Prize–winning novel *The Grapes of Wrath* was banned in scores of school districts. Though no Communist, the author portrayed destitute farmers abused by giant agricultural corporations, which offended some conservatives. Yet, too often, textbooks with favorable views of slavery remained in students' hands. According to Ralph V. Harlow's *Story of America,* "Most planters treated their slaves fairly. The owners were kindly, humane men. The Negroes had to be encouraged [i.e., forced] to work because many of them were irresponsible, if not lazy." Herbert Townsend's *Our America* portrayed farmwork as hard, but softened by after-hours watermelon feasts, banjo playing, and dancing. "It was true," Townsend declared, "that most of the slaves were happy. They did not want to be free." It was not true. Saying enslaved people were happy in bondage is nonsense; saying they did not want to be free is nonsense on steroids.[21]

American colleges and universities had their own version of the loyalty craze. Institutions of higher learning prided themselves as bastions of academic freedom, defenders of the right of professors to speak and publish freely in their areas of expertise. Nevertheless, academic freedom has its limits. It was never intended to protect *all* speech, especially speech harmful to the school. During the Cold War, defending "politically sensitive" or "unorthodox" opinions could harm a school's bottom line. Alumni donations closed budget gaps and funded new buildings; government grants and contracts paid for laboratories and special research projects. Rather than risk financial loss, schools became overly cautious. That is why Harvard, Dartmouth, Cornell, Vassar, and Princeton barred Earl Browder from speaking when he was invited by student groups; police officers stood by to escort the CPUSA leader off campus if he dared show his face. Other schools blocked concerts by Paul Robeson and lectures by novelist Howard Fast. As the president of Wayne State University ex-

plained, "It is now clear that the Communist is to be regarded . . . as an enemy of our national welfare."[22]

Like public school teachers, college professors had to prove their loyalty. Taking the Fifth was not an option. The presidents of the nation's thirty-seven top universities issued a statement declaring that academics had an "obligation of candor." In other words, when questioned about their political beliefs, they had to answer fully and truthfully. It was said that "the right of the Communist to

Paul Robeson joins shipyard workers in singing "The Star-Spangled Banner" to protest their working conditions. (1942)

teach should be denied because he has given away his freedom in the quest for truth," surrendering his mental independence to Moscow. To prove his worthiness, the professor must name names, turning in colleagues he knew to be, or thought might be, Communists. Refusal brought dismissal and blacklisting. Though informal, blacklists followed people throughout their academic lives. Unable to find jobs, many left the teaching profession or took positions in all-Black Southern colleges, which were happy to hire qualified teachers with doctorates.[23]

The effects of the loyalty campaigns haunted America during the late 1940s and early 1950s. Columnist Drew Pearson called these an affliction, "a disease of fear." Novelist Norman Mailer thought the nation suffered from "a collective failure of nerve." People played it safe. Rather than risk being labeled as a Communist, it seemed best to keep your head down and your opinions to yourself. A government employee expressed this attitude best: "If Communists like apple pie and I do, I see no reason why I should stop eating it. But I do." When a reporter in Madison, Wisconsin, asked passersby to sign the preamble to the Declaration of Independence, the part saying "All men are created equal," nine out of ten turned him down. A reporter for the *St. Louis Dispatch* had a similar experience; people refused to sign the preamble to the Constitution. As for academic freedom, an anonymous poet wrote "Ode to Hysteria: University Division." Though written in a humorous vein, it was deadly serious:

> *I am the very model of a member of the faculty,*
> *Because I'm simply overcome with sentiments of loyalty. . . .*
> *The thoughts I think are only thoughts approved by my community.*
> *I pledge allegiance to the flag at every opportunity.*
> *I haven't had a thing to do with Communist conspirators,*
> *And neither have my relatives, descendants, or progenitors.*[24]

HUAC GOES TO HOLLYWOOD

Congressman Martin Dies Jr. saw himself as a patriot. With war clouds gathering over Europe, the Texas Democrat urged the House of Representatives to appoint a committee to investigate the actions of homegrown Nazis and Communists. In May 1938, he became chairman of a temporary House Un-American Activities

Martin Dies Jr., who would become the first chairman of the House Un-American Activities Committee. (1935)

very beginning HUAC faced harsh criticism. Conservatives concerned about civil liberties were leery of all congressional investigating committees. Columnist George E. Sokolsky spoke for them. A firm anti-Communist, he thought such committees inherently unfair and un-American. Sokolsky wrote:

Civil liberties are always impaired by Congressional committees. . . . You will say that Congressional committees only investigate; they do not try. These committees put a man on the

Committee (HUAC). Dies's appointment brought pledges of support from across the land. Among them was a telegram from what we may call a Dies fan club, the race terrorists of the Ku Klux Klan. "Every true American, and that includes every Klansman," the telegram said, "is behind you and your committee in its effort to turn the country back to the honest, freedom-loving, God-fearing American to whom it belongs." Translation: Klansmen believed America belonged only to white Protestants, and that it was impossible for Catholics, Jews, and Muslims to be loyal citizens.[25]

Despite the Klan's blessing, from its

Cartoon showing HUAC as an out-of-control car running over multiple people, with the caption "It's okay— we're hunting Communists." It was published soon after the Hollywood hearings. (c. 1947)

spot, bring in the reporters, camera men, newsreelers and demand to know, yes or no, whether it isn't true that he did so and so. He says that he would like to read a statement proving that he is being maligned and his conduct misunderstood. Nothing doing! You can't read statements! Well, he says, have I done anything that is against the law? That isn't the point. They've given the public the impression they want to give, and the defendant is almost helpless unless he has a good publicity man of his own or he shouts down the Congressmen, who don't like to be exposed to shouts. What about the civil liberties involved in this technique?[26]

Nevertheless, HUAC initially served a useful purpose. During its first year, the committee's investigators exposed the German-American Bund (League), a New York–based group linked to Hitler's intelligence services, whose members wore Nazi uniforms at rallies in Madison Square Garden and shouted anti-Semitic slogans. Like the CPUSA, the Bund ran summer camps. "A mental world of Hitlerism is embedded in these unsuspecting minds," a wit-

ness testified. "The camps are completely Nazi German. The flaming swastika of Germany is the important flag. [Campers] eat, sleep, talk, and dream Nazi-ism with the same fervor of the regimented youth of Germany." President Roosevelt used the committee's report as the basis for a crackdown on Nazi-front groups and German agents posing as businessmen.[27]

HUAC next turned to Hollywood. Chairman Dies had become interested in Communist influence in the motion picture industry when investigators found actors' names in Party publications. Yet his decision to hold hearings in September 1938 blew up in his face. A rumor that child star Shirley Temple (age ten) might be questioned was met with ridicule. HUAC had taken leave of its senses, observed Interior Secretary Harold Ickes. It came to Tinseltown, he quipped, "and there discovered a great red plot. It found dangerous radicals there, led by Shirley Temple. Imagine the great committee raiding her nursery and seizing her dolls as evidence." With luck, Dies's sleuths might yet discover the CPUSA membership card of Donald Duck! Embarrassed, the chairman backed down. No hearings were held in Hollywood, and his committee was sidelined during World War II.[28]

HUAC took on new life in 1945. Martin Dies Jr. had retired by then, and Congressman John E. Rankin became its sponsor. Nicknamed "the Great American Earache," the Mississippi Democrat was a verbose crackpot. A hater from the ends of his hair to the tips of his toes, Rankin declared that communism was "Yiddish," blaming Jews for the Bolshevik Revolution—this when Lenin and his followers were militant atheists. The congressman further believed that slavery had been a blessing for the enslaved; its abolition was a national tragedy, in his opinion. Rankin loved the Ku Klux Klan, and Klansmen loved him. "After all," he'd say, "the KKK is an old American institution," just like lynching. Nevertheless, Rankin convinced the House to make HUAC a permanent committee, with a regular budget and full powers to investigate "subversion." In 1947 and 1951, it returned to hunting Communists in the film industry. We will focus on its first set of hearings, as these were the most infamous.[29]

But first we must understand Party thinking about motion pictures. Students of film at the time believed that most people are "eye-minded"—that is, more than anything, the things they see are the things that form their ideas about the

Mississippi congressman John E. Rankin helped establish HUAC. (1938)

world. Thus, Lenin viewed films as an essential propaganda tool. "Communists," he wrote, "must always consider that of all the arts the motion picture is the most important." Stalin agreed that "the cinema is [a] channel through which to reach the minds and shape the desires of people everywhere." Though Soviet studios made adventures and comedies, each year also saw a slew of pictures on the joys of labor in the "workers' paradise" and the ills of "decadent capitalism." Stalin himself was a movie buff; no film could be released in the USSR without his approval. A prudish man, he was infuriated by the least hint of nudity, a high skirt or a plunging neckline.

After signing death lists, he'd relax in his private Kremlin theater with a Charlie Chaplin comedy, a cowboy thriller, or, of all things, *Tarzan the Ape Man*. Adolf Hitler had a collection of American films and especially liked *It Happened One Night*.[30]

American films ruled the silver screen. By the 1930s, regarded as Hollywood's golden age, they'd become the standard by which the art form was judged everywhere. Knowing this, the Comintern decided that controlling the content of American films would give it influence the world over. On its orders, in the fall of 1935, CPUSA organizers left dreary Manhattan for sunny Hollywood.[31]

They struck pay dirt. Like other Depression-era Americans, movie people struggled to understand what was happening and why. They, too, wanted to crusade for justice, equality, peace, and a better world. The CPUSA came to such people as a godsend. It said it had all the answers—glib answers, easy to understand. Screenwriter Richard Collins recalled those heady days: "When I joined the Party, I was handed ready-made friends, a cause, a faith, and a viewpoint on all phenomena. A one-shot solution to all the world's ills and inequalities."[32]

The Party played to less wholesome instincts as well. In a time of widespread misery, it allowed those who'd made it big in pictures to enjoy the privileges of wealth with a clear conscience. They could, a critic observed, signal their moral superiority while enjoying "Communism with two butlers and a swimming pool." For self-styled "cinema rebels," wrote Eugene Lyons, the first American newsman to interview Stalin, communism created "an intoxicated state of mind, a glow of inner virtue, and a sort of comradeship in supercharity." Well-heeled performers met in plush living rooms to talk Marxist theory and bemoan capitalist abuse of fellow "toilers." To speed the revolution, they'd stand "by their swimming pools with clenched fists" raised in salute to "Uncle Joe Stalin." One New Year's Eve, fancy-dressed rebels gathered in a Beverly Hills mansion. Liveried butlers moved among them silently, balancing trays of champagne glasses. At the stroke of midnight, the guests rose, raised their glasses, and belted out "The Internationale":

Arise ye prisoners of starvation!
Arise ye wretched of the earth . . .

As a celebrity left a party in his chauffeured car, he tossed loose change to "a small crowd of Negroes" who were asking for handouts.[33]

Any film is the end product of the combined efforts of many skilled craftspeople. While the public idolizes actors, it seldom credits the screenwriters who furnish their scripts and the directors who guide their performances. During Hollywood's golden age, Communists were among the best of these. Between 1935 and 1946, an estimated 146 screenwriters, 60 actors, and 25 directors were dues-paying members of the CPUSA.[34]

A Communist true believer, screenwriter John Howard Lawson headed the Party's Hollywood branch. His son Jeff remembered him as a cold, egotistical man who "believed that Russia was a paradise and could do no wrong." Those who knew Lawson said, "He speaks with the voice of Stalin and the bells of the Kremlin." The men and women he led were organized into secret twelve-person subgroups called "cells," a precaution to keep them, and the authorities, from learning the identities of more than a few comrades. The Party leadership in New York considered movie people so valuable that they were excused from routine chores such as marching in parades and selling *People's World,* the West Coast's version of the *Daily Worker.*

Instead, these so-called "commissioned officers" of the Revolution were to promote Soviet interests by forming front groups and penetrating non-Communist organizations. Before August 1939, for example, the Hollywood Anti-Nazi League campaigned against the menace of Hitlerism, a most worthy cause. But during the Hitler-Stalin Pact, the front changed its name to the Hollywood League for Democratic Action, attacking FDR's supposed plot "to lead America to war." When Hitler's armies invaded the USSR in June 1941, it became the Hollywood Democratic Committee, demanding all-out aid in the "people's war against fascism."[35]

Like Lenin and Stalin, Lawson valued film as a weapon. "It is your duty," he told acting students, "to further the class struggle by your performance." Even if they were lowly extras in a lavish country-club scene, they must try to appear snooty and decadent. "If you are an extra on a tenement street, do your best to look downtrodden, do your best to look a victim of existing society." Similarly, Lawson advised comrades not to write entire Communist scripts, but to slip five minutes of Marxist ideology or the Party line into every picture. Those five minutes should be put into a scene with a big set, many extras, and a top star like Gary Cooper. ("Coop" was Hollywood's highest-paid actor in 1937, earning $370,000 a year, equal to $6.6 million in today's money.) That way, if a studio executive caught on, he would find it too expensive to cut the scene or shoot it over. This was Lawson's intention; whether it was ever realized is quite another matter. Many people have a hand in the final preparation of a script. To get Communist propaganda into a picture would have involved an entire creative group being in cahoots, about as likely as a July blizzard in Hollywood.[36]

The Party's main thrust was censoring what the public saw. Communist story analysts read incoming scripts, deciding whether the studio should buy the film rights to them. Scripts with anti-Nazi themes passed easily; those with anti-Soviet or anti-Communist story lines were rejected. Communist talent agents ruined the careers of their own clients who held "wrong" ideas, and Party members circulated informal "Red Lists," branding anti-Communists unfit to work in films. Such a list, film journalist John Cogley noted, "was as elusive an undertaking as a rumor whispered over a luncheon table. . . . The reason given would always be that [an actor] was not right for the part, that he was too tall, too short, too young or too old— never that he was too anti-Communist."[37]

Comrade Lawson enforced Party discipline. Here the man spoke out of both sides of his mouth. From one side, he pretended to be devoted to Thomas Jefferson's motto "Eternal hostility against every form of tyranny over the mind of man." From the other side, he preached unwavering devotion to Stalin, the USSR, and the CPUSA. His creed: "When the Party makes a decision, it becomes your opinion." This meant that members were not supposed to think for themselves, have their own ideas, or express themselves as conscience dictated. Indeed, there were lists of books Party members were forbidden to read; nor were they allowed to consult psychiatrists, because they might speak too freely. Similarly, certain expressions were taboo: "whitewash" and "black sheep," for example, were deemed "white chauvinism." Moreover, Lawson viewed "individualism" as a serious character flaw in a Communist, akin to mental illness. Writers who bucked the Party line risked standing trial, not in public like "white chauvinists" in Harlem, but secretly, in posh Beverly Hills mansions.[38]

Albert Maltz was branded a "literary deviationist." In 1946, the acclaimed screenwriter published an article titled "What Shall We Ask of Writers?" Maltz argued that the Party's notion of art as a weapon acted as a "straitjacket," a bar to creativity, and thus a barrier to spreading the Communist message. The artist, he insisted, must not be bound by the political needs of the moment, but be free to explore the eternal, most profound aspects of human life. True enough, but his plea ran counter to Party directives.[39]

When Maltz was put on trial by the Hollywood branch of CPUSA, people he had always regarded as comrades turned on him as if he were some loathsome creature. Writer Leopold Atlas, who was there, recalled how "they worked him over with every fang and claw" in a ferocious display of "intellectual cannibalism." When Maltz tried to defend himself, "almost instantly all sorts of howls went up in protest." Comrade Lawson, never doubting his own virtue, lashed out at the hapless man for sabotaging the "class struggle" and rejecting the "fundamental principles of Marxism." Stunned, Maltz groveled before his accusers, confessed his "errors," begged forgiveness, and wrote a follow-up article saying that people with bad politics could not be good writers. Never again, he promised, would he stray

Screenwriter Albert Maltz. (Date unknown)

from the Party line. Why did such a talented person, at the height of his powers, submit to such a degrading assault? Did he doubt his own ideas? Had he lost every shred of self-respect? Years later, Maltz admitted that he was emotionally chained to the Party; like so many others, he could not imagine a life worth living outside it. Indeed, he never regretted his action, saying it was his "desire not to be made to become a renegade—not to be expelled from the Party." Fellow writer Robert Rossen was made of sterner stuff. Rossen was the writer-director of *All the King's Men* (1949), the screen version of Robert Penn Warren's novel about a scheming politician and the evils of one-man rule. Since the film's theme that "power corrupts" could be taken as an exposé of Stalin's tyranny, soon after its debut, Rossen was put on trial in, of all places, Maltz's own Beverly Hills mansion. Rather than bow to such an indignity, he told his accusers, "Stick the whole Party up your ass!" and stormed out. Rossen later gave HUAC the names of fifty-seven Hollywood Communists.[40]

In the fall of 1947, HUAC held nine hearings in Washington. Today, there is a tendency to confuse these with the hearings held in the early 1950s by Wisconsin senator Joseph McCarthy's Committee on Government Operation. While both committees aimed at "unmasking" Communists, McCarthy had little interest in the media; his focus was on subversives and spies in the federal government, especially in the State Department and the armed forces.

HUAC chairman J. Parnell Thomas, a Republican from New Jersey, set three goals: investigate CPUSA influence in the film industry, hear the opinions of industry leaders who opposed communism, and get Party members to name other members and fellow travelers. As Martin Dies Jr. had before the war, HUAC soon ran into opposition. Top-notch performers, box-office gold like Humphrey Bogart, Judy Garland, Gene Kelly, and Burt Lancaster, denounced the forthcoming hearings as assaults on civil liberties. Hit singer Frank Sinatra asked: "Once they get the movies throttled, how long will it be before the Committee goes to work on freedom of the air? How long will it be before we're told what we can say and cannot say into a radio microphone? If you make a pitch on a nationwide radio network for a square deal for the underdog, will they call you a Commie? . . . Are they going to scare us into silence? I wonder."[41]

The hearings opened with testimony from studio heads Jack Warner and Louis B. Mayer. These titans of Tinseltown deplored the fact that "un-Americans" had bored into their industry like "ideological termites." Walt Disney, the king of animated cartoons, added fuel to the fire, telling how the Communist-dominated Screen Cartoonists Guild sought to make Mickey Mouse spout the Party line. The executives were followed by an actor named Ronald Reagan.[42]

Though rosy-cheeked Reagan looked younger than his thirty-six years, as presi-

Ronald Reagan, a well-known actor at the time and, decades later, president of the United States, testifying at the HUAC hearings. (1947)

dent of the Screen Actors Guild, he'd often clashed with Party loyalists. After one encounter, he got a phone call warning that if he did not lay off Communists, a "squad" would throw acid in his face "so that I would never be in pictures again." Another time, Comrade Lawson wagged his finger under Reagan's nose, shouting that "a two-party system is in no way necessary or even desirable for democracy." After all, the USSR was a "people's de-

mocracy," and it allowed only one party. When the actor tried to answer, Lawson's cronies pelted him with curses: "fascist," "capitalist scum," "enemy of the proletariat," "red-baiter." Though Reagan told HUAC he "detested communism," he opposed outlawing the Party as a matter of principle. "In opposing these people," he declared, "the best thing to do is make democracy work. . . . As a citizen, I would hesitate to see any political party outlawed on the basis of its political ideology. We have spent 170 years in this country on the basis that democracy is strong enough to stand up and fight against the inroads of any ideology." The press praised the actor's moderation, noting that Americans should not allow fear to overcome their devotion to democracy. None predicted that Reagan would become the fortieth president of the United States.[43]

Next, forty-one screenwriters and directors were called to testify. Most answered HUAC's core question: "Are you now or have you ever been a member of the Communist Party?" As proof of their sincerity, these "friendly" witnesses were then required to name other Communists or fellow travelers they knew. Ten refused to cooperate. These "unfriendly" witnesses, dubbed "the Hollywood Ten," were Alvah

Bessie, Herbert Biberman, Lester Cole, Edward Dmytryk, Ring Lardner Jr., John Howard Lawson, Albert Maltz, Samuel Ornitz, Adrian Scott, and Dalton Trumbo.

We should note that the forty-nine movies the Ten scripted during the war, including Lawson's *Action in the North Atlantic,* Maltz's *Pride of the Marines* and *Destination Tokyo,* and Trumbo's *Thirty Seconds over Tokyo,* were as patriotic as the Office of War Information could have wished for. Similarly, a careful study by film scholar Dorothy B. Jones remains the last word on their later films' lack of Communist bias. "My analysis of the content of films credited to the Hollywood Ten during the years immediately following the close of World War II and during the early years of the Cold War showed that none of these reflected in any manner the current viewpoint of the Communist Party. On the contrary, the films of the Ten during those years were, with a few exceptions, escapist Hollywood fare. In the case of films which undertook to treat social themes [like racial discrimination], the ideas expressed were those being treated and discussed generally throughout the country in magazines, newspapers, and postwar novels."[44]

Yet the Ten were not lambs cast into a wolves' den. They were steadfast Stalinists guided by Party lawyers; only two of their seven attorneys were not members. During the long train ride from Los Angeles to Washington, the lawyers devised a two-part strategy. First, it was agreed that nobody would take the Fifth, since that would be as good as admitting they were Communists. Instead, they must claim to be champions of the First Amendment. Here they stood on solid ground, as the First Amendment to the Constitution is the bedrock of American liberty; it bans Congress from passing laws restricting freedom of speech, freedom of the press, and the right to peacefully relate to whomever one wishes. Never mind that the comrades did not believe in free speech for those with opposing views. At the same time, the Ten were to follow the timeworn tactic of disrupting the proceedings, turning them into assaults on the American system of government. Witnesses, the Party taught, must be aggressive and even insulting, while claiming their rights as patriots. In 1958, screenwriter Dalton Trumbo admitted that he'd taken part "in a circus orchestrated by CP lawyers."[45]

John Howard Lawson testified first. It was a brilliant performance. Before answering any questions, he insisted upon

Screenwriter John Howard Lawson.
(Date unknown)

wannabes that used Nazi scare techniques to choke free expression. After that, the man who'd led the tormenting of Albert Maltz wrapped himself in the Bill of Rights. That sacred document, Lawson cried, "was established precisely to prevent the operation of any committee which could invade the basic rights of Americans." When Lawson continued in this vein, Chairman Thomas had him dragged, shouting, from the witness chair.[46]

Dalton Trumbo was the second act. Described as a "waspish, feisty man," he was the highest-paid screenwriter in the industry, earning $4,000 a week ($56,600

reading a written statement. Chairman Thomas glanced at the first sentence and refused to let him continue, saying it had no bearing on the hearing. The offending sentence damned HUAC for staging an "illegal and indecent trial of American citizens" based on evidence from "a parade of stool-pigeons, neurotics, publicity-seeking clowns, Gestapo agents, paid informers, and a few ignorant and frightened Hollywood artists," an obvious swipe at Ronald Reagan. Then the fireworks began. Lawson described HUAC as a bunch of Hitler

Screenwriter Dalton Trumbo at the HUAC hearings. (1947)

in today's money) when working on a script. Yet this Hollywood aristocrat had imagined himself a "proletarian wage slave," and screenwriters as "industrial workers toiling under monopoly capitalism." A devoted Stalinist, Trumbo called the dictator "one of the democratic leaders of the world" and boasted about how he'd personally blocked production of anti-Communist films. When called to testify, Trumbo, like Lawson, asked to read a statement. His request denied, Trumbo danced around questions, refusing to give straight answers. When Chairman Thomas dismissed him, Trumbo roared, "This is the beginning of an American concentration camp." Nobody thought to ask him about Stalin's slave-labor camps.[47]

Albert Maltz went next. What a change! For anyone in the know, his testimony was a stunning turnaround. The man who'd groveled at his Party trial became aggressive, loosing a torrent of clichés about patriotism seasoned with personal insults. "I am an American," Maltz declared, "and I believe there is no more proud word in the vocabulary of man." As an American, the Stalinist claimed to take his ideals from Thomas Jefferson and Abraham Lincoln. Then, in words he'd dared not utter at his Party trial, he declared: "I claim and

I insist upon my right to think freely and to speak freely . . . to publish whatever I please; to fix my mind or change my mind, without direction from anyone." However, the committee made sure to have the last word. After each witness was excused, an investigator read from his dossier. This document included a list of his writings and front-group memberships and the number of his CPUSA registration card: John Howard Lawson, No. 47275; Dalton Trumbo, No. 47187; Albert Maltz, No. 47196. How these numbers were obtained was never divulged, though it was likely from an FBI burglary of a Party office.[48]

The behavior of the Hollywood Ten enraged representatives of both parties. On November 24, 1947, the day the first round of hearings ended, the House of Representatives voted to hold them in contempt. (Convicted by a court, all were later fined $1,000 and sentenced to up to a year in federal prison.) That same day, the heads of the major studios met at the Waldorf-Astoria Hotel in New York. These were frightened men. The narrative promoted by the hearings, that the studios tolerated Communists, threatened to cut into their profits. As Louis B. Mayer of Metro-Goldwyn-Mayer put it, their duty was "to protect the industry and to draw the greatest possible number of people into the theaters." A two-page press release made his view official: The studios would fire anyone who did not disavow communism under oath, and they would not knowingly employ a Communist or anyone else who called for the overthrow of the United States government. This statement marked the birth of the Hollywood blacklist, a system that lasted through the 1950s. Some thought it poetic justice. In its essence, they claimed, the blacklist was simply payback for the Party's Red Lists: Both punished people for their beliefs. To show their patriotism and boost box-office receipts, the major studios made a slew of B-grade propaganda dramas like *I Married a Communist* (1949), *The Red Menace* (1949), *I Was a Communist for the FBI* (1951), and *The Atomic City* (1952). The last film, released shortly after the trial of "atomic spies" Julius and Ethel Rosenberg, showed how vulnerable America's nuclear secrets were to theft by foreign agents and traitors.[49]

The Hollywood Ten were merely the best-known targets of HUAC. Before long, however, the hunt for "subversives" spread beyond the film studios into the world of theater, music, television, and broad-

Poster for *I Married a Communist,* one of the many Hollywood films that promoted anti-Communist messages. (1949)

cast journalism. Here, the vehicle was the printed word in the form of a pamphlet titled *Red Channels.* This was the work of former FBI agent Theodore (Ted) C. Kirkpatrick and his aides, among them HUAC informant J. B. Matthews, who later became research director for Senator Joseph

McCarthy. *Red Channels* listed the names of 151 individuals, along with their supposed Communist leanings and affiliations based on information gleaned from newspaper articles, petitions, and, likely, leaks by HUAC staff. The pamphlet created such a stir that unless a person could clear himself or herself by confessing to HUAC and naming names, no producer would hire them for fear of losing sponsors.

Though *Red Channels* was used as a reference by Hollywood studio heads, not everyone was cowed into silence. There were individuals who vehemently protested its smearing people without giving them the chance to clear their name. Among these was Raymond Gram Swing, a renowned radio newscaster and commentator. On October 19, 1950, in a speech to the Radio Executives Club in New York, Swing blasted *Red Channels* as "utterly un-American":

> The technique used is that of the blanket smear, against which . . . there is no adequate disinfectant or deodorant. A person once named, however innocent he may be, can never quite be rid of the taint, the taint not of his guilt, but of his having been named. It is the power of

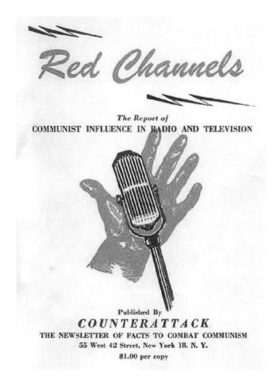

Cover of *Red Channels,* a pamphlet listing the names of alleged Communists in Hollywood. (1950)

> people using these methods that an ounce of insinuation overweighs a ton of fact. It is conviction by private committee without a trial. Certain persons are declared guilty without weighing the evidence and then punished for life without possibility of sufficient redress even if the most flagrant wrong has been done.[50]

Nevertheless, *Red Channels* took its pound of flesh. Without proof of clear, or of any, Communist affiliation, scores of talented people lost their jobs or found it nearly impossible to get bookings. Conductor Leonard Bernstein and composers Marc Blitzstein and Aaron Copland were banned from concert halls. So were singers Paul Robeson, Harry Belafonte, Lena Horne, Burl Ives, Pete Seeger, and Woody Guthrie. Bestselling author Howard Fast found publishers turned off to his novels. The careers of actors Edward G. Robinson and Orson Welles took a downturn. Because film studios and concert halls depended on banks for financing and banks were leery of lending to institutions that might be boycotted, their heads played it safe, in effect censoring what the public viewed.

Several women saw their careers evaporate in the blink of an eye. Upon returning from Paris, where she'd had a pleasant dinner with Eleanor Roosevelt, Marsha Hunt was expecting to sign a contract to host her own TV talk show. The offer never came. Her reaction when told that she'd been smeared by *Red Channels,* she recalled, was "Well, that ended my career." Actress Karen Morley was practically impoverished. She explained: "It was really murder to find work after being blacklisted, not just for me particularly, but for all actors who were prominent, because their faces were well known. I couldn't work anyplace where people might spot me. I couldn't even work as a saleslady in a fancy shop, for example, which I might have done in New York."[51]

Unable to find work in his chosen profession after being named in *Red Channels,* Philip Loeb, a union activist and actor, lost his career, and his life fell apart. In September 1955, he checked into a New York hotel under a false name, lay on the bed, and swallowed a bottle of sleeping pills. Loeb's friend, actor and comedian Zero Mostel, also blacklisted, honored the victim in the 1976 film *The Front,* in which the Loeb character he played jumps out of a window.[52]

As with Prohibition, the banning of alcoholic drinks after World War I, the blacklist and *Red Channels* spawned a lucrative racket. The only way to get off the hook was to hire a "clearance man," also called a "fixer." These were usually men with Washington connections who knew all the right moves; Ted Kirkpatrick, for example, ran a so-called "screening service for employers." For a fee, a fixer would set up an FBI interview in which the blacklisted person declared his patriotism and repented his sins. To prove his sincerity, he named names, implicating others who might or might not have been involved with the Party. If all went well, a call from a clearance man to a booking agent signaled that it was all right to hire the performer. Ronald Reagan fixed at least one case we know of. In the early 1950s, actress Nancy Davis learned that her name had been mistakenly placed on a blacklist. When she asked "Ronnie," as president of the Screen Actors Guild, to have it removed, he did; they later married.[53]

Writers fared better than performers. Faced with a shortage of material, producers winked at the budding black market in screenplays. Unable to find work, some writers used false names or turned to "fronts." A front was a writer who, as a favor or for a share of the fee, put their name on the screenplay the blacklisted author had actually written. After serving his prison term, Dalton Trumbo, for example, moved to Mexico, where he wrote thirty scripts under assumed names. Trumbo's *Roman Holiday* (1953) won an Academy Award for Best Story, but nobody came onstage to receive the Oscar. Trumbo could not claim it because he'd written the script under the name Robert Rich. "It was kind of a wondrous thing," his daughter Mitzi recalled. "But we couldn't tell anybody."[54]

The Hollywood blacklist lasted until 1960. That year, Kirk Douglas, the star and producer of *Spartacus,* took a bold step. Based on the novel by Howard Fast, *Spartacus* is a deeply moving story about the leader of a Roman slave revolt that ended with the crucifixion of all the surviving rebels. Douglas detested the blacklist: "I even hated the name," he said. He'd spent months trying to figure out a way to break it when the answer suddenly came to him. Since Dalton Trumbo had written the film adaptation, Douglas told him, "Not only am I going to tell them that you've written it, but we're putting your name on it . . . your name, Dalton Trumbo, as the sole writer." Years later, Douglas recalled the moment: "I could feel my heart pounding. Even as I was saying the words, I was still trying to convince myself that this was worth the risk." It was. The election of John F. Kennedy as president in 1960 sounded the death knell for the blacklist. *Spartacus* got the blessing of the new president when he calmly crossed an American Legion picket line to view it. After that, official Washington could not support the blacklist without an implied insult to the man in the White House. Also in 1960, director Otto Preminger announced that Trumbo had written the screenplay for the blockbuster *Exodus,* a fictionalized account of the founding of the State of Israel.[55]

Critics of HUAC have called its probe of the film industry "the greatest propaganda victory ever achieved by the CPUSA." It was a victory of sorts, because we are still living with its legacy. Many in today's film industry who were not alive during the blacklist era revere the Hollywood Ten as "rebels" and "martyrs," high-minded champions of free speech subjected to a witch hunt by frantic nitwits. In October 1997, on the fiftieth anniversary of the start of the hearings, the industry elite held a gala called Hollywood Remembers the Blacklist at the Academy of Motion Picture Arts and Sciences in Beverly Hills. The program featured contemporary film clips, live commentary, and dramatic re-creations of the hearings, ending with thunderous applause for the group's surviving members and the presentation of plaques engraved with the text of the First Amendment.[56]

Yet the Hollywood Ten were hardly victims of a witch hunt. In colonial New England, Puritan zealots hunted beings that did not exist and hanged innocents for acts no human could possibly perform. Nobody, after all, can speak to Satan through a dog, fly on a broomstick, or sicken people by staring at them with an "evil eye." While there were no witches in Hollywood, there were CPUSA activists operating in secrecy. And these activists were committed to using their craft to shape public opinion according to their Marxist ideology. Their success or failure in this effort is not at issue. Almost certainly, they did far less harm than they were blamed for. Yet we may ask: Were they martyrs

Flyer from the National Committee to Abolish the House Un-American Activities Committee. (1960)

to free speech? Closed-minded and rigid Stalinists, they staged struggle sessions in which they tormented their own for daring to express "deviant" opinions. While testifying before HUAC, they sought to defend themselves by invoking the Bill of Rights, which the CPUSA would in all likelihood have snuffed out if it took power. At the same time, the Ten were, whether consciously or not, acting in the interests of the USSR, a foreign foe bent on defeating the United States in the Cold War. From the government's standpoint, therefore, they represented a national security threat that it could not ignore or tolerate.

That said, something about HUAC and Hollywood does not smell right. The screenwriters broke no law. They were, in fact, attacked for their beliefs by congressmen with sins of their own. J. Parnell Thomas, a smug hypocrite, was also a crook who later served time in federal prison for swindling the government; John E. Rankin was a ranting bigot. This leaves the larger issue of whether a free society can allow freedom for those who would abolish freedom—a serious issue in the age of terrorism in which we live.

OF ATOMIC BOMBS
AND SPIES

The Soviet espionage offensive . . . indicated that the Cold War was not
a state of affairs that began after the Second World War, but a
guerrilla action that Stalin had secretly started years earlier.
—John Earl Haynes and Harvey Klehr, *Venona* (1999)

IMAGINING DOOMSDAY

President Truman's loyalty program and HUAC were early responses to the Cold War. Nevertheless, throughout the 1940s the American homeland faced no direct foreign military threat. So long as the United States had a monopoly on the atomic bomb, another Pearl Harbor was inconceivable. Yet time does not stand still. On September 23, 1949, the White House announced that the USSR had exploded its first atomic bomb the previous month.

The Soviet test shocked Americans. However, anyone informed about science may explore nature's mysteries. It was common knowledge that atoms are the smallest building blocks of matter. If, scientists reasoned, a single atom of uranium, a rare silvery-white metal, could be split, its high-speed "fission" particles would strike adjoining atoms, splitting them in turn and causing a chain reaction that would release enormous amounts of energy. The problem was not one of atomic theory, but of technology. To turn out enough purified uranium and determine how to use it in a bomb required vast research facilities employing thousands of scientists, engineers, and machinists. Here, the United States, the world's leading industrial power, had a definite advantage. Though Washington policy makers knew that the USSR would eventually build its own version of the weapon, they did not expect it to do so before repairing the massive damage the country had suffered during the war, an effort expected to take at least a decade. But it was not to be.

Stalin knew the Americans were developing a radically new type of weapon. Almost from the moment work began in 1939, his spies had been collecting information about the top-secret Manhattan Project. Nevertheless, Soviet research moved at a snail's pace due to lack of resources and the need for scientists' expertise on urgent wartime projects. The destruction of Hiroshima came as a wake-up call. When the news reached the Kremlin, an official recalled, "Stalin was frightened to the point of cowardice." The next day, the tyrant summoned his chief scientists to his dacha outside Moscow. Everyone was so worried, his daughter, Svetlana, who'd just had a baby, recollected that "my father paid hardly any attention to me." Stalin ordered the scientists to build a Soviet atomic bomb quickly, no matter what the cost. "Hiroshima has shaken the world," he said solemnly. "The balance has been broken. Build the bomb—it will remove a great danger from us."[1]

The test of what Americans called "Joe-1" on August 29, 1949, created what one scientist called "soul-wrenching terror," raising questions we must address in this chapter. First: How could the United States protect itself from the horrors of a nuclear holocaust, especially when scientists were experimenting with ways of placing nuclear warheads on rockets? Soon the short-range rockets, with a range of a few hundred miles, that were first deployed by Germany in World War II would evolve into intercontinental ballistic missiles (ICBMs), aimed by sophisticated guidance systems and capable of striking targets thousands of miles away. Second: How was the USSR able to develop its bomb in such a short time?[2]

One way of protecting the nation was through deterrence—that is, being so strong that even if an enemy nation struck a devastating first blow, it knew the United States would still be able to destroy it. To that end, in January 1950, President Truman gave the go-ahead to build "the super." Officially known as the hydrogen bomb, it would use the explosion of an atomic bomb as a trigger to release energy from the radioactive element plutonium. Dubbed "the hell bomb," its earliest versions were designed to equal the explosive power of 10.4 million tons of TNT, one thousand times greater than the atomic bomb that destroyed Hiroshima. Truman's decision prompted Albert Einstein, the foremost scientist of the day, to warn that using this "doomsday machine" could end life on earth. His warning had no effect; the United States set off the first hell bomb on November 1, 1952, on Eniwetok, an atoll in the Pacific. Within seconds, the weapon produced a fireball three miles wide; after fifteen minutes, the mile-wide

The world's first successful hydrogen bomb test was conducted in the Pacific by the U.S. (1952)

coral island on which it had been detonated was vaporized, leaving a crater two hundred feet deep and more than a mile across. The USSR followed suit. On August 12, 1953, it exploded "Joe-4," its first hydrogen bomb—"Joe-4" was an American nickname, with "Joe" referring to Joseph Stalin—in the Soviet Republic of Kazakhstan.[3]

This was a very worrisome development. Until the 1950s, the United States lacked an effective civil defense program. It hadn't needed one; during World War II, Americans felt safe at home. Apart from Hitler's U-boats prowling off the Atlantic coast, its enemies had no long-range bombers capable of reaching its shores. The only serious precautions existed along the coasts, where nighttime blackouts prevented enemy submarines from seeing ships silhouetted against the lit shoreline. Aside from that and twenty-four-hour beach patrols, the nation had no program to build air-raid shelters, let alone evacuate cities at a moment's notice. Local fire departments were beefed up, schools held more fire drills, medical supplies were stockpiled, and rescue workers were trained, but that was all.

Washington sought to reassure the nation about the looming nuclear threat. Government printing presses churned out millions of ten-cent pamphlets titled *How to Survive an Atomic Bomb* and *Survival Under Atomic Attack.* According to the latter, "Not even hydrogen bombs could blow the earth apart or kill us all by mysterious radiation." Why, even the survivors of Hiroshima and Nagasaki were now doing just fine, it said in a breezy, matter-of-fact style. "[They] live in new houses built right where their old houses once stood. The war may have changed their way of life, but they are not riddled with cancer. Their children are normal. Those who were temporarily unable to have children because of radiation are now having children again." Unless you were directly under a nuclear blast, you had an excellent chance of staying alive if you followed a few simple rules, the pamphlet noted. "Should you unexpectedly be caught out-of-doors, seek shelter alongside a building, or jump into any handy ditch or gutter." After a blast, "select your food and water with care," "do what you can to keep from being showered by radioactive waste ma-

Facts About Fallout, issued by the Federal Civil Defense Administration. (Date unknown)

terials," and "should you find your body radioactive, scrub yourself from head to foot." Last, "take these precautions, but don't worry." To be on the safe side, citizens were urged to build bomb shelters and stock them with canned food, water, and tranquilizers.[4]

Such advice was so unrealistic that it amounted to official lying. The authors neglected to say that thousands of Japanese survivors bore hideous burn scars all over their bodies and, yes, many were still dying in agony from multiple types of radiation-induced cancer. Nor did the authors answer basic questions about bomb shelters. How long would people have to stay in them after a blast? What kind of world would they find when they emerged? It would not be a pleasant world, experts knew, but they spoke about it only among themselves. During a meeting of army reserve medical officers in New York, Colonel Wilfred A. Steiner detailed the emergency medical supplies needed to care for *one* burn victim for just a few days: 42 tanks of oxygen, 2.7 miles of gauze bandages, and 40 pints of blood. Steiner estimated 100,000 burn victims in the city. "Where," he asked, "would New York get forty million pints of blood?" Audience members gasped. Some may have thought

those killed instantly would be luckier than the survivors.[5]

Meanwhile, schoolteachers held "duck and cover" drills. The name came from the title of a government film meant to instruct children about what to do in the first seconds of a nuclear attack. Just as its cartoon hero Bert the Turtle instinctively hid in his shell to protect himself, children had to take shelter under their desks. According to the jolly Bert the Turtle song, this wise little turtle knew exactly what to do when danger presented itself:

> *He'd hide his head and tail and four little feet*
> *He'd duck and cover!...*[6]

Yet "duck and cover" was nothing to sing about. "Obediently," novelist Mary Mackey recalled, "we would fold our bodies into that attitude of prayer and supplication known only to the children of the fifties: legs folded, head between the knees, hands raised to protect the fragile, invisible nerve that floated somewhere in the blackness behind our eyes." However, not all teachers were as sensitive as they could have been. If a child did not get entirely under his or her desk, the teacher, also stressed, might snap: "Your right arm

"Duck and cover" drills at a Brooklyn middle school. (1962)

is burned off! Your right leg is gone! And half your face is burned away!" Some children became hysterical; the boy under the desk next to mine wet his pants. In one case, a principal, as subtle as a hammer dropping on an egg, told a parent, "He needs to be talked to like that. Now he won't forget." Afterward, a child might have recurrent nightmares, awakening screaming, or become terrified of the sky itself. Issuing "dog tags" often heightened anxiety. Modeled on the metal identification discs that members of the military wore around their necks, these gave the child's name, date of birth, parents' names, and address. The reason for the tags, a wise fourth grader observed, was "that people will know who I am if my face is burned away." In New York, press reports noted that the tags had a melting point of 1,400 degrees Celsius, meaning they could withstand temperatures that

Children were issued dog tags to identify their bodies in case of a nuclear attack. (1951)

vaporized human bodies. My mother threw my tag away.[7]

STALIN'S SPIES

The answer to how the USSR built its atomic bomb so quickly seemed obvious. Though it had first-class scientists, they could not have made such rapid strides without outside help. One did not have to be a genius to figure out that spies had stolen American secrets. But before seeing who did this, we must explore the larger issue of Soviet espionage.

When President Roosevelt granted the USSR diplomatic recognition in 1933, he unintentionally opened America's doors to the Committee for State Security—or KGB, from its Russian initials. The KGB was Stalin's foreign intelligence service. KGB men called "legals" were attached to the Soviet embassy in Washington and consulates in the nation's major cities. Since they had diplomatic immunity, they could not be jailed if discovered, only expelled from the country. Other KGB men, called "illegals," had no legal cover; they usually entered the country disguised as seamen from Soviet freighters docked in New York Harbor. Once ashore, they went undercover, posing as private citizens working at various trades, often for years or even decades. New York was ideal for the KGB illegal. In a city of immigrants, few paid attention to an agent's Russian accent and ignorance of American ways. Yet neither legals nor illegals could have spied on their own; rather, they passed Moscow's orders to, and received stolen information from, American citizens. This information was sent to the "Moscow Center," KGB headquarters, by coded telegraph cables or in diplomatic mailbags, which could not be searched by American authorities. The United States had no spy networks in the USSR until the start of the Cold War and the creation of the Central Intelligence Agency.

The CPUSA earned its Moscow gold because the KGB could not have functioned without its assistance. As historians John Earl Haynes and Harvey Klehr explain, the Party "was an auxiliary service of Soviet intelligence." While the vast majority of its members never spied, spies were almost always members or fellow travelers. Historians point to General Secretary Earl Browder as the "pivotal figure—indeed, a linchpin of Soviet espionage in the United States." Browder, not the KGB, selected "virtually all" Soviet "sources, couriers, and group handlers"; indeed, he personally recruited eighteen spies for the KGB, assisted by his younger brother, Bill. With Browder's help, the KGB contacted those willing to furnish safe houses, secret places where agents could hide and photograph stolen documents, and those who could provide passports, driver's licenses, and other identity papers. What's more, Browder inspected stolen government documents and dickered with the KGB over agents' assignments. Spying was a Browder family enterprise. Earl's lover, Kitty Harris, worked for the KGB, as did his younger sister Margaret, who was a full-time KGB agent in Europe. His niece, Helen Lowry,

was married to and aided an important KGB illegal in his work. None of these people were ever charged—or punished— for their activities.[8]

By the late 1940s, some five hundred Americans had spied at some point for the KGB. The Party's agents or contacts were in key branches of government: the State Department, Commerce Department, Treasury Department, Justice Department, and War Department. They passed confidential documents to the KGB, revealed American negotiating strategies, and helped shape policy in ways favorable to Soviet interests. Spies in private firms specializing in electronics, chemical, and aviation research made off with blueprints, technical handbooks, and experimental data worth billions of dollars.[9]

Spies came from all walks of life: rich and poor, city dwellers and small-town folk, the self-taught and graduates of elite universities. Despite their varied backgrounds, spies had certain things in common. All Soviet spies (those who have been identified) were white people. Unlike post–Cold War spies such as Aldrich Ames, a senior CIA officer who received $2.7 million for his treachery, they shunned financial rewards. Self-styled idealists, the spies of the 1930s and 1940s believed their serving the USSR served the cause of peace. For them, spying was a moral duty—or that is how they justified it to themselves.[10]

America's entry into World War II made it and the USSR allies but not friends, at least not in Moscow's view. When engineer Victor Kravchenko arrived in the United States in 1943, his boss warned: "Hold fast to the knowledge that as a Communist you are the sworn enemy of the capitalist society whose world you enter today in America. Communism and capitalism can never be reconciled! . . . Today we regard our relations with capitalist America as diplomatically and militarily useful. This does not mean that our interests can ever coincide. . . . If you bear that in mind, you will understand why we must remain vigilant, suspicious and aloof."[11]

While American media whitewashed "our heroic Soviet ally," thousands of Soviet lend-lease technicians, inspectors, and advisers poured into the country on official business. Their hosts, overflowing with the spirit of American-Soviet "friendship," took them on guided factory tours, allowed them to copy plans, and gave them nearly everything they asked for. Once a week, a Soviet plane took off from Gore Field in Great Falls, Montana, on the first leg of its return via Alaska to the USSR. Every flight carried crates of sensitive materials; one plane had hundreds of pounds of unrefined uranium ore. Such careless generosity shocked Victor Kravchenko. "Who cared what we took?" the engineer wrote. "Had we taken the Empire State Building and put it on a ship, nobody would have cared. . . . Nobody opened boxes and checked." No wonder the war years were a bonanza for the KGB. With the FBI devoting the lion's share of its resources to tracking German agents, it had little time for Moscow's spies.[12]

Yet 1945 saw a run of bad luck for the KGB. That year, Igor Gouzenko, a twenty-six-year-old code clerk in the Soviet embassy in Ottawa, Canada, learned that he and his family were to be sent home. This was ominous news; he knew of other embassy staff ordered home and never seen again. Fearing the worst, Gouzenko turned to his wife, Svetlana. She advised him, "Go into the vault and steal every secret thing you can put your hands on, and change the combination on the vault and lock the door. It'll take six weeks for the Russians to send somebody over to chisel the door of the safe open to find out you've taken all these things. Turn yourself over to the Canadians." Gouzenko recalled that when he finally left the embassy on

September 5, "there were almost a hundred documents, some of them small scraps of paper and others covering several large sheets of stationery. . . . The documents felt like they weighed a ton and I imagined that they were bulging out from under my shirt." Upon examination by Canadian authorities, the documents proved beyond doubt that Soviet spies were operating in North America. Because KGB hit men were searching for Gouzenko, Canada gave him a new identity. For the rest of their lives, Gouzenko and his family were protected by the Royal Canadian Mounted Police. To be sure, his young son and daughter did not know their true family name. Gouzenko occasionally gave interviews, but always with a hood over his face.[13]

Two months after Gouzenko's flight, Elizabeth Bentley, a CPUSA member since 1936, had a change of heart. Operating under the code names "Good Girl" and "Wise Girl," the Vassar graduate was the contact for several highly placed spies in the U.S. government, whose information she passed to her KGB handler. A heavy drinker disillusioned with her role, Bentley confessed to the FBI on November 7. In a 107-page statement, she exposed a ring headed by Russian-born Nathan

Gregory Silvermaster, a senior economist with the United States War Production Board. Among the ring's members were two of the most influential fellow travelers in Washington. Senior Treasury Department official Harry Dexter White was the KGB's highest-ranking source. Not only did White promote a dozen fellow spies to sensitive positions within the government, he advised the Soviets on ways to counter American diplomatic moves. White even met with a KGB agent during the

Elizabeth Bentley. (1948)

San Francisco conference establishing the United Nations, giving him the American negotiating position on several issues. Another spy, Lauchlin Currie, was described as "a powerful Washington insider with access to every top official from FDR down." As White House economic adviser, Currie worked closely with the president, whose confidence he had, and handled the most important documents. In all, Bentley named more than eighty people, of whom twenty-seven held government jobs. The Moscow Center panicked. Due to Bentley's revelations, it shut down one network after another. By March 1951, the KGB had no functioning agents in America whatsoever.[14]

The public had only Bentley's word for her charges. The hard evidence to back them up lay in the files of the Venona Project. Venona was a seldom-used girl's name adopted by Colonel Carter W. Clarke of the Signal Security Agency, the army's code-breaking division. Clarke distrusted Stalin. Early in 1943, he'd heard rumors of secret Soviet-Nazi peace talks, a disastrous turn of events if true. The notion that Stalin might abandon his Allies was quite plausible; Lenin had done exactly that during World War I. We also know that the tyrant regretted the end of Soviet-Nazi

"friendship" (his term). Stalin's daughter, Svetlana, remembered her father repeating, even after the war, "Together with the Germans we would have been invincible."[15]

Upon deciding to investigate, Clarke turned to the FBI. Since 1939, the bureau had been quietly collecting copies of every coded Soviet telegram leaving or entering the United States. To confirm his suspicions, the colonel formed a team of expert code breakers, largely women with mathematical ability and patience—lots of patience. Nonetheless, the work proved so stressful that several had nervous breakdowns, one developed a phobia of bathing and was awful to be near, and another killed herself; a male linguist became an alcoholic. Yet by early 1946, the team had broken the first batch of cables. Though the war had ended by then, these showed that Stalin had not sought a separate peace with Hitler. What they did show was that the Soviets had at least 349 Americans actively spying for them. Since analysts decoded only a tiny fraction of the more than three thousand cables they had, it was logical to assume there were many other spies still to be found. To track them down, the army shared its findings with the FBI's counterintelligence division tasked with neutralizing security threats from foreign espionage services.[16]

Another problem: The decoded cables usually gave only a spy's code name. Fortunately, the FBI had photographed documents during a burglary of a Soviet diplomatic office in New York. However, even with this information, the Venona team could identify only half the roughly two hundred individuals behind the code names. Among them was "Helmsman," code for CPUSA chief Earl Browder. But who was "Muse," and what had he given the KGB? Where had "Bibi" worked? Was "Donald," a navy captain, still in uniform? What about Source No. 19, who was so highly placed he attended a closed-door meeting with FDR and Winston Churchill? And "Mole," "Dodger," "Grandmother," "Fakir"—who were they? Where were they? Were they still active?

Who were their handlers? And even if they were unmasked, Venona evidence could not be used in court without revealing the project's existence to the KGB. Desperate for a solution, the FBI chief decided that the only way to use Venona was to catch a spy and get him to identify his contacts. Even if he did not know the identities of those behind specific code names, his naming names would lead to other spies, who might be pressured into talking.[17]

It so happened that several Venona cables mentioned a man called "Antenna," later changed to "Liberal." Though the FBI did not know it at the time, these were the code names of Julius Rosenberg, head of one of the KGB's all-time most productive spy rings. The arrest, trial, and execution of Julius and his wife, Ethel, began a debate that still sparks controversy.

VII

THE ROSENBERG SPY RING

The truth is too simple: one must always get there by a complicated route.
—George Sand, letter to Armand Barbès, May 12, 1867

JULIUS AND ETHEL: A LOVE STORY

Julius Rosenberg was born on May 12, 1918, the youngest of the five children of Harry and Sophie Rosenberg. Immigrants, his parents had joined the exodus of Jews fleeing anti-Semitism in czarist Russia in the early 1900s. If they'd come to America expecting to find *die Goldene Medina*—Yiddish for "the Golden Land"—they were sorely disappointed. There were no gold nuggets in the streets ready for the taking, as the gullible imagined. Like the majority of Eastern European immigrants, they could only afford to live in a tenement on New York's Lower East Side, the most densely populated district on the planet. Jews were its largest ethnic group, followed by Italians in the Little Italy section. Communist novelist Michael Gold described everyday life there in *Jews Without Money* (1930):

I can never forget the East Side . . . a tenement canyon hung with fire-escapes, bed-clothing, and faces. Always these faces at the tenement windows. The street never failed them. It was an immense excitement. It never slept. It roared like a sea. It exploded like fireworks. People pushed and wrangled in the street. There were armies of howling push-cart peddlers. Women screamed, dogs barked and copulated. Babies cried. A parrot cursed. Ragged kids played under truck-horses. Fat housewives fought from stoop to stoop. A beg-gar sang. . . . East Side mothers with heroic bosoms pushed their baby carriages, gossiping. . . . A tinker hammered at brass. Junk bells rang. . . . Excitement, dirt, fighting, chaos! The sound of the street lifted like the blast of a great carnival or catastrophe.[1]

Though Harry Rosenberg found a job in a small garment factory, he barely earned enough to afford a proper meal for his family. "I remember," one of Julius's sisters recalled, "we were so poor my mother hard-boiled the eggs, so she could divide one among us." Like his

Julius Rosenberg grew up in a Lower East Side tenement in New York City, not unlike this one on Hester Street. (Date unknown)

siblings, Julius attended the local public schools. At the end of the school day, he'd walk to the Downtown Talmud Torah on East Houston Street, where he studied Torah, God's law as revealed to Moses and recorded in the first five books of the Hebrew Scriptures. Torah was the youngster's soul candy; he could not get enough of it. Abiding by its sacred laws and rituals anchored him in the world, giving him an absolute certainty about good and evil, right and wrong, justice and injustice. The boy became so pious that his parents had hopes of him becoming a rabbi, a great honor for the family.[2]

Yet that was not to be. By his early teens, Julius began to have doubts. The rabbis who taught him often seemed like *luftmenschen*—Yiddish slang for "people with their heads in the clouds"—detached from the realities of Depression-torn America. This became all too apparent to the sensitive youngster. On his way home, he'd stop and listen to the soapbox speakers on Delancey Street, the Lower East Side's main shopping street. Besides demanding federal programs to fight poverty, they called for the release of Tom Mooney, a labor leader framed for a bombing that killed ten people, and justice for the Scottsboro Boys. In 1934,

a five-month strike began at two local department stores that saw violent clashes between workers and police. When Julius asked his rabbis to join him on a picket line, they turned him down. Their refusal to take sides in what he saw as a clear matter of right and wrong soured him on religion; thereafter, he appears to have lost interest in Judaism. Torah study, prayer, and synagogue attendance became things of the past.[3]

Julius found others more attuned to the times. By the 1930s, playwright Lionel Abel joked, the Lower East Side was "the most interesting part of the Soviet Union." The CPUSA had deep roots in the neighborhood. Circulation of the daily *Morgen Freiheit* (*Morning Freedom*), a Yiddish-language Communist newspaper, topped that of the *Daily Worker* by several thousand copies. May Day was a festive holiday, with marchers, often accompanied by their young children, carrying portraits of Marx and Engels, Lenin and Stalin. Party speakers addressed mass meetings in Union Square, dubbed "New York's Red Square." The Party, too, ran scores of cellar clubs, where teenagers hung out, played cards for pennies, read Communist pamphlets, and sang revolutionary songs like "The Red Flag":

The people's flag is the deepest red,
It shrouded oft our martyred dead,
And ere their limbs grew stiff and cold,
Their hearts' blood dyed its ev'ry fold.

Then raise the scarlet standard high.
Within its shade we'll live and die,
Though cowards flinch and traitors
  sneer,
We'll keep the red flag flying here.[4]

By the time Julius (or "Julie," as his friends called him) graduated from Seward Park High School in 1934, he was an ardent Marxist. Like so many others, he found in its teachings the clarity and energy lacking in traditional religion. Author Ilene Philipson explains:

> The careful attention Julie previously had paid to the Torah and the Prophets was turned to the works of Marx, Lenin, and Stalin. His belief in a better world through the coming of the Messiah was replaced by a belief in the historical inevitability of socialism. When he spoke of socialism, it was with the same ardor and piety that one could imagine him formerly using to describe the return to Zion.

The USSR had become his promised land.[5]

That same year, at the age of sixteen, Julius enrolled in the engineering school of the City College of New York (CCNY). Located in Harlem, CCNY was the crown jewel of the city's five public colleges. Unlike private colleges, it charged no tuition, only a modest registration fee, and accepted all qualified male applicants. (Hunter College served female students.) For the cost of textbooks and a nickel subway ride, one got a fine education and, with luck, a path out of the tenements. Ivy League colleges, like Columbia a mile to the south, on Broadway, had quotas limiting the number of Jews admitted each year. Politically, students and faculty at Ivy League schools were typically Democrats or Republicans. CCNY, however, was a CPUSA stronghold. The Party boasted its own faculty unit and newsletter, *Teacher and Worker.* Like the *Daily Worker,* this publication supported Stalin's Moscow Trials and mass purges of "traitors."

The CCNY lunchroom was a hub of student activity. It had a dozen alcoves, U-shaped side rooms with a bench along the wall and a table in the middle. Followers of Leon Trotsky, Catholics, Orthodox

THE KREMLIN

Students with Stalinist inclinations at City College of New York (CCNY) had their own alcove, dubbed "the Kremlin." (1936)

Jews, chess fanatics, and jocks: each had their own alcove. Between classes, students gathered in their respective alcoves to eat and socialize. Alcove No. 1 belonged to the Trotskyites. Alcove No. 2, dubbed "the Kremlin," was Stalinist turf. Kremlin students debated the fine points of Marxist theory, adored Stalin, and cursed anyone they disapproved of as fascist. From time to time, Trotskyites and Stalinists had shouting matches, ending in black eyes and bloody noses.

The Kremlin became Julius's home away from home; on some days, he became so absorbed in discussions that he forgot to go to class. He was a firm believer in Soviet-style communism; arguing with him was like debating a stone wall. "Fellow students who chanced to disagree with him," a classmate recalled, "found him a doctrinaire and inflexible opponent." From the Kremlin, Julius organized and led the Steinmetz Club, the CCNY branch of the Young Communist League, composed of electrical engineering students. In later years, several club members would join the Rosenberg spy ring. According to Morton Sobell, a college friend of Julius's, half the CCNY engineering class in the late 1930s were Communists.[6]

During the 1936 Christmas break, Julius attended a benefit for the International Seamen's Union in an East Side tenement. The moment he stepped through the door, he saw a petite woman with "the saddest eyes" and "the face of an angel." It was love at first sight. Her name was Ethel Greenglass. Born on September 28, 1915, Ethel was the oldest of the three children of Barney and Tessie Greenglass, immigrants from Russia and Austria. Like the Rosenbergs, her family barely scratched out a living; Barney repaired sewing machines, not the busiest trade in the Depression-ridden garment industry. Though Ethel showed talent as a singer, upon graduating from Seward Park High School in 1933, she had to find a job to help support her family. While working as a clerk in a shipping firm, she became involved in social and political causes, even leading a strike, for which she was fired.[7]

The youngsters began dating. Their idea of a date was not eating out or taking in a movie, but going to rallies and meeting like-minded people. Though Julius had fallen behind in his studies, Ethel encouraged him to buckle down; to keep him focused, she typed and edited his lab reports. In February 1939, he graduated from CCNY with a degree in electrical engineering, finishing near the bottom of his class, seventy-ninth out of eighty-five. The couple married in June. It was a good marriage; they were not shy about showing affection, calling each other "darling," "honey," and "bunny" in public. Nor could they keep their hands still. "Always they were touching each other," Julius's mother recalled. And after they'd been apart for a few hours during the day, "they couldn't wait to get into the bedroom, that's how much in love they were." In 1943, Ethel

Julius and Ethel Rosenberg. (Date unknown)

gave birth to their son Michael; Robert arrived in 1947.[8]

Julius had to settle for part-time jobs, but not for long. In the fall of 1940, his luck changed. Hitler's armies had already overrun France, and Britain was feeling the fury of the Nazi air force. With President Roosevelt's rearmament program gaining momentum, engineers were in demand, regardless of their class standing. The U.S. Army Signal Corps hired Julius to inspect electronics parts made by private companies under contract to the military. On his job application, the engineer stated that he'd never belonged to a subversive group. That was a lie. Julius had become a CPUSA member while courting his future wife. We can say this with confidence, because army intelligence officers later found his membership card, No. 6603, and an acquaintance told the FBI that they'd been in Party Branch 13B. Ethel likely joined at around the same time, though the authorities never turned up her membership card. According to a psychologist who treated Ethel later in life, communism fulfilled a deep emotional need, offering her "a window to the world," a cause to believe in with every fiber of her being. (Leaking such information was highly irregular, a violation of doctor-patient confidentiality.)[9]

WORKING FOR THE KGB

Sometime in the early spring of 1941, Julius decided to volunteer for "special work"—code for spying for the USSR. This was during the Hitler-Stalin Pact, while the dictators were working to destroy the independent nations of Eastern Europe and Stalin was doing his utmost to derail FDR's defense buildup. As followers of the Party line, Julius and Ethel "heartily supported" what critics dubbed "the Pact of Blood." Whatever crimes Stalin committed, the couple accepted Moscow's explanation on faith. According to a Russian contact, Julius was convinced that a perfect society could never be born without mass terror. "For him," the contact said, "the bloody episodes in the building of Socialism didn't change the fact that the system was much more equitable than capitalism." Accordingly, Julius approved of what we might call "necessary killing," just as Lenin and Stalin did. It is impossible to know if he would have acted on that belief, had he the means and the power. However, Hitler's invasion of the USSR on June 22 only deepened his resolve to aid the Communist nation.[10]

Contacting the KGB was difficult; it did not advertise for spies in the *Daily Worker*. Julius simply kept telling CPUSA officials what he wanted to do until one steered him to the right person. After a security check more thorough than the one by the Signal Corps, it accepted him for espionage work. From that moment, Julius began a secret life. All official ties to the Party were cut. He was relieved of rank-and-file duties, his *Daily Worker* subscription canceled, his name stricken from Party membership rolls and entered in a "special register" kept under lock and key. To avoid slipups, he was ordered to avoid pro-Soviet rallies, as the FBI might photograph these, and cut ties with Communist friends. Family members were not to be let in on his secret. He was also briefed on *konspiratsya,* the KGB term for tradecraft. To avoid being "tailed," he learned to get on and off buses and subways, to duck into buildings with an entrance at either end, and to practice the art of "brush past," passing documents to his handler in the street or some other busy place like Grand Central Station.[11]

Julius's handler was Alexander Feklisov, a military electronics specialist attached to the KGB unit in the Soviet consulate in New York. Born in 1914, Feklisov was a gifted operator; in 1998, Russia paid tribute to him by issuing a postage stamp in his honor. He and Julius hit it off from the very beginning. They met fifty times, usually in busy cafeterias, where they could talk without attracting attention. Deeply impressed with his contact, Feklisov saw Julius as a committed Communist, well read in the works of Marx and Engels, Lenin and Stalin. His espionage work, Feklisov noted, was "a kind of religious calling"; indeed, Julius "was a true revolutionary who was willing to sacrifice himself for his beliefs." Julius, in turn, told his handler, "Our meetings are among the happiest moments of my life," because they were a direct link to his beloved USSR. Proud of his selflessness, the engineer refused to take any money except for the twenty-five dollars a month he needed for travel expenses and the restaurant bills he paid for his contacts. "If I can do anything to help," he'd say, "you can count on me."[12]

Feklisov did count on him—a lot. Julius, he reported, was an "extremely valuable agent." His KGB superiors in Moscow agreed. Out of a total of three thousand Venona cables that have been made public, nineteen relate to Julius and his activities. According to one cable: "He always regards any assignment with a sense of responsibility. . . . 'Liberal' is highly politically developed and devoted to our cause. He considers helping our country to be the principal aim of his life." The term "politically developed" was KGB-speak for a committed Stalinist who could be trusted.[13]

Another cable is especially informative about Ethel Rosenberg. Dated November 27, 1944, it was sent from the KGB's New York "residency" (outpost) to the Moscow Center. The cable specifically mentions Julius's wife by name: "ETHEL, 29 years old, married five years . . . a FELLOWCOUNTRYWOMAN [CPUSA member] since 1938. Sufficiently well developed politically. Knows about her husband's work. . . . In view of delicate health does not work. Is characterized positively and as a devoted person." "Does not work" can be interpreted two ways. It might mean that Ethel was not physically up to spying and, as a homemaker, had pressing duties—or that she did not choose to work as a spy, which seems more likely. That she knew what Julius was doing, however, is evident from the cable. The phrase "devoted person" is KGB shorthand for a loyal Stalinist. Though Alexander Feklisov claimed that they'd never met, she once signaled him that the coast was clear for a late-night meeting in their apartment. Ethel also hid money and spy equipment for Julius. Equally important, she evaluated potential recruits for his spy ring.[14]

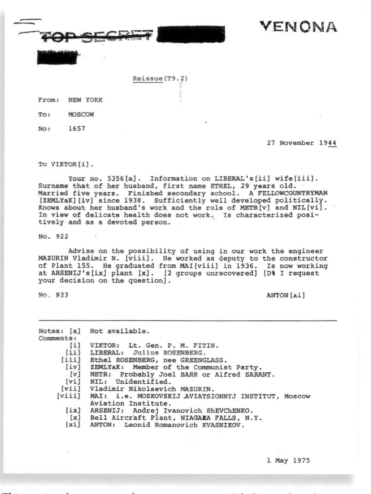

This previously top-secret document mentions Ethel Rosenberg by name. (1944)

Julius proved himself an able manager of spies. His ring's specialty was not atomic research, but cutting-edge military technology. Those he recruited were chiefly men he'd known during his student days who shared his political views. Since graduating from CCNY, they had risen to trusted positions in university research laboratories and firms involved in electronics, aircraft, and weapon design. According to Steven T. Usdin, an authority on Soviet technical espionage, Julius ran "a complex, sophisticated operation that stole industrial secrets on an industrial scale." The astonishing fact is that his ring "gave the Red Army blueprints for every major U.S. military technology development during the Second World War."[15]

CCNY classmate Morton Sobell was a "Red diaper" baby, a child of parents who were CPUSA members. Jewish immigrants from Russia, Louis and Rose Sobell were keen activists steeped in Marxist ideology; one of Morton's uncles was a secret courier, carrying messages between Party higher-ups in New York and the KGB's Moscow Center. "People like me," Morton later explained, "were attracted to communism because it seemed to offer a rational explanation for what was wrong with society. Capitalism wasn't rational." As an engineer at the General Electric Laboratory in Schenectady, New York, he secretly photographed thousands of pages of plans for, among other things, a new electronic device called sonar for tracking submerged U-boats and an early-generation computer for aiming antiaircraft guns. Other members of the ring included Joel Barr and

Alfred Sarant, friends who worked at Bell Laboratories and Western Electric, both of which were prime war contractors. Between 1943 and 1945, they handed Julius precisely 9,165 pages of secret documents relating to over a hundred projects, including plans for night-navigation radars and the Norden bombsight. One of the most closely guarded U.S. secrets of World War II, the bombsight allowed planes to drop explosives within a 100-foot radius from an altitude of 20,000 feet. In addition, the duo stole the design manual for the P-80 Shooting Star, America's first jet fighter. William Perl, another CCNY graduate, was an aeronautical whiz. Perl worked at the Lewis Flight Propulsion Laboratory in Cleveland, from which he stole experimental designs for supersonic jet aircraft. Julius microfilmed many of these documents with a special camera provided by the KGB, or handed them directly to Feklisov.[16]

When it came to spying, Julius was no slouch himself. On Christmas Eve 1944, he met Feklisov in a cafeteria in Times Square. Despite the war, this area of movie houses was brightly lit, and New Yorkers rushed to do last-minute shopping. The spy had been "shopping," too. As the KGB man nodded for him to sit down, Julius gave him a neatly wrapped cardboard box, saying, "I have a Christmas present for the Red Army." Feklisov smiled and gave Julius a watch for himself, a leather handbag for Ethel, and a stuffed teddy bear for Michael. Afterward, Feklisov took the box back to his office. Upon opening it, he was shocked to find a fully working proximity fuse, plus spare parts. One of the major achievements of U.S. technology, this was the world's first "smart" weapon. World War II–era antiaircraft guns were not very accurate. To down an enemy plane, their shells had to strike it directly or explode nearby, puncturing it with metal fragments. So gunners fired thousands of rounds at a single plane, most, if not all, of them wasted. But fitted with a proximity fuse, a shell could track a given plane with its miniaturized radar set and usually detonate within the kill zone. As a result, ships were less likely to run out of antiaircraft shells while on long cruises and could better defend themselves against air attacks. Used against ground troops, shells fitted with proximity fuses could explode just feet above their heads, even if they were in trenches. As a Signal Corps inspector, Julius Rosenberg regularly visited the Emerson Radio Corporation, the fuse's manufacturer. With each visit, he'd sneak a part

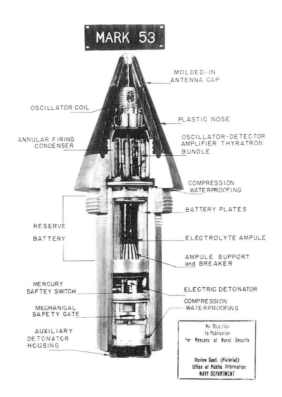

Diagram showing a proximity fuse, similar to the one smuggled to the Soviets by Julius Rosenberg. (Date unknown)

in his briefcase, until he could assemble a complete sample.

After getting over their initial surprise, Feklisov's superiors were furious; Julius had taken such a risk that he'd endangered his entire ring, they grumbled. When Feklisov told Julius about their reaction, he replied: "I calculated the risks very carefully. What I was taking was only one-hundredth of what a Red Army soldier risks when he attacks a tank." Note that Julius never compared himself to an American service-man taking the same risks in combat with German or Japanese troops. Developing the proximity fuse cost American taxpayers over a billion dollars. Julius gave it to the KGB for nothing. "I think," Feklisov wrote, "my 1944 Christmas present was the most expensive one individual ever received from another!" It was expensive in terms of blood as well. During the Korean and Vietnam Wars, Soviet-made proximity fuses were used with deadly effect against American forces.[17]

THE MANHATTAN PROJECT

The Rosenberg ring might have escaped detection if not for Julius's role in passing atomic bomb data to the Soviets. That was not what he'd planned on doing when he volunteered for espionage work; rather, it was something he became involved with because of his wife's youngest brother.

Born in 1922, David Greenglass was his sister's favorite sibling. Like Ethel, "Davy" was an ardent Communist, as was his wife, Ruth, whom he married in 1942, when she was eighteen years old. David had hero-worshipped Julius for years; his brother-in-law had persuaded him to join the Young Communist League when he was fourteen. Communism had become

so ingrained in David that to remind Ruth of his undying love, he'd coo: "I love you with all the love of Marx and the humanity of Lenin." And like Julius, he excused atrocities committed for the noblest of motives. "I believe," David wrote to his wife, "that every time the Soviet Government used force they did so with pain in their hearts and the belief that what they were doing was to produce good for the greater number." He had no qualms about defending Stalin's mass arrests and executions during the 1930s.[18]

A graduate of Haaren High School in Manhattan, where he majored in aviation mechanics, David was a machinist by trade. After being drafted into the army, in July 1944 he was assigned to a workshop in one of the huge government plants at Oak Ridge, Tennessee. Though only key managers knew their purpose, this and other plants were purifying uranium ore for use in the atomic bomb. However, after just a week on the job, David was promoted to sergeant and transferred to a facility at Los Alamos, a site thirty miles northwest of Santa Fe, New Mexico. Located on a 7,200-foot-high mesa surrounded by desert and patrolled by armed soldiers on horseback, the facility employed hundreds of scientists and engineers tasked with designing, building, and testing the atomic bomb. Sending David to this vital installation was a colossal blunder by army intelligence officers, who had failed to look into his Communist background. "Nobody ever asked if I was a Communist," he said. To make matters worse, David was not silent about his political beliefs. During conversations, a co-worker recalled, he took the "side of communism one hundred percent" and was "definitely pro-Russian." Another man noted that the machinist would "invariably adopt the communist line. He never made any secret of his politics."[19]

Nevertheless, security was a top priority at Los Alamos. Giant billboards blazed the slogan "Silence Means Security." Bulletin boards had signs showing a bare-bottomed boy asking: "HEY! Are Your Drawers Closed? Have You Left Anything Out of the Safe?" David soon realized that he'd become part of something big. Almost daily, researchers came to his workshop with drawings of metal parts to fabricate, though he had no idea what they were for. When he wrote to Ruth about his mystery job, she told her brother-in-law, who perked up at once.

Alexander Feklisov, Julius's handler, had already told him to be on the lookout for anything to do with "Enormoz," the Soviet code word for the American ef-

fort to build the atomic bomb. Not only did Moscow know about the Manhattan Project's existence, but a leading Los Alamos scientist was feeding it information. Feklisov suggested that Julius ask Ruth to persuade her husband to become a spy. At first Ruth balked, but Ethel asked, forcefully, whether spying might be something David wanted to do, something she should let him decide. Venona cable 1340 (September 21, 1944) mentions Ruth by name. It reads in part: "LIBERAL and his wife recommend her as an intelligent and clever girl," a "TOWNSWOMAN" (American citizen) and a "GYMNAST" (member of the Young Communist League). When David, code-named "Kalibr" (Caliber),

Security poster at Los Alamos. (1946)

had a few days' leave in Santa Fe, Ruth, code-named "Ossa" (Wasp), visited him. He gladly agreed to her proposal. Julius was thrilled. Indeed, he told Feklisov, "I'll give my right hand to be chopped off if he lets us down!" Yet the Rosenbergs would give a lot more than a hand for drawing David into espionage.[20]

An intelligent man with an easygoing manner, David had no need to break into safes; he simply stayed alert. "Guys were all around me," he recalled years later. "I just listened. Stuff was in the shop; I didn't miss it. I visualize things—that's what I do for a living. I just stored it in my head." As luck would have it, he worked in a section where explosives molded into various shapes were studied for use as triggers to set off a chain reaction. Occasionally, he'd slip into scientists' discussion groups, taking mental notes on all sorts of bomb-related matters. He also jotted down scientists' names, noting their backgrounds, their interests, and, as far as he could tell, their political views. David's problem was not getting hold of information, but getting it into Soviet hands.[21]

In January 1945, while on leave in New York, he and Ruth had dinner at the Rosenberg home, a one-bedroom apartment in Knickerbocker Village, a middle-income development on the Lower East Side. After the meal, Julius made an offer they could not refuse. If Ruth moved to Albuquerque, he said, she could rent a small apartment where David would stay whenever he got time off. He, Julius, would see that all Ruth's expenses were paid, in cash. From time to time, he added, a courier would collect David's reports and deliver them to the KGB. Julius then took a box of Jell-O from the kitchen cabinet, emptied it into the sink, and tore a side panel into two jagged pieces. He gave Ruth one piece, saying he would get the other piece to a KGB courier.

Unexpectedly, in February, the Signal Corps fired Julius after an FBI check revealed that he'd lied about his CPUSA ties on his job application. Almost immediately, he was hired by the Emerson Radio Corporation—the same firm from which he'd stolen the proximity fuse—which was ignorant of his Communist ties. To be on the safe side, the KGB broke the Rosenberg ring into smaller units, each with its own handler. It needn't have worried, for the FBI dropped the ball, failing to keep tabs on Julius after his dismissal. He continued working for the Soviets.

On the morning of Sunday, June 3, 1945, a man showed up at the Greenglasses' Albuquerque apartment. Identify-

Replica of the Jell-O box Julius Rosenberg used as a recognition signal between David Greenglass and Harry Gold. (Date unknown)

ing himself as "Dave from Pittsburgh," he gave the recognition signal. "I come from Julius," he said, and showed the other half of the Jell-O box's panel. David asked him to come back in a few hours, as he was not ready to turn over his notes. When the stranger returned, David handed him the papers, and he gave David an envelope containing $500 in cash for "expenses." But when David offered to recruit other "young men" at Los Alamos for spying,

"Dave" cut him short. "The devil you can," he snapped. KGB agents were instructed never to allow a source to recruit unvetted people on their own, as this might blow an entire operation. His mission completed, the stranger left. The final delivery took place three months later, on September 11. Japan had surrendered nine days earlier, and the couple had returned to New York to await David's honorable discharge from the army. That afternoon, they had lunch with the Rosenbergs. Afterward, David gave Julius another batch of papers, including, he boasted, "a pretty good description of the atom bomb." He exaggerated. What he handed over was some handwritten notes and a rough sketch of the bomb's triggering mechanism. These revealed nothing the Soviets didn't already know, only in precise detail, thanks to another spy at Los Alamos.[22]

THE UNMASKING

The Rosenberg ring seemed to have gotten away scot-free. After the war, Joel Barr and the others went about their lives as if they'd never betrayed their country. Julius left his job with Emerson Radio and opened a machine shop with his brother-in-law. The business did poorly, causing heated quarrels over money. And then their world fell apart.

In September 1949, the FBI sent MI5, Britain's secret intelligence agency, a recently decoded Venona cable. The document revealed that the Soviets had planted a spy, code-named "Rest," at Los Alamos. MI5 suspected he might be physicist Klaus Fuchs, a German refugee the British had sent to work with the Americans. A warm, gentle man, Fuchs was popular with fellow scientists, whose children he babysat so their parents could go out on nights off. After the war, he returned to Britain, taking a post at Harwell, the country's main atomic research laboratory. According to Alexander Feklisov, who handled Fuchs as well as Julius Rosenberg for a time, he gave "everything what was needed to create" the USSR's first atomic bomb. Klaus Fuchs was an idealist, a dedicated Communist willing to do anything to advance the cause he believed in. He'd spied, Feklisov said, because "he considered that communism is the highest stage of human society."[23]

MI5 put Fuchs under surveillance and in January 1950 arrested him. Almost immediately he broke, confessing to spying and detailing what he'd given the KGB. Fuchs also described his courier; the man had never mentioned his name, but Fuchs said he seemed to know a lot about chemistry. The FBI took it from there. Agents

Klaus Fuchs. (Date unknown)

pored over old files, searching for known Communists with backgrounds in chemistry. When MI5 showed Fuchs FBI photos of these men, he identified Philadelphia-based chemist Harry Gold. Upon his ar-

The arrest of Harry Gold. (1950)

rest, Gold admitted that he had been involved in espionage since 1934, adding, "I am the man to whom Klaus Fuchs gave the information on atomic energy." On May 23, Gold's picture and news of his confession were plastered on front pages across the nation.[24]

Fearing further exposures, Moscow ordered the former members of the Rosenberg ring to flee to the USSR by way of Mexico, where the KGB had "rat lines," escape routes linked to visiting Soviet freighters. "You're hot," a frightened Julius told his brother-in-law. The Greenglass family, like his own, must leave for Mexico at once! But that was impossible. The couple already had a young son, and Ruth was due to give birth to their second child any day. Moreover, she was hospitalized with burns suffered in a household accident. David said he would stand by his beloved, whatever the cost.[25]

It was already too late to leave. Under FBI questioning, Harry Gold revealed that he'd also received information from David Greenglass while in Albuquerque. On June 15, agents burst into the Greenglass apartment and arrested him while he was preparing formula for his newborn, a daughter. By evening, David confessed to espionage. Though he said he'd done it "for the Cause," that did

not stop him from mentioning that he'd been recruited by his brother-in-law. Moreover, he noted that Julius had often boasted about his network of "boys" all over the country. After shadowing Julius for a month, FBI agents arrested him on July 17. A few days later, while sharing a jail cell with Harry Gold, David said the Soviets had secretly awarded him and

Julius Rosenberg was arrested by the FBI after being accused of spying for the Soviet Union. (1950)

Julius the Order of the Red Star, a military decoration for valor.[26]

Meanwhile, Julius's other accomplices fled, though how they were tipped off and by whom is unknown. Joel Barr was in Paris, studying music; he vanished with just the clothes on his back. Alfred Sarant, who was working at Cornell University's nuclear physics laboratory in Ithaca, New York, drove to Mexico and disappeared. Sarant was accompanied by his lover, Carol Dayton, the wife of a close friend; each abandoned their spouses and two small children. Two years later, the spies surfaced in the USSR. Working under assumed names, they became pioneers in military electronics and computer research, founders of Zelenograd (Green City), a secret city on the outskirts of Moscow dubbed the "Soviet Silicon Valley." Aeronautics engineer William Perl refused to run; a court sentenced him to five years in prison for lying under oath about knowing Julius Rosenberg. Morton Sobell flew to Mexico with his wife, Helen; Sydney, her eight-year-old daughter by a previous marriage; and Mark, their one-year-old son. Mexican security police, acting on an FBI tip, seized the family at gunpoint and drove them to the Texas border, where agents took Sobell into custody.

TRIAL AND CONVICTION

J. Edgar Hoover knew from Venona that Julius Rosenberg had led a major spy ring. Yet the government could not use the secret material in court without making the KGB suspicious about the source of its information. The FBI director realized that he had to safeguard the Venona Project at all costs, even if it meant allowing a spy to escape; that is why William Perl never faced trial for espionage. But the stakes in the Rosenberg case were so high that Hoover felt bound to proceed by other, less ethical means. He was certain that Julius had critical information on his own ring and, likely, on other spies masked by code names. Julius, however, stubbornly insisted that he knew nothing about espionage, as did Ethel. Shortly after his arrest, she gave an interview to the Associated Press in which she portrayed herself as an everyday American housewife. She even posed for photos at her kitchen sink, dish towel in hand. Ethel insisted that she had no idea why the FBI should be interested in Julius. "Neither my husband nor I have ever been Communists," she said, "and we don't know any Communists.

Ethel Rosenberg, in a display of domesticity in her kitchen, after Julius's arrest. (1950)

The whole thing is ridiculous." Stymied, Hoover decided to turn up the heat. The bureau, he told aides, must use Ethel as a "lever." Put bluntly, she would be taken hostage to pressure her husband into telling all he knew about KGB activities. On August 11, agents arrested Ethel as she was walking to the subway.[27]

The couple were charged with conspir-

acy to commit espionage—not treason, as is commonly believed. The Constitution (Article 3, Section 3) defines treason as "levying war against the United States" and giving "aid and comfort" to its enemies. Because the penalty for treason is death, "two independent witnesses" must testify to each and every act cited in the government's charge. The Rosenberg ring had not committed treason; indeed, the USSR was an ally while it was most active. However, a charge of conspiracy favored prosecutors. As stated in the Espionage Act of 1917, when it came to spying, there was no legal difference between friend or foe, ally or enemy. What mattered was that information stolen in wartime *might* be used to harm the United States or to aid a foreign power—*any* foreign power. To win a conviction, prosecutors simply had to link the accused to each other, since the law held each responsible for the illegal actions of any of the conspirators. The penalty for conspiracy to commit espionage is thirty years in a federal prison or death—nothing else.[28]

Hoover reckoned that threatening Julius with death for himself and his beloved wife would force him to cooperate. He misjudged his man. Julius was caught in a double bind. On the one hand, cooperating

The Rosenbergs share a fervent kiss after their arraignment on atomic spy charges. (1950)

would go against his idea of decency. He surely realized that confessing would be the easy part. After that, he would have to give up other agents, who'd trusted him with their lives, and then testify at their trials for betraying the United States. Moreover, he and Ethel were steadfast Communists. Alexander Feklisov described Julius as "an unreconstructed idealist . . . who did not want to betray his Russian comrades." The KGB man was right; the couple truly, if naively,

saw the USSR as the hope of the world. Death? Julius thought it honorable to die, as he styled himself "a soldier for Stalin." It seems never to have occurred to him that Stalin could be a monster and the propaganda image of the USSR a pack of lies.[29]

By the time of Julius's arrest, the Second Red Scare had reached fever pitch. Barely three weeks earlier, on June 25, North Korean troops invaded South Korea. Stalin encouraged the dictator Kim Il Sung to strike with words and trainloads of weapons, including tanks and MiG-15 jet fighters. These state-of-the-art warplanes incorporated features detailed in the plans stolen by William Perl—features the Americans had been slow in taking advantage of. Until they did, the enemy deprived them of air superiority; indeed, some North Korean planes were flown by Soviet pilots. President Truman, Stalin felt, dared not retaliate against the USSR, which now had the atomic bomb.[30]

Stalin was playing with fire; he knew it, but played anyhow. If the Third World War was inevitable, he said in private, "let it be waged now and not in a few years," when American power had grown in Asia. In this way, Korea became the first hot war of the Cold War. After U.S. forces intervened, driving the invaders back, Chinese Communist leader Mao Zedong sent masses of "volunteers" to North Korea's aid. The CPUSA showed where its allegiance lay. Its press outlets portrayed the war as a Wall Street–backed plot to enslave all of Asia and bring down the governments of the USSR and the People's Republic of China. In following the Party line, screenwriter Dalton Trumbo portrayed the victim as the aggressor, accusing South Korea of starting the war. Folk singer Woody Guthrie called upon American soldiers to "lay down their killing irons and walk home"—that is, desert in the face of the enemy. In the meantime, the public was agitated by the antics of Senator Joseph McCarthy, who charged the government with continuing to harbor Communists. Confronted with the prospect of nuclear war, some Americans thought living under communism preferable to dying and took the motto "Better Red Than Dead." Others countered with "Better Dead Than Red." By the time the shooting stopped in July 1953, the Korean War had claimed the lives of over 36,500 Americans, plus 7,600 missing in action and over 103,000 wounded.[31]

The trial of the Rosenbergs and Morton Sobell began in New York on March 6, 1951. The defendants pleaded innocent. On his lawyer's advice, Sobell did not testify, hoping the fact that he'd not passed atomic secrets would save him from the electric chair; the case against him was based only on the testimony of electrical engineer Max Elitcher, a fellow Communist who charged that Sobell tried to recruit him into the Rosenberg ring. Emanuel Bloch, the couple's lawyer, was a CPUSA activist; during a wartime rally, the FBI noted he'd refused to carry the Stars and Stripes, claiming a sore back, but at another rally proudly carried the Soviet flag. The prosecutor was Irving Saypol, U.S. attorney for the Southern District of New York, a man who heartily despised Communists. Irving Kaufman, the presiding judge, longed for a seat on the U.S. Supreme Court; according to an FBI memo, he "worshiped J. Edgar Hoover." Moreover, the prosecutor and judge were biased against the defendants from the outset. Somehow—just how is unclear—they'd learned about Venona, which colored their entire approach to the case. Years later, assistant prosecutor Roy Cohn let the cat out of the bag. He told Harvard law professor Alan Dershowitz, "Since the FBI knew Julius was guilty and that he would get away with it if they played by the rules, the FBI 'enhanced' evidence, got witnesses to 'improve' their stories and worked hand in hand with the judge." Cohn added: "Irving [the judge] was in on everything. He knew all about the secret intercepts and that we couldn't use them."[32]

Without Venona, the prosecution had no evidence of a conspiracy. Its only links to the Rosenbergs were the Greenglasses. Thus far, David had tried to shield his sister, claiming she was ignorant of her husband's spying activities. Roy Cohn did not buy that. With Saypol's permission, ten days before the trial began, he asked Ethel's sister-in-law to "rethink" her role in the case. As the mother of two young children, Ruth held their future in her hands, he implied, none too delicately. If she did not do her duty, the little ones would likely grow up with both parents in jail or as orphans.

Ruth was ready to "rethink." By then, she'd come to despise her sister-in-law. Soon after Julius's arrest, Ethel had visited Ruth, who, she said, must be exhausted after her hospital stay and giving birth. Since Ruth needed a break, Ethel offered to babysit her son and daughter for the weekend. Ruth claimed to have been outraged, saying the "favor" was really a trick to kidnap the children and hold them "hostage" for David's silence.

David agreed. When he learned of the incident, he recalled a conversation in which Julius repeated Stalin's maxim that, in a war, massive losses did not matter "so long as you win."

"Oh," David said, "I see, my life and my wife's life, and my children's lives, are not that important."

"Well," Julius replied, "nobody's important compared to the overall idea." Clearly, the Greenglasses now believed, their relatives would do whatever it took to protect Julius's spy network.[33]

Ruth dropped a bombshell when she took the witness stand. She "remembered" how, at that September 11, 1945, luncheon at the Rosenberg apartment, David gave Julius his final notes on the atomic bomb. But since Julius could not read his handwriting, she said, Ethel, who was used to her brother's scribbles, typed them for him; Julius then burned the papers in a frying pan. That was untrue. A decoded Venona cable said the KGB received *only* David's handwritten notes, which Julius gave to his new contact, Feklisov having been reassigned elsewhere. Nevertheless, Ethel's "typing" directly linked her to the alleged conspiracy, and thus made her eligible for the death penalty. In his testimony, David confirmed his wife's account.[34]

"The truth never dies, but lives a

wretched life," says a Jewish proverb. Despite efforts to suppress it, the truth eventually finds a way to reveal itself. Many years after the Rosenbergs' trial and execution, America learned the behind-the-scenes story. Though David and his wife lived quietly, under assumed names, he gave journalist Sam Roberts a series of interviews in 1996 for a book Roberts was writing, *The Brother: The Untold Story of the Rosenberg Case.* In 2001, the spy, his face and voice disguised, appeared on CBS's *60 Minutes II* television show. In these interviews, David admitted that he'd lied under oath. Yet he had no regrets. He'd tried to shield Ethel at first, he said, "but my wife put her in it [the conspiracy]. So, what am I gonna do, call my wife a liar? My wife is my wife. My wife is more important to me than my sister. Or my mother or my father, okay? And she is the mother of my children." Asked if he had a troubled conscience, David replied, "I sleep very well," though he also had a recurring nightmare. "But every time I'm haunted by it, or say something, my wife says, 'Look, we're still alive. We have our kids. Everything is okay.'" Ruth died in 2008, David in 2014.[35]

The Rosenbergs hurt rather than helped their own defense. Julius testified

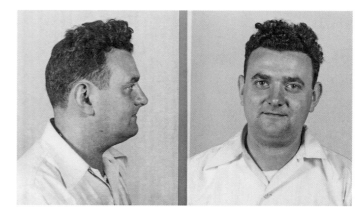

David Greenglass's mug shot. (1950)

first. Claiming to be a patriotic American, the soldier for Stalin declared himself "heartily in favor" of the U.S. Constitution and Bill of Rights. Still, even as young Americans were being maimed and killed daily by Soviet weapons in Korea, he could not resist praising Stalin's government, telling the court that it "improved the lot of the underdog . . . has made a lot of progress in eliminating illiteracy, has done a lot of reconstruction work and built up a lot of resources." Aside from this, he offered a string of denials. Julius denied encouraging his brother-in-law to spy, receiving information about the atomic bomb, and using the Jell-O box trick. When asked if he'd ever belonged to a group that discussed the Soviet political system, such as the CPUSA, he took the Fifth Amendment. From then on, Julius defiantly used the

Julius and Ethel Rosenberg arrive at federal court. (1951)

activities. Beneath her apparent calmness, Ethel's tone and body language signaled what onlookers took as scorn for the entire proceeding. The American woman of the 1950s was not supposed to act that way. As the title of feminist Betty Friedan's 1963 book *The Feminine Mystique* suggests, decent women of that era were assumed to be warm, cuddly homebodies whose "only fight [was] to get and keep their husbands. They had no thought for the unfeminine problems of the world outside the home; they wanted the men to make the decisions." This was not Ethel Rosenberg! She did not whimper or play the demure "little woman." Instead, she came across not as the loving wife and mother she was, but as cold, tough, and crafty, "like a Red Spider," as newsmen described her. Indeed, this "deceptively soft-looking dumpy little woman" seemed to be stronger than her husband and, thus, the brains behind the conspiracy. Obviously, she "felt a need to dominate a man."[37]

Fifth as if it were an escape hatch. It wasn't; the jury of eleven men and one woman assumed he was hiding something.[36]

The jurors might have been more sympathetic toward Ethel had she presented herself as an innocent caught up in a tragedy. Like her husband, however, she repeatedly took the Fifth, refusing to answer basic questions about herself and her

On March 29, 1951, the jury gave its verdict: guilty of conspiring to pass secret defense information, including material related to the atomic bomb, to the USSR. Before passing sentence on April 5, Judge Kaufman tongue-lashed the Rosenbergs, saying they'd caused the Korean War by "putting into the hands of the Russians the A-bomb" years before they could have gotten it on their own. Kaufman reserved his sharpest remarks for Ethel, whom he scolded as a bad wife. Instead of deterring Julius "from pursuing his ignoble cause, she encouraged and assisted the cause. . . . She was a full-fledged partner in his crime." Finally, His Honor blamed the couple for "sacrificing their own children" out of fanatical "love for the cause that dominated their lives." He might have said, instead, that they loved both their children and their cause, but decided they must keep their secrets. Nor did the couple cause the Korean War; Stalin encouraged North Korea to strike its neighbor. And if anyone gave the Soviets key atomic secrets, it was Klaus Fuchs, not David Greenglass. No matter; Kaufman ordered the Rosenbergs sent to Sing Sing Prison in Ossining, New York, until their appeals ran out and they went to the electric chair.[38]

Morton Sobell received a thirty-year sentence. David Greenglass got fifteen years as a reward for his cooperation and was out on parole in ten; Ruth was never charged. Both men felt they'd been punished too severely. Not Harry Gold. Sentenced to thirty years by another judge after pleading guilty to receiving stolen

Daily News headline announcing the death sentence of Julius and Ethel Rosenberg. (1951)

secrets, he took responsibility for his actions. During his early months in prison, the former courier wrote about his "horrible sense of shame and disgust, which I can never lose, concerning my deeds. . . . I must be punished, and punished well, for the terribly frightening things I have done. I am ready to accept this penalty. There shall be no quivering, trembling or further pleas for mercy. What was, was, and now I am prepared to pay the price." These were not just words; Gold was genuinely sorry. To make amends, he volunteered as a human guinea pig. During the Korean War, many wounded Americans developed jaundice, a life-threatening illness, after receiving blood plasma. To allow scientists to develop an antidote, Gold allowed himself to be injected with tainted plasma. He became deathly sick, and though he recovered, he suffered from fatigue, chest pains, and shortness of breath for the rest of his life. A model prisoner, he was paroled in 1965, having served just under half of his sentence. Harry Gold died in 1972. Mourners remembered a decent, gentle man, always eager to help others.[39]

THE CONTINUING BATTLE

Within days of their sentencing, the two-year campaign to save the Rosenbergs got under way. It was fought on several fronts. Emanuel Bloch battled in the courts, arguing that his clients had been framed. Others took the fight into the arena of public opinion. Groups such as the National Committee to Secure Justice in the Rosenberg Case (NCSJRC) set out to create a grassroots movement to protest the death penalty as inhumane and press for a retrial for those they called "innocent Jewish peace activists." Nevertheless, mainline civil rights groups and high-profile individuals kept their distance. Since the Rosenbergs had been convicted fairly, said the American Civil Liberties Union, their case "raised no civil liberties issue." Without a doubt, it added, the death sentence was "the proper way to deal with Communist totalitarianism." Eleanor Roosevelt, the late president's widow, refused to sign a clemency petition, because "that would mean that the courts were wrong and the Rosenbergs right." Albert Einstein took a hands-off approach, claiming groups like the NCSJRC were "Communist-inspired."[40]

It was more complicated than that. At first, Communists were cautious; the *Daily Worker* said nothing about the trial while it was in progress. John Gates, the paper's editor, recalled years later: "We didn't want to be associated in any way, shape or form with espionage." Given the Party's links to the KGB, there was good reason to lie low. Similarly, when members of the NCSJRC approached Party leaders for help, they were told that the couple were "expendable." Yet when it became clear that they would rather die than tell all, Moscow sought to use them for its own advantage.[41]

The Soviets had no interest in the Rosenbergs as human beings. In this regard, General Pavel Sudoplatov, the KGB officer in charge of atomic espionage, was brutally frank. "The Rosenbergs," he wrote in his memoir, "behaved heroically and did not admit their guilt. . . . More important than their spying activities was that the Rosenbergs served as a symbol in support of communism and the Soviet Union. Their bravery to the end served our cause, because they became the center of a worldwide Communist propaganda campaign." Here the tactic was to accuse the foe of doing exactly what the USSR was doing. The general added, "We claimed that the Rosenberg case proved the United States had a consistent policy of anti-Semitism . . . while actually a very real anti-Semitic campaign was gaining momentum in the Soviet Union." So, on April 14, just days after the trial's end, Moscow issued its first instructions to foreign Communist parties on the points to make in their propaganda. They were told to stress that the real aim of the trial was to stir up anti-Semitism in order to "frighten the populace" into accepting a fascist dictatorship. Moreover, sentencing a mother of two to death should be portrayed as "the latest word from American civilization" and proof positive of "the immorality of a country capable of passing such a sentence."[42]

The focus on anti-Semitism is a classic example of Soviet *dezinformatsiya*—disinformation—the deliberate spreading of falsehoods to shape public opinion and conceal unpleasant truths. For Moscow and its allies, the idea that the Rosenbergs were victims of religious bigotry served a dual purpose. As with the Scottsboro Boys, their ordeal provided evidence that America's ruling class was racist, and the justice system a farce intended to keep it in power. Equally important at this time, the charge of anti-Semitism was meant to deflect attention from Stalin's latest series of crimes.[43]

The Rosenberg case coincided with the vilest outbreak of Russian anti-Semitism since czarist times. Though expressing hatred of Jews was illegal in the USSR, the founding of the State of Israel in May 1948 infuriated Stalin. The Jewish state, he raged, was an American puppet! By extension, in his mind, Soviet Jews, as Jews, were disloyal. He told his henchmen that "every Jew is a potential spy for the United States." Actions followed words. That fall, Jews in responsible positions—military officers, educators, bureaucrats, Soviet Communist Party officials—were fired en masse. On Kremlin orders, the state-controlled news media spewed anti-Semitism, reawakening and legitimizing age-old prejudices. Jew-hatred acted as a potent stimulant. As one Soviet writer put it: "Anti-Semitism makes your vodka stronger and your bread more appetizing." Jewish schoolchildren were beaten up by classmates. "This is just like Hitler," one child said. Indeed, the popular humor magazine *Krokodil* (*Crocodile*) went overboard, printing anti-Semitic cartoons as ugly as any that had appeared in the Nazi press.[44]

At the Tel Aviv Museum of Art, David Ben-Gurion, who would become the first prime minister of the Jewish state, proclaims the creation of the State of Israel in 1948. The portrait is that of Theodor Herzl, the father of modern political Zionism. (1948)

It was as if Hitler's ghost had taken possession of Stalin. In 1951, as the Rosenberg trial began, he shut down Jewish newspapers, publishing houses, schools, and theaters and set quotas on the number of Jews admitted to universities. New identity cards bore the notation "Nationality: Jewish." On August 12, 1952, while the Rosenbergs sat on death row, the dictator ordered what has become known as "the Night of the Murdered Poets." Within hours, NKVD men shot thirteen eminent Jewish poets for conspiring to "topple, undermine, or weaken the Soviet Union." Outraged, American journalist I. F. Stone, a low-level KGB source in the 1930s, pointed to the difference between the USSR and a free society: "No picket lines circled the Kremlin to protest the execution of Jewish writers and artists," he wrote. "They did not even have a day in court; they just disappeared." Only in the USSR, Soviet writers whispered, did the authorities take writers seriously—seriously enough to kill them. In November 1952, eighteen leaders of the Czechoslovak Communist Party, most of them Jewish, were tortured into confessing they were Israeli spies; they were then tried, convicted, and immediately hanged.[45]

It got worse. In January 1953, "the

Doctors' Plot" shook the USSR. Stalin took personal charge of the whole dirty business; nothing could have happened without his say-so. Nine doctors, seven of them Jews, were accused of plotting with the CIA to murder Kremlin leaders, including Great Stalin himself. Before long, a wave of arrests of Jewish doctors swept the country. Fueled by newspaper articles with titles such as "Murderers in White Coats" and "Spies and Murderers Under the Mask of Doctors," hysteria over the "[Yid] ghouls" became an epidemic. Terrified Russians were convinced that babies delivered by Jewish doctors would be born blue because these "vampires" sucked out their blood. On the pretext of avoiding anti-Semitic riots, prominent Jews were forced to sign an appeal to Stalin to save their people by deporting them to camps in Siberia. The few Jews allowed to remain in Moscow would have to wear a Nazi-style yellow-star armband on their sleeves.[46]

Moscow needed to change the subject, and Communist parties throughout the world obliged. In the United States, Party activists infiltrated existing Rosenberg defense groups and formed numerous front groups, whose members joined in good faith. These "Rosenberg committees" collected signatures on clemency petitions,

held candlelight vigils, marched, chanted, sang, shouted, wept, picketed, pasted up wall posters, and handed out millions of pieces of literature. To gain the widest audience, they hammered away at emotional themes. Irrational fear of communism and spies had made Americans mentally ill! The Rosenbergs were victims of lynch law! For the umpteenth time, the nation was turning fascist and hell-bent on war with the USSR! "Gangsters, grafters, and murderers" ruled in Washington! Above all, the Rosenbergs were victims of the crazy ideology that inspired Hitler to murder six million Jews![47]

Now the CPUSA press, leaders, and activists went all out. The *Daily Worker* declared: "The Rosenberg case is a ghastly frame-up, a new Scottsboro boys' case. It was arranged to provide blood victims to the witch-hunters, to open the door to new violence, anti-Semitism, and court lynchings of peace advocates as 'spies.'" Party national secretary William L. Patterson thundered: "The lynching of these two innocent American Jews . . . will serve as a signal for a wave of Hitler-like genocidal attacks against the Jewish people throughout the United States." Communist novelist Howard Fast urged American Jews to rise up in righteous rage against the "judicial murder of two innocent, brave, and good people . . . [who] had no knowledge of what crime they had been charged with or why they were arrested." This modest couple, Fast continued, heroes in "the struggle for peace," were being offered as a blood sacrifice "by the men of war, the men of death, the lords of the atom, the lords of pain, of greed, of hunger, and destruction." The slogan of the day was "Stop the anti-Semitic legal lynching of Ethel and Julius Rosenberg."[48]

These calls sparked a backlash within the Jewish community. Many condemned the couple's betrayal of their country as a *shanda,* Yiddish for a shame or a scandal that dishonored the entire Jewish people. Moreover, they resented efforts to weaponize anti-Semitism. The CPUSA, they charged, was cynically using "moral blackmail" in its "war against America." Mainstream Jewish organizations, fearing the public might tar all Jews as disloyal, sought to counter the propaganda. The Anti-Defamation League of B'nai B'rith, a worldwide Jewish service organization, said bluntly: "The Communists aren't interested in the Rosenbergs as Jews. They are not concerned with the welfare of the Jewish community. They're yelling anti-Semitism for their own, partisan purpose." Not only did the American

Jewish Committee refuse to speak up for the doomed couple, it supported Judge Kaufman's sentence. Along with the Jewish War Veterans, it also cooperated with HUAC, opening its files to investigators. Leading rabbis declared that "a true judgment was passed upon the Rosenbergs in accord with our American principles of evidence." Longtime Jewish members of the CPUSA dismissed these claims as Cold War propaganda by sellouts to American "fascism." Besides, said the loyalists, nobody could have spied for the USSR in the first place, because the "Stalin constitution" of 1936 banned espionage![49]

Meanwhile, the movement to save the Rosenbergs went global. Asia, Africa, Latin America, even Australia and New Zealand: all saw demonstrations on their behalf. Protests behind the Iron Curtain were, as ever, state-run affairs; workers were ordered by their unions to appear and show enthusiasm. A play staged in East Berlin drew large audiences and rave reviews in the state-controlled press. Titled *In God's Own Country,* the play portrayed the condemned as victims of Wall Street hangmen. The Hungarian press registered shock at America's "bloodthirsty inhumanity" and "brutal cannibalism." Poland offered the couple political asylum.[50]

Rosenberg committees sprang up across Western Europe. We should not write off this outpouring of sympathy as merely the result of Communist influence. Protests were often organized by Communists but not always. Thousands who sincerely believed in the couple's innocence or opposed capital punishment picketed U.S. embassies and flooded them with petitions for clemency. Religious leaders joined the outcry more out of disappointment than anger. The Reverend Charles E. Raven, chaplain to Queen Elizabeth II, grieved over Americans' perceived betrayal of their ideals. "This savage verdict," he preached from the pulpit, "underlines the conviction that America, instead of leading the world to a more righteous and liberal way of life, is becoming so hysterical in its dread of communism, as to betray the very principles upon which the Constitution is based." France fairly quivered with indignation—no surprise in a nation with over a million Communist Party members, the largest outside the USSR itself. On a single day, the U.S. embassy in Paris received 7,598 clemency petitions. Party member Pablo Picasso, Europe's greatest living artist, made delicate line drawings of Julius and Ethel, which were enlarged and used on picket signs. Giant photos of the couple captioned "Save the Rosenbergs" decked speakers' platforms.

Lithograph by Pablo Picasso depicting Ethel and Julius Rosenberg. (1952)

Angry Parisians plastered city walls with a poster titled "His Famous Smile," showing President Dwight D. Eisenhower smiling, but with rows of electric chairs in place of teeth. Crowds in the Place de la Concorde, the largest public square in Paris, chanted, "We demand justice for the Rosenbergs" and "The Rosenberg case is U.S. legal murder." Yet there was not a word about the upsurge of Soviet anti-Semitism.[51]

Back in the States, the self-described "soldier for Stalin" and his wife tried to help their defenders by writing more than five hundred letters to each other, many of which were released for publication. These "death-house letters" expressed the writers' love for each other and their sons, but also echoed current propaganda themes. Such phrases as "monstrous frame-up," "political prisoners," "American fascism," and "legal lynching" appear constantly. Calling themselves advocates of "American democracy, justice and brotherhood," the condemned insisted: "We are in the death house today as warning to all ordinary men and women . . . that there are forces today which hope to silence by death those who speak for peace and democracy."[52]

Their execution was stayed pending appeals. Nevertheless, seven times, courts, including the U.S. Supreme Court, saw

French poster protesting the execution of the Rosenbergs. The caption reads "They electrocuted two innocents, Ethel and Julius Rosenberg. May the assassins be forever cursed." President Dwight D. Eisenhower is portrayed in the poster with electric chairs for teeth. (1953)

no reason to review the case, since judges had ruled that the Rosenbergs had gotten a fair trial. With the execution date drawing near, on June 16, 1953, Ethel appealed directly to the White House. Having served as commander of Allied forces in Western Europe during the war, President Eisenhower surely understood the plight of "a condemned wife as well as a condemned husband," she wrote. Now "the great democratic United States is proposing the savage destruction of a small unoffending Jewish family, whose guilt is seriously doubted throughout the length and breadth of the civilized world!"[53]

Coming from Ethel, this may seem surprising, since neither she nor her husband had ever involved themselves with a specifically Jewish interest or cause, religious or secular. At any rate, her letter fell on stony ground; if anything, it enraged the normally placid president. Toward the end of the war, General Eisenhower had seen Jewish bodies piled like cordwood in Hitler's concentration camps, so, he reckoned, Ethel needn't instruct him on the destruction of unoffending Jewish families. What's more, as a believer in "the feminine mystique," the president saw her as a coldhearted manipulator. With the stakes so high, he thought granting clemency would show weakness, which would be portrayed as a Communist victory. Sparing Ethel in particular, he reasoned, would also encourage the Soviets to recruit more female spies. Finally, Eisenhower said, "by immeasurably increasing the chances of atomic war, the Rosenbergs may have condemned to death tens of millions of innocent people all over the world." Like it or not, they must be held to account![54]

Yet all was not lost. While Tessie Greenglass did not know about J. Edgar Hoover's lever scheme, she tried to persuade her daughter to tell what she knew about Julius's spying. "If you don't talk," Tessie screamed, "you're gonna burn with your husband!" Ethel replied, "But I've lived with him; I know he didn't do those things." Another time, Tessie, furious at Ethel's obstinacy, called her a "dirty Communist." For the sake of their children, she urged her to divorce Julius and tell the truth. Ethel, enraged, called her mother a "witch," adding, "Don't mention the children. Children are born every day of the week."[55]

The execution was set for the evening of Friday, June 19, the couple's fourteenth anniversary. That afternoon, they wrote a final letter to their sons. After expressing love for Michael and Robert, their "dearest boys," they closed with these revealing words: "Always remember that we were innocent and could not wrong our conscience." Was this a lie, a cynical last-minute betrayal? I think not. The parents, I believe, were telling their sons the truth *as they understood it*. Their understanding, however, illustrates the power of ideology to capture minds and drive self-destructive behavior. The Rosenbergs likely believed they'd done nothing wrong by aiding the USSR, a wartime ally and, to them, humanity's hope for a better future. Sadly, they actually were soldiers for Stalin—Stalin, the persecutor and killer of fellow Jews. How they justified this to themselves, if they thought about it at all, we'll never know.[56]

Up to the last moment, the couple held their fate in their own hands. The night before the execution, Special Agent Robert Lamphere, the FBI's ace spy chaser, had his team outfit a room near the death chamber with a direct phone line to headquarters in Washington. "I wanted very much for the Rosenbergs to confess—we all did," he wrote in his memoir, for that would have spared their lives. Two stenographers stood by to take down their statements, even as each was being strapped into the electric chair. It was wasted effort; the call never came. Julius died first, saying nothing. While guards walked Ethel to the death chamber, Rabbi Irving Koslowe, Sing Sing's Jewish chaplain, begged her to tell what she knew and save herself for her children's sake. "No," the doomed woman replied, "I have no names to give, I'm innocent." When it was over, Lamphere went home. "I felt, not satisfaction, but defeat," he wrote. "I knew the Rosenbergs were guilty, but that did not lessen my sense of grim responsibility at their deaths." This was the worst outcome, because the FBI did not want them to die: it desperately wanted Julius's information about Soviet espionage. But getting him to talk was impossible, given the couple's commitment to Communist ideology. Lamphere said it best: "They died for what they believed in." Yet he might have said the same about

Boston Herald headline announcing the Rosenbergs' death. (1953)

fanatical Nazi racists executed for crimes against humanity. Sacrificing oneself for an ideology may explain a person's motive, but it does not justify one's actions, nor does it make that ideology true or noble.[57]

The executions were followed by outpourings of sadness and joy. In the United States, Rosenberg supporters saw their deaths as perversions of justice amid a climate of Cold War hysteria and atom-bomb panic. On cue, the June 23 issue of the *Daily Worker* denounced the "brutal act of fascist violence" as proof of the ongoing "Hitlerization of America." W. E. B. DuBois, the eminent Black historian–turned–fellow traveler, wrote a scathing verse:

> *We are the murderers hurling mud*
> *We are the witch hunters drinking*
> *   blood.*[58]

Then again, others were glad to see the "traitors" receive their just deserts. Motorists honked their horns in approval. Outside the White House, people carried signs reading "Death to the Communist Rats." Happy passersby screamed at anti-execution demonstrators, "Let's have fried Rosenberger" and "Fry the Reds." There was also an outpouring of joy in the Middle East, where hatred of Israel often translated into hatred of Jews in general. Editorials in the Arab press declared that "the Rosenbergs' action was typically Jewish in the betrayal of the nation to which they were supposed to owe allegiance and in its contribution to the Communist cause."[59]

A shudder of horror and a thrill of joy rippled across Europe. The reaction behind the Iron Curtain was predictable, given its captive press. TASS, the official Soviet news agency, charged that the Rosenbergs

Protesters siding with the death penalty for the Rosenbergs near those supporting clemency. (1953)

were executed "in defiance of the protests of world opinion," neglecting to mention that a good many protests were inspired and led by Communists. Poland's national news agency blustered that the execution was "a murder carefully prepared beforehand and staged in detail by the thugs of the FBI."[60]

In Western Europe, ordinary nonpolitical people gathered outside U.S. embassies, many of them in tears. However, in Italy, Communist demonstrators at the U.S. embassy in Rome sang and shouted with delight, now that the couple was "safely dead" and could be treated as martyrs, carrying their secrets to the grave, as literary critic Leslie Fiedler noted. Yet the most intense Western reaction came from France, where philosopher Jean-Paul Sartre spoke out. Moscow's disinformation campaign had sought to damage relations between the United States and its NATO partners. The Rosenberg case, Sartre declared, signified America's unfitness to lead any alliance. The executions, he added, were a "legal lynching which smears the whole nation with blood. . . . Whenever innocent people are killed it is the business of the whole world. . . . Watch out! America has the rabies! Cut all the ties which bind us to her, otherwise we will in turn be bitten and run mad!" This came from a prominent thinker, who'd also said "an anti-Communist is a dog" and excused Stalin's crimes as necessary for ensuring "the superiority of the socialist camp." Others were not taken in by such talk; they saw Sartre and his ilk as Stalinist stooges. Simone Signoret, one of France's greatest film stars, wrote: "While the world and I were fighting for the Rosenbergs, there were heaps and heaps of Rosenbergs in the USSR. And those who orchestrated the anti-American witch hunt here knew perfectly well what was going on in Soviet Russia."[61]

In the years after Morton Sobell's conviction, his wife, Helen, picketed the White House with a sign reading "Bring My Innocent Husband Home" and shouted that concentration camps were ready for any who defied the nation's fascist rulers. The KGB likely supported her as a way of keeping up the propaganda about the Rosenbergs; a decoded message mentions sending money to the "wife of Stone," one of Sobell's code names. After his early release from prison in 1969 for good behavior, the couple visited Moscow and were treated like rock stars, with a private suite in a luxury hotel, complete with a maid, a cook, and a chauffeur, and a mink coat for Helen. The KGB knew how to say thank you.

Yet Morton still claimed to be innocent. With the passing years, however, perhaps as a bid for attention toward the end of his life, he decided to come clean. In 2008, at age ninety-one, the engineer admitted that all the shrill cries of innocence were a hoax. The convicted spy and his supporters, including his wife, had lied all along. Of course he and Julius had been spies. "I did it for the Soviet Union," he explained. As for Helen, she "approved of it," and Ethel knew exactly what her husband was doing. Still unrepentant, Sobell approved of the Red Terror, the Moscow Trials, and the Soviets' other crimes against humanity. Without the least trace of remorse, in 2018 he told interviewer David Evanier: "Well, that comes with the territory"—that is, the end justified the means, as Lenin always preached. Asked about the secrets he'd stolen, Sobell split hairs. "Stole?" he replied irately. "I *transmitted* them." His only regret, apparently, was getting caught. Morton Sobell died shortly after the interview, at the age of 101.[62]

After their parents' executions, the Rosenberg sons were adopted by Communist poet and songwriter Abel Meeropol and his wife, Anne, whose last name they took.

Morton Sobell (left) visiting East Germany. (1976)

For most of their lives, Michael and Robert asserted their parents' innocence. However, evidence to the contrary began to mount. In 1990, Nikita Khrushchev, Stalin's successor, claimed that he'd overheard his boss mention, "with warmth," the couple's services to the USSR. And when faced with Morton Sobell's admission and evidence from the Venona cables, declassified in 1996, the sons accepted their father's guilt, but rightly claimed that their mother had been the victim of a prosecution scheme. As children, they alone emerged from the tragedy unblemished—though not undamaged. All the adults involved were tainted in one way or another.[63]

Today, the facts are undeniable. Julius Rosenberg ran a highly effective spy ring for the KGB. His wife knew about his activities, approved of them, and helped recruit her brother for espionage, but was no spy herself, as evidenced by the fact that the KGB never gave her a code name. When questioned about her Communist sympathies, she lied, saying neither she nor Julius knew anything about the CPUSA, let alone belonged to it. Though the Rosenberg spy ring did not steal "the secret" of the atom bomb, its electronics and aviation information enabled the Soviets to forge ahead in these technologies, which cost American lives in Korea and Vietnam. People working for the U.S. government, notably assistant prosecutor Roy Cohn, pressured Ruth Greenglass into giving false testimony at the trial, which her husband confirmed out of loyalty to her. Technically, what Cohn did is called "subornation of perjury," persuading or pressuring a witness to lie under oath, a serious crime.

J. Edgar Hoover once described the Rosenberg case as "the crime of the century." He had a point, for it lives in American memory, decades after its end, as a watershed event in Cold War history. Lawyers study it in minute detail and discuss their findings in scholarly journals. The case has also been kept alive through frequent references in the entertainment media. In the 1989 film *Crimes and Misdemeanors,* for example, actor-director Woody Allen had his character say of his annoying brother-in-law: "I love him like a brother—David Greenglass." Tony Kushner's 1991 play *Angels in America* included a scene in which Roy Cohn is haunted on his deathbed by the ghost of Ethel Rosenberg, though in fact he had no misgivings. In 2018, the Boston Playwrights' Theatre staged its first opera, *The Rosenbergs,* a Danish work that asked the question "Would you die for love?"[64]

The Rosenberg case remains important because it raises a basic issue. The *New Republic* magazine explained it best: "In its moment of crisis, American democracy apparently could not defend itself without violating precisely those demanding principles and values that distinguish it from its tyrannical enemies." Might this sad history repeat itself in our day, when terrorists slay innocents without compunction and government officials feel obliged to do anything, even break the law, to prevent their outrages?[65]

VIII

A LITTLE LIST:
JOE McCARTHY INVESTIGATES

As some day it may happen that a victim must be found,
I've got a little list—I've got a little list
Of society offenders who might well be underground.
—Gilbert and Sullivan, *The Mikado* (1885)

STARTING OUT

Joseph Raymond McCarthy was born on his parents' farm near the town of Grand Chute, Wisconsin, on November 14, 1908, the fifth of the seven children of Timothy and Bridget "Bid" McCarthy. Neighbors remembered him as a "gawky ugly duckling" so full of nervous energy that he "couldn't sit still." An excellent student, though easily bored, Joe quit school at fourteen to raise chickens on an acre of land rented from his father. The chickens died. Joe tried to rebuild his business from scratch, but that, too, failed after a few years. While searching for a path in life, the youngster knocked about, doing odd jobs. Finally, Bid told her son, "Go out and be somebody. Take a chance. Nobody starves in America."[1]

Joe decided to go to college. But before an admissions officer deigned to look at him, he needed a high school diploma. So, at twenty-one, he went back to school—a one-room country school with the same teacher for all the grades. Nearly six feet tall and weighing 170 pounds, he towered above the kids he sat among in class. Yet Joe did not sit there long; he buckled down, cramming four years' work into one. Choosing a college was easy. The University of Wisconsin at Madison, a state school, would likely have accepted him; he had real-life experience and a fine student record. However, his parents disapproved, because the school was too secular for their liking. A family friend recalled, "The state university was a godless place, filled with atheists and Communists. You send your kids there . . . and they wouldn't go to church anymore." As staunch Roman Catholics, they wanted their son to go to a Catholic college. Marquette University in Milwaukee, run by the Jesuit order, fit the bill. Joe always revered the Church, though in later life he often skipped ser-

vices. Nevertheless, he respected priests, and they liked him.[2]

While at Marquette, Joe burned the candle at both ends. Determined to get ahead, he attended classes in the law school and plugged away at his assignments. When not studying, he washed dishes, ran elevators, flipped hamburgers, gambled at poker, and worked as a part-time boxing coach— anything to earn a few bucks. Nicknamed "Smiling Joe," he amazed fight fans with his "pile-driving lefts and rights" and his ability to take a punch. Still, there was something about Joe that puzzled those who knew him. Yes, he was easy to like; generous to a fault, he could not hold on to money. "If somebody needed a loan," a friend recalled, "Joe would give it to him and often forget to ask for repayment." At the same time, he had a quick temper and might interpret a word or a gesture, however innocent, as an insult. At such times, he spat insults and balled his fists. Before long, however, the words turned to honey. "Joe was like that," an attorney who knew him told an interviewer. "He'd do something nasty and then make it up to you. He couldn't stand to have people stay mad at him. It upset him no end." Alas, whatever made Joe tick, his deepest feelings and ambitions are unknowable. Historians have never quite been able to figure him out. Why a man of his intelligence, with so many appealing qualities, should have gone so far astray remains a puzzle.[3]

McCarthy graduated from Marquette in 1935. After four years in private law practice, he won election to Wisconsin's Tenth Judicial Circuit. Almost everyone, lawyers and clients alike, thought the judge fair and sympathetic. "You could call on him any time if you had a problem," said an attorney. "Joe was full of vitality. . . . He opened the courtroom windows and let in a little fresh air." His Honor shone in

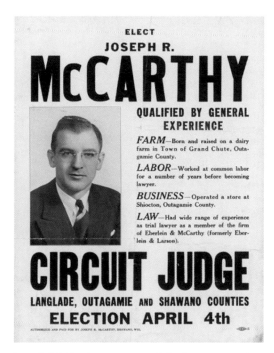

Joseph McCarthy ran successfully for circuit judge in his early thirties. This was his campaign poster. (1939)

divorce cases, because he thought it cruel to lock couples into unhappy marriages. Usually, in those days, a husband would almost have to beat his wife to a pulp for a judge to consider granting her a divorce. McCarthy, however, had the reputation of being the state's most lenient judge in divorce cases, especially when it came to abused wives. In that respect, a colleague said, "I think he was ahead of his time."[4]

When the United States entered World War II, the government drafted millions of men for the armed services. McCarthy, as a judge, was exempt from the draft; nobody would have criticized him for not being in uniform. Nevertheless, he took a leave of absence from the bench; on June 4, 1942, he received a commission as a first lieutenant in the Marine Corps. His reason for joining was likely a combination of patriotism and ambition. Like other volunteers, he genuinely loved his country. Yet he also knew the value of a good war record to an aspiring politician. Throughout American history, politicians have capitalized on their military service. George Washington, Andrew Jackson, Ulysses S. Grant, Theodore Roosevelt, Dwight D. Eisenhower, and John F. Kennedy won the presidency largely on their military records.

McCarthy served as an intelligence

officer with a dive-bomber squadron on the island of Bougainville in the South Pacific. Upon their return from raids on Japanese-held islands, he debriefed the pilots, questioning them about what they'd seen and done. From time to time, when they expected an easy run, pilots took him along as a tail gunner. It was great fun. During his dozen flights, McCarthy blazed away at buildings with twin machine guns, coming under light return fire at least once. Mostly, though, he riddled coconut trees with bullets, prompting buddies to give him a mock medal as the squadron's top tree destroyer. McCarthy laughed with

McCarthy posing in full flying gear as a tail gunner. (1943)

them, but also sent hyped-up accounts of his exploits to the newspapers back home. When a stack of clippings arrived weeks later, he'd go around camp waving them and yelling, "This is worth fifty thousand votes to me."[5]

In 1944, while still on Bougainville, McCarthy entered the Wisconsin Republican primary for the party's nomination to the U.S. Senate. For starters, he invented a glowing record for himself. He wrote up a citation, forged his commander's signature, and sent it to Admiral Chester W. Nimitz, the commander in chief of the U.S. Pacific Fleet. Shamelessly, he claimed to have gotten a serious leg wound during a combat mission, resulting in a permanent limp. This was a flat-out lie; had he been wounded in the line of duty, he would automatically have received the Purple Heart. McCarthy's "wound" came during horseplay while crossing the equator for the first time; he fell down a ship's ladder, fracturing his foot. Admiral Nimitz, who approved thousands of citations, likely signed McCarthy's without reading it. Armed with this phony award, McCarthy got a month's leave in order to campaign. The judge put on a good show, shaking voters' hands, kissing babies, and playing the limping war hero. Posters pictured "Tail-Gunner Joe" in full flying gear, sitting behind his trusty machine guns. Nevertheless, he lost the primary to the incumbent, Alexander H. Wiley, who appealed to Republicans and Democrats alike. McCarthy returned to the Pacific and applied for another leave to, he said, deal with pressing court business. Denied leave, he resigned his commission and received an honorable discharge in February 1945.

McCarthy's next primary race, in 1946, found him opposing Senator Robert La Follette Jr., the son of a Wisconsin legend. Nicknamed "Fighting Bob," Robert M. La Follette Sr. was a three-term governor who'd gone on to serve nineteen years in the U.S. Senate. Upon his father's death in 1925, "Young Bob" won the vacant seat. After so many years, his being a senator seemed almost a part of the natural order. Certain of victory, Young Bob stayed in Washington, tending to his duties, returning home to campaign only two weeks before Republican voters went to the polls. That was a mistake. Dipping into his bag of tricks, Tail-Gunner Joe had used the time to brand his opponent a scoundrel. To drive home the point, he hired men to wear rubber masks that were the spitting image of the incumbent. They'd walk down streets, deliberately bumping into pedestrians, then ask who they thought they were to get in the way of so grand a person as a United States senator. McCarthy won the primary with 207,935 votes to La Follette's 202,557. Since Wisconsin was a Republican stronghold, he easily defeated Democrat Howard J. McMurray by 620,430 votes to 378,777. At age thirty-eight, Joe became the youngest member of the U.S. Senate.[6]

SENATOR JOE

Wisconsin's junior senator showed two faces to those he met in Washington. McCarthy could be a good guy, especially to ordinary folks. Unlike so many senators, he did not put on airs. He felt for the little people, taking time to learn the names of the humblest workers in the Senate Office Building; he asked them to call him "Joe." Ruth Watt, a clerk, thought him a lovely man. "He was extremely friendly," she recalled, "and very concerned with our feelings. If I made a mistake, it was always, 'Don't worry about it, Ruthie. It's no big deal. Don't let it bother you.' No one, absolutely no one, was better to us." Ever generous, he was melted by nearly any hard-luck story, and he opened his wallet. McCarthy also became friendly with two other freshmen, Representatives Richard

M. Nixon and John F. Kennedy. He'd met Kennedy during the war. The navy lieutenant, "a hell of a nice guy," took the marine for a ride on his PT boat, and he happily "got to shoot the machine guns."[7]

McCarthy's other face was not so nice. Fellow senators often saw him as a crude wheeler-dealer, a bandit in a rumpled suit, faded shirt, and gravy-stained tie. Not that he was alone in his greed; like too many other senators, McCarthy used his position and the inside information that came with it to feather his nest. Yet he seemed not to care what the elite thought, let alone apologize for anything. "Whatever he could get," colleagues said, "whatever he could take, was good because Joe McCarthy wanted it. His effrontery was both breathtaking and invincible." Brazenly, he sported the nickname "Pepsi-Cola Kid" for taking a $20,000 loan from an executive of the soft-drink company, then urging the Senate to end sugar rationing, a wartime carryover.[8]

Another carryover was the matter of the Malmédy massacre. On December 17, 1944, German troops murdered eighty-four American captives near the Belgian town of Malmédy. The killings were so outrageous that front line officers ordered their men to stop taking German prisoners for a while—that is, shoot them. After the war, American military police rounded up former members of the German unit; a military court found seventy-three of them guilty of war crimes, sentencing forty-three to death and the rest to life in prison. Though examining physicians said the defendants had not been physically abused, they claimed to have been tortured to make them confess. Early in 1949, the Senate Armed Services Committee held hearings on the Malmédy affair.

Joe McCarthy sided with the Malmédy killers. Whether he did so out of ignorance or to curry favor with Wisconsin's German American voters, some holding Nazi sympathies, is unclear. But whatever the reason, he behaved shamefully. During the hearings, the former judge bullied witnesses, made ignorant statements, "and turned almost every session into a barroom brawl." To make matters worse, he ignored the fact that the Malmédy killers were SS troops, Nazi fanatics bent on destroying racial "inferiors"; SS kill squads had slaughtered millions of Jews in Eastern Europe. In their defense, McCarthy accused the U.S. Army of a cover-up. Warming to his argument, the senator described its interrogators as "non-Aryan refugees" and "refugees from Hitlerism," none-too-subtle references to Jews who'd fled Ger-

American soldiers
murdered at the
Malmédy massacre.
(1944)

many in the 1930s. Those poor SS men, he moaned, were merely "innocent GI Joes of the German army" and "patriots whose only crime was attempting to win the war" for their beloved Führer and Fatherland. As for American military judges, McCarthy thought them "brainless" and "imbecilic." The committee disagreed, stating in its final report that the torture claims were bogus. Whether justice prevailed, however, is another matter. As the Cold War intensified, Washington wanted a loyal West German ally as a counterweight to Soviet-dominated East Germany. To satisfy West German public opinion, the death sentences were commuted and all the SS men eventually released, a triumph of politics over justice.[9]

By the end of 1949, McCarthy was in political hot water. After three years in the Senate, he had no achievements to point to. He'd authored no important piece of legislation nor done much for his home state. Quite the opposite: a poll of the

Senate press corps voted him the worst U.S. senator in office. The midterm elections of 1950 would not be a problem, because he was not up for reelection. But 1952 was not far off. When it came, the country would elect a president, the entire House of Representatives, and one-third of the Senate. McCarthy would then have to account for his lackluster record. Given his situation, he needed a rousing vote-getting issue to campaign on—an issue, as he put it, with "some real sex appeal."[10]

On January 7, 1950, the senator had dinner at the elegant Colony Restaurant with three Washington friends, among them Edmund A. Walsh, a Jesuit priest and the dean of Georgetown University's School of Foreign Service. While aiding Eastern European famine victims after World War I, he had seen the "Red Menace" close up. So when McCarthy explained his problem, Father Walsh asked, "How about communism as an issue?" McCarthy perked up. "That's it," he said, smiling. "The government is full of Communists. We can hammer away at them." Until then, he'd given little thought to communism. Of course, he denounced it as a wicked ideology—as every "right-thinking" American did. Now rooting "subversives" out of the government be-

came his passion, the basis of his fame, and finally his shame.[11]

THE SPEECH

McCarthy jumped on the anti-Communist bandwagon with both feet. Early in February, schedulers booked him for a series of Lincoln's Birthday speeches, an annual event at Republican fund-raisers. But since he seemed like such a flop, they decided not to put him in front of important groups. On February 9, McCarthy took the podium to address the Ohio County Women's Republican Club of Wheeling, West Virginia. If the schedulers thought his remarks would be bland and soon forgotten, they were mistaken—terribly mistaken.

Titled "Enemies from Within," McCarthy's speech focused on the Cold War as a make-or-break test of democracy. The struggle, he said, pitted the values of "our western Christian world" against "the atheistic Communist world" and its "religion of immoralism." Communism was on the march! Since the end of World War II, the USSR had taken over the nations of Eastern Europe, while in 1949 it got the atomic bomb and the armies of Mao Zedong overran Nationalist China, a U.S. ally. These disasters, McCarthy insisted, were not due to any American weakness, but to a massive betrayal. "The reason why we find ourselves in a position of impotency is . . . the traitorous actions of those who have been treated so well by this Nation . . . those who have . . . the finest homes, the finest college education and the finest jobs in the government." Those privileged ingrates, the senator railed, had enslaved themselves to an inhuman ideology. To drive the point home, he held up a paper, saying, "I have here in my hand a list of 205 [Communists who] are still working and shaping policy in the State Department."[12]

McCarthy was bluffing; he had no list. The number he cited likely came from an outdated State Department report on employees "separated from the service" for various reasons, which gave no names and did not mention CPUSA membership. More puzzling still, the number 205 was not carved in stone. In later speeches,

McCarthy's speeches were often inflammatory and filled with hyperbole and smear tactics. (1950)

McCarthy claimed to have the names of 57, 81, 116, 122, and 126 traitors in high government positions. When reporters asked to see the lists, a reasonable request, he made excuses for not producing them.[13]

And no wonder, for when McCarthy gave his speeches, Communist penetration of the federal government was on the wane, if not totally eliminated. Thanks to Elizabeth Bentley's disclosures in 1945, the KGB began shutting down its operations. By the early 1950s, the Truman loyalty program and the FBI had combed thousands of "security risks," real and imagined, out of the government. Despite the ruckus the senator made during the next four years, his effort was a dismal failure. He unmasked exactly zero Communists, though his accusations ruined scores of individuals' careers and, in some instances, their lives. To be sure, the CPUSA itself had already been dealt a series of stunning blows. In 1949, eleven members of its executive board, including Peggy Dennis's husband, Eugene, were convicted under the Smith Act, a federal law making it a crime to advocate the violent overthrow of the U.S. government, and sentenced to up to five years in federal prison. The Supreme Court's upholding of the convictions in 1951 was followed by a wave of arrests of lesser Party officials, forcing scores of others to go into hiding.

None of this impressed Joe McCarthy. On February 11, two days after the Wheeling speech, he sent a telegram to the White House. In it, he urged President Truman to crack down on Communists in the State Department. Failure to do so, he added ominously, would brand the Democratic Party "the bedfellow of international communism." That the Republican senator should be making national security a political issue infuriated the man in the Oval Office. Truman did not mince words, replying that he'd never "heard of a Senator trying to discredit his own Government before the world." As for the telegram, it was a pack of lies, proof "that you are not even fit to have a hand in the operation of the Government of the United States." The president pitied the good people of Wisconsin; they must be "extremely sorry" to have elected "a person who has so little sense of responsibility as you have."[14]

The rebuke rolled off McCarthy like water off a duck's back. Truman's fellow Democrats, however, were incensed. Since they held both houses of Congress, in March the Senate's Tydings Committee, named for its chairman, Maryland's

Millard E. Tydings, began hearings on McCarthy's charges. Tydings was a genuine war hero, a former army major awarded the Distinguished Service Cross for his exploits in World War I. The time had come, Tydings said, for McCarthy to make his case or slither away in disgrace; even some Republicans echoed his demand. But McCarthy did neither. A few days into the hearings, he startled the committee by naming "Moscow's top spy," Owen Lattimore of Johns Hopkins University.

Though no diplomat, from time to time Lattimore had advised the State Department on Asian affairs, his academic specialty. While not a Communist or fellow traveler, the professor was easily duped. In the summer of 1944, he visited the Kolyma labor camps as part of an inspection team led by Vice President Henry Wallace. It was a total farce; the thugs who ran the camps took the visitors for, in Lenin's words, "useful idiots." They kept their slaves hidden while burly, well-dressed NKVD men pretended to be "typical" inmates undergoing reeducation to take their proper roles in Soviet society. Upon returning to the States, Lattimore wrote a glowing report on what he'd seen for the *National Geographic* magazine, comparing Kolyma to the Tennessee Valley Authority, FDR's Depression-era project to rehabilitate the impoverished region.[15]

McCarthy went after Lattimore not for his naivete about Stalin's slave labor, but for his advice concerning China. In the late 1940s, Mao Zedong's Communists seemed poised to defeat the Nationalists under U.S.-backed General Chiang Kai-shek. The professor thought it best to work with them, thereby drawing them away from the USSR, America's main Cold War foe. McCarthy, however, smelled treason; he accused the scholar of engineering Mao's victory by deliberately giving Washington bad advice.[16]

McCarthy's tactics gave Americans a new word. On March 29, the *Washington Post* ran a piece by Herblock, the pen name of Herbert L. Block, a cartoonist with a knack for skewering shady politicians. Overnight, the cartoon became an icon, still reproduced in books on history and politics. It shows Republican senators pulling and shoving an elephant, the symbol of their party, toward a platform labeled "McCarthyism," atop a wobbly stack of tar buckets. The wide-eyed elephant asks: "You mean I'm supposed to stand on that?" The word stuck. Since then, the term "McCarthyism" has been a synonym

"You Mean I'm Supposed To Stand On That?"

First instance of the term "McCarthyism," coined by cartoonist Herbert Block. This cartoon features an elephant, representing the Republican Party, refusing to mount the shaky platform of a tar and smear campaign, representing McCarthy's tactics. (1950)

for character assassination, destroying a person's reputation by insults, innuendo, rumors, and outright lies.

McCarthy faced a challenge from a prominent member of his own Republican Party. Margaret Chase Smith of Maine, then the only female member of the Senate, was deeply offended by her colleague's baseless accusations and outrageous buffoonery. On June 1, she addressed the crowded chamber in terms as biting as they were true. As McCarthy looked on, she began: "Mr. President, I would like to speak briefly and simply about a serious national condition. . . . The United States Senate has long enjoyed worldwide respect as the greatest deliberative body. . . . But recently that deliberative character has . . . debased to a form of hate and character assassination." For the next fifteen minutes, she proclaimed every American's right to criticize, to protest, and to hold unpopular beliefs. "Freedom of speech is not what it used to be in America," she declared. "It has been so abused that it is not exercised by others," fearful of attack. She asked fellow Republicans not to ride to victory on "The Four Horsemen of Calumny— Fear, Ignorance, Bigotry, and Smear." As Senator Smith finished, she introduced a statement called her "Declaration of Conscience," signed by herself and six other Republican senators. McCarthy, true to form, only sneered, calling her and the other signatories "Snow White and the Six Dwarfs."[17]

The Tydings Committee issued its report on July 17, 1950. Though it cleared Lattimore of all charges, McCarthy had inspired a vicious campaign by self-styled "patriots." Lattimore fought back as best he could. Later that year, he published *Ordeal by Slander,* an account of his torment and a warning about the threat McCarthyism posed. The senator's reckless attacks, he wrote, and not Marxism, were the greater enemy of democracy. "We ourselves can cause the decay of capitalism and democracy. The sure way to do this is to destroy the wellspring from which capitalism and democracy derive their vitality: namely, freedom of research, freedom of speech, and freedom for men stoutly to maintain their diverse opinions. . . . If the people of this country can differ with McCarthy only at the risk of the abuse to which I have been subjected, freedom will not long survive. . . . He who contributes to this process is either a fool or an enemy of his country." It was a losing battle. Exhausted and broke, the scholar fled the United States to become the first professor of Chinese studies at the University of Leeds in England.[18]

Senator Tydings went on to brand McCarthy "a fraud and a hoax," a brutal practitioner of Adolf Hitler's "big lie" technique, which involves telling a lie so bizarre, and telling it so often, that people eventually come to believe it. Tydings had a point. The Wisconsin senator was a fan of Hitler's, though not a follower. "As far as I know," his campaign manager recalled, "Joe looked at only one book in his whole life." That was *Mein Kampf* (*My Struggle*), in which the Nazi leader outlined his racist ideology and plans for world conquest. Yet McCarthy "had no use for Hitler or for anything the Nazis did. But when he looked at *Mein Kampf,* it was like one politician comparing notes with another. Joe was fascinated by the strategy, that's all." Still, he seemed never to have understood that repeated lies, told forcefully and with conviction, can erode democratic values.[19]

McCarthy did not take the criticism lying down. His foes, he sneered, were a pack of "egg-sucking phony liberals," whose "pitiful squealing" had sold China into "atheistic slavery." Amazingly, his popularity grew. The Senate post office began leaving sacks of mail with his office staff. Many of the letters contained money, the lifeblood of politics. Donations came in the form of small amounts of cash, but also as $1,000 checks. Fellow senators received letters from voters, asking, "If you aren't too busy, please take a moment to tell Joe McCarthy that the plain people of America are grateful to him." Shouts of "Let 'em have it, Joe" followed the senator everywhere.[20]

McCarthy's support did not grow out of thin air; millions of Americans were primed to receive his message. The former judge personified what historian Richard Hofstadter termed "the paranoid style in American politics." Hofstadter defined this as a state of mind typified by "heated exaggeration, suspiciousness, and conspiratorial fantasy." It is a simplistic way of seeing the world in terms of a plot by evil forces to destroy everything good and decent. By 1952, the fear of nuclear annihilation, the cracking of the Rosenberg spy ring, and bloody setbacks in Korea had cast doubts on the abilities and motives of the nation's leaders. For many, McCarthy's charges made sense: hidden traitors must be pulling the strings in favor of the enemy. Viewed in this light, the senator was a truth teller, not a phony. His outbursts seemed heartfelt, signs of sincerity rather than deception. Furthermore, McCarthy attracted his share of kooks, quacks, and eccentrics who saw Communists behind public health schemes designed to poison "all of the material, mental and spiritual resources of this GREAT REPUBLIC!" Dubbed "the Unholy Three," these al-

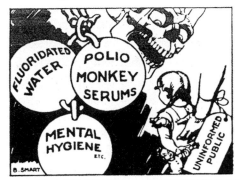

Poster suggesting fluoridation and polio vaccination are part of a Communist plot to impose a world government. (1955)

leged schemes involved Jonas Salk's polio vaccine, mental hygiene, and government introduction of fluoride into the water supply to fight tooth decay. The hysteria over fluoridation reached such proportions that it inspired a dark satire on the Cold War. Titled *Dr. Strangelove or: How I Learned to Stop Worrying and Love the Bomb*, this

1964 film has Jack D. Ripper, an insane bomber-base commander, launch a nuclear attack on the USSR, a move certain to bring retaliation and the end of human life on earth. General Ripper acts because he believes Moscow has been fluoridating America's water "to sap and impurify all of our precious bodily fluids," thereby destroying our "life essence."[21]

McCarthyism, too, forged links to organized religion. Marxists, the Wisconsin senator charged, correctly, were atheists, people who denied the existence of God. This made him the natural ally of conservative religious leaders. Among Protestants, Baptist minister Billy Graham, Dwight Eisenhower's friend and spiritual adviser, hammered at the theme that Communists aimed to "destroy the American home and cause . . . moral deterioration," leaving the country exposed to Soviet subversion. Politicians, in turn, used religious symbols to counter "atheistic communism." In the mid-1950s, Congress added the phrase "one nation under God" to the Pledge of Allegiance and adopted "In God We Trust" as the national motto, declaring that it must appear on all American currency. Monuments depicting the Ten Commandments went up in courthouses, city halls, and parks across the nation.[22]

McCarthy also enjoyed the support of respected leaders in his own Roman Catholic Church, notably Cardinal Francis Spellman of New York. Equally important, conservative Catholic laypeople, parish priests, and journalists often spoke of "Senator Joe's" having undertaken a sacred mission. He was, people said, "a deeply religious man" fighting Communist devils. Devout women regularly wrote to Catholic periodicals pledging to pray for McCarthy. "Every day I pray a Rosary for you and your staff, bearing in mind that the Rosary is more powerful than the Atomic bomb," a woman wrote in an open

McCarthy holding up a newspaper. The headline reads "McCarthyism is treason to America." (Date unknown)

letter to McCarthy. Others wrote to praise him for "driving the Reds out of places of importance, similar to the way our dear Lord lashed the money changers out of the temple." Indeed, Catholic McCarthyites compared his zeal to that of John the Baptist, Isaiah, Jeremiah, and "all the prophets and all the apostles."[23]

McCarthy's growing appeal translated into votes. During the 1950 midterm elections, he campaigned for his party's candidates in fifteen states. Though Democrats lost heavily, they managed to eke out majorities in both houses of Congress. Despite that, Republicans had a good year, winning seats in every state McCarthy visited. When the dust settled, he got much of the credit for these victories. His face appeared on the covers of *Time* and *Newsweek,* glossy, mass-circulation newsmagazines. Gone were the days when Republican senators could poke fun at him behind his back. As Arkansas senator J. William Fulbright, a Democrat, put it: "The Republicans looked upon him as the new messiah. . . . He was the same old McCarthy, as odious as ever. But, oh my, how things had changed."[24]

A FORCE TO RECKON WITH

High on praise, McCarthy turned his attention to George C. Marshall. Appointed army chief of staff by President Roosevelt, General Marshall had been America's head war planner. To lead "Operation Overlord," the invasion of Nazi-occupied France in 1944, he promoted Dwight D. Eisenhower over dozens of generals with greater seniority and battlefield experience. Eisenhower, a natural team builder, seemed best suited to unite the Allies, getting them to work toward common goals. Late in 1945, President Truman sent General Marshall to China to broker a peace deal between Mao Zedong and the Nationalists, only to have both sides reject his proposals. As Truman's secretary of state (1947–1949), he devised the Marshall Plan to rebuild war-ravaged Europe.

Where others saw selfless patriotism, McCarthy saw an arch-conspirator. On June 14, 1951, he tore into Marshall in a sixty-thousand-word Senate speech later published as *America's Retreat from Victory: The Story of George Catlett Marshall.* In tones of spite and hatred, he accused the former secretary of state of multiple crimes. The Marshall Plan, he said, was "an evil hoax on the generosity, good will and carelessness of the American people . . .

the product of a will and intention hostile to this free society." In a classic expression of the paranoid style, after declaring that "the feeling of America's weakness is in the very air we breathe in Washington," he asked: "How can we account for our present situation unless we believe that men in high places in this Government are concerting to deliver us to disaster? This must be the product of a great conspiracy, a conspiracy on a scale so immense as to dwarf any previous such venture in the history of man. A conspiracy of infamy so black that, when it is finally exposed, its principals shall forever be deserving of the maledictions of all honest men." The aim of the conspiracy, McCarthy declared, was "to diminish the United States in world affairs, to weaken us militarily, to confuse our spirit with talk of surrender in the Far East and to impair our will to resist evil. To what end? To the end that we shall be contained and frustrated and finally fall victim to Soviet intrigue from within and Russian military might from without." Eye-deep in the conspiracy, he charged, was George C. Marshall. That wicked man, that scoundrel, "made common cause with Stalin" and formed the policy that, "destroying China, robbed us of a great and friendly ally." In Korea,

George C. Marshall. (1939)

the senator stormed, Marshall had personally "turned that war into a pointless slaughter."[25]

George C. Marshall, ever the gentleman, kept silent; the award of the 1953 Nobel Peace Prize said all that needed saying. Dwight Eisenhower kept silent, too, at least in public. "Ike," as friends called him, was preparing to run for the presidency in 1952. Though critical journalists condemned his craven behavior, calling him "yellow" for not defending Marshall, he thought it best not to "get into the gutter with that guy," McCarthy. Though he despised the senator, he saw him as useful in the upcoming elections. There would be time enough to deal with him later if need be, Ike thought.[26]

The 1952 general election was a turning point in American politics. Ever since FDR's landslide victory in 1932, the Democrats had held the White House and both houses of Congress. That changed, in part due to McCarthy. While he did not campaign in Wisconsin, since he was now a shoo-in for reelection, he stumped the country for the Republican ticket. His favorite tactic was to brand Democrats guilty of "twenty years of treason." When mentioning Ike's opponent, Illinois governor Adlai Stevenson, he'd mispronounce his first name as "Alger," a not-so-sly reference to Alger Hiss, a former State Department official accused of espionage.[27]

The one state McCarthy avoided was Massachusetts. He stayed away as a favor to Joseph P. Kennedy, the former ambassador to Great Britain, whom he'd met in Washington. The two Joes got along famously. From time to time, the older man invited him to the family estate on Cape Cod, where he palled around with Kennedy's sons John and Robert and dated two of his daughters, Patricia and Eunice. "He had a certain raw wit and charm when he had not had too much to drink," Eunice recalled. Already he was suffering from al-coholism, which was destroying his health. In 1952, Representative John F. Kennedy, who'd taken him for PT boat rides, ran as a Democrat for the Senate seat held by a popular Republican, Henry Cabot Lodge. Given McCarthy's own popularity, his campaigning for Lodge would likely have led to JFK's defeat. Thanks to his bypassing the state, the three-term congressman defeated Lodge by a slim margin. McCarthy's absence may well have changed the course of American history by allowing JFK to take his first steps on the path to the White House.[28]

JOE AT HIGH TIDE

Eisenhower handily defeated Stevenson, while fellow Republicans won both houses of Congress. The leaders of the majority party in the Senate and the House of Representatives appoint the heads of each body's committees and subcommittees. These act as Congress's eyes and ears, monitoring government operations, some of them secret; collecting and evaluating information; and recommending action. Certain committees—Armed Services, Ways and Means, Judiciary, Intelligence, and Foreign Affairs—deal with matters essential to national well-being. Other committees are less important, meaning their heads have less influence. Though Republican lawmakers valued McCarthy as a vote getter, they also saw him as a "loose cannon," a man so reckless there was no telling what harm he might do if unleashed. To be on the safe side, Senate leaders decided to "bury" McCarthy by making him head of the Permanent Subcommittee on Investigations of the Committee on Government Operations. Despite its mouthful of a name, this subcommittee was hardly "sexy," as McCarthy might have said. Since it usually investigated fraud and waste in federal agencies, Indiana senator William Jenner thought the appointment a stroke of genius on the leadership's part. "We've got McCarthy where he can't do any harm," Jenner crowed. In reality, it was the height of arrogance to assume that a human dynamo like Joe McCarthy would be content with dull, routine probes. Unintentionally, the Republican wiseheads gave him a license to investigate just about anything.[29]

Chairman McCarthy assembled his team. As chief counsel, he hired Roy Cohn. We met Cohn during the Rosenberg trial and must now get to know him better. Born in 1927, the only child of Albert Cohn, a politically connected New York judge, and his wife, Dora, Roy was a legal

Roy Cohn, nearly ten years after assisting with McCarthy's investigations against suspected Communists. (1964)

wizard. Upon graduating from Columbia Law School at nineteen, he had to wait two years before coming of age to take the bar exam. Slender and baby-faced, with slicked-back black hair, he stood five feet eight inches tall. Despite his boyish looks, Cohn was anything but innocent. Hard as nails and cynical as Satan, he believed that people were innately selfish, guided only by greed and self-interest. Roy, an aunt recalled, was a boy who "when he wanted it, he wanted it. And it didn't matter what anyone else said." Foes described him as "one of the most loathsome characters in American history," a fellow without conscience, who'd stop at nothing to win. Yet, like McCarthy, he had a softer side. Roy Cohn, a reporter observed, "notices and is kind to doormen, chauffeurs, little people." The lawyer also loved dogs because, unlike people, "you know they're sincere."[30]

McCarthy's assistant counsel was twenty-seven-year-old Robert F. Kennedy, JFK's younger brother. "Bobby" despised Cohn for beating him out for the chief counsel's job. Frustrated at having to play second fiddle, he resigned from the subcommittee in July 1953, but always liked McCarthy. However, he observed, the boss had his flaws: "[He] didn't anticipate the results of what he was doing. He was very thoughtful of his friends, and yet he could be so cruel to others." Joe did not understand or care how his words and actions affected other people, needlessly turning them into enemies.[31]

Another man served on the subcommittee as an unpaid consultant. Born the same year as Roy Cohn, G. David Schine, his best friend, was tall, blond, and as handsome "as a Greek god." A Harvard College graduate, Schine was heir to a fortune; his father owned a chain of luxury hotels and vacation resorts. Yet wealth and wisdom do not necessarily go

G. David Schine. (1954)

together. Schine imagined himself an expert on communism. He wrote a six-page pamphlet titled *Definition of Communism* and had copies of it placed in every room of his father's hotels, next to the Gideon Bible. Sloppily written and riddled with factual errors, it was a hilarious display of ignorance. Some wondered exactly *what* he'd learned at Harvard. It got Lenin's first name and the date of the Bolshevik Revolution wrong! Why, Schine declared ignorantly, Communists even lifted the words "security" and "equality" from the Bible— words absent from the Good Book. FBI readers thought the pamphlet childish and advised J. Edgar Hoover against endorsing it.[32]

McCarthy's team had twenty-five paid investigators, professionals skilled in tracking down information for use in the hearings, including former FBI agents. Besides these, the senator counted on a spy network he dubbed "the Loyal American Underground." This shadowy group consisted of scores, perhaps hundreds, of workers in the government, including the Army Intelligence Agency, who gave him leads, tips, names, and documents he had no business having. Moreover, McCarthy and J. Edgar Hoover knew each other well, often dining together in Washington restaurants. "I view him as a friend and believe he so views me," the FBI director told a reporter. "He is earnest and he is honest." It should be no surprise that Hoover looked away when information passed quietly from FBI headquarters to the subcommittee's offices.[33]

Though a former judge, the senator flouted the law whenever it suited him. While government employees are supposed to be discreet, he urged them to "leak" to him. The senator announced: "I would like to notify two million federal employees that it is their duty to give us the information

they have about graft, corruption, Communists, and treason. I just will not abide by any secrecy directive by anyone." In short, rules did not apply to Joe McCarthy, who, deep down, likely thought himself above the law. If reporters asked about his sources, he'd say his mind was too full of information to fuss over minor details. Those who persisted with their questions became enemies. McCarthy could be quite brutal. Once, during a speech, he spotted an unfriendly reporter in the audience. The senator aroused his supporters to such hatred of this Communist "spy" that the reporter fled, fearing for his life. Another time, at a dinner party, McCarthy attacked columnist Drew Pearson, kneeing him in the groin and knocking him to the ground. "If I hadn't pulled McCarthy away," claimed newly elected senator Richard Nixon, "he might have killed Pearson." Had Nixon held back, few would have missed Pearson; politicians in both parties loathed the columnist for his tell-all articles.[34]

In February 1953, McCarthy's subcommittee began its first series of investigations. It focused on the Voice of America (VOA), the State Department's overseas broadcasting service. VOA had been set up to counter Soviet propaganda, but informants in the Loyal American

Underground charged that its broadcasts soft-pedaled Soviet crimes, while highlighting American "injustices." McCarthy wanted to know if, and to what extent, Communists influenced VOA's programming. His hearings, however, proved a waste of time; witnesses had nothing to offer but rumors and hearsay. What the hearings did accomplish was to damage agency morale. Raymond Kaplan, a radio engineer, committed suicide during the hearings. In his note to his wife, Kaplan wrote: "You see, once the dogs are set on you everything you have done since the beginning of time is suspect. I have never done anything that I consider wrong but I can't take the pressure upon my shoulders any more." Edwin Kretzman, an agency adviser, thought it VOA's "darkest hour when Senator McCarthy and his chief hatchet man, Roy Cohn, almost succeeded in muffling it."[35]

McCarthy turned next to the State Department's overseas library program. In the early 1950s, some 230 libraries and information centers in Europe were visited by 27 million people a year. The program's stated aim was "to advance American ideas in the struggle with communism." The books and magazines available to visitors ranged from American novels and poetry to popular science, history, politics, and current affairs. Yet the program seemed self-defeating, for its shelves also held works by CPUSA stalwarts like William Z. Foster, plus titles by Communist sympathizers and fellow travelers. McCarthy accused the State Department of wasting taxpayer dollars on anti-American propaganda.[36]

Roy Cohn and David Schine romped through Europe, searching library catalogs for books by "inappropriate" authors. During their time abroad (April 3–20), they visited nine major cities, starting in Paris. Cohn would later describe the tour as "a colossal mistake." He was right; their antics resulted in a public relations disaster. Dubbed by the European press "quiz kids" and "a pair of juvenile comedians," the visitors acted like teenagers in need of parental supervision. On a shopping spree, they stocked up on French perfume and silk stockings, which they charged to the American embassy. Riotous pillow fights in their room disturbed other hotel guests. Schine chased his friend around the lobby with a rolled-up newspaper, giggling while smacking him over the head. After they left for Germany (without paying the hotel bill), housekeepers found their room utterly trashed.[37]

Meanwhile, librarians were so terrified they removed thousands of books from shelves, even burned some, before the terrible duo arrived. Upon their return to Washington, McCarthy made such a fuss that the State Department ordered the removal of all books "of any Communists, fellow travelers, et cetera." Almost immediately, more than three hundred titles by forty authors were banned. Though the State Department fired 830 VOA employees as possible subversives, nobody ever learned who had ordered the offending books in the first place. President Eisenhower criticized McCarthy and his boys without mentioning their names. In an address at Dartmouth College, he told graduates: "Don't join the book burners. . . . Don't be afraid to go to your library and read every book, as long as [it] does not offend our ideas of decency. That should be the only censorship."[38]

THE LAVENDER SCARE

While "McCarthy's gumshoes" were traipsing around Europe, at home rumors spread that they were more than best friends—they were lovers. That may or may not have been the case; we will never know for sure. In 1955 David Schine married Hillevi Rombin, a Swedish-born Miss

Universe; they would have seven children and stay married until their deaths in 1996 in a private airplane crash. Roy Cohn never married. Though he denied being gay, he was a regular at gay clubs in New York and Washington; Cohn died in 1986 from complications of AIDS.

If McCarthy knew of his aides' sexual preferences, he kept it to himself. Having an admittedly gay man on his staff would have been hard to explain, since he openly expressed hatred of such people. Words like "queer" and "homo" came easily to his lips. The State Department, a favorite target, took the brunt of these insults. Without a shred of evidence, McCarthy smeared the department as a haven for "fruits," "Russian-loving pansies," and "lace-panty diplomats." In speeches and committee hearings, he blithely paired "Communists and queers" as security risks. An unnamed intelligence officer, McCarthy informed the Senate, told him that "practically every active Communist is twisted mentally or physically in some way" and that gay people had "peculiar mental twists." Though McCarthy was not directly involved in persecuting gays, his statements helped fuel the so-called Lavender Scare, which in turn inflamed the Second Red Scare.[39]

The color lavender has traditionally

been associated with gays and lesbians. It is the color we get by mixing baby blue, symbolizing boys, with pink, symbolizing girls. The term "Lavender Scare" refers to the hunt for gay people in the U.S. government. During the early years of the Cold War, the nation's capital had a flourishing same-sex culture. Public spaces such as Lafayette Square across from the White House were meeting spots for gay men. In addition, gays and lesbians favored certain restaurants, bars, movie houses, and nightclubs. Since many of these were government employees, security concerns were raised at a time of high anxiety in the country at large.

There were several reasons for suspicion. Homophobia—the irrational fear of gays and lesbians—was rampant in 1950s America. During the Cold War era, physicians labeled homosexuality a "perversion"—that is, a condition innately abnormal and therefore evil. In 1952, the American Psychiatric Association published its *Diagnostic and Statistical Manual of Mental Disorders,* listing every known type of mental illness and its symptoms. Homosexuality, the manual said, was a serious personality disorder. Recommendations for "treating" it were nothing short of barbaric. These included "aversion therapy," delivering electrical shocks to the patient's genitals whenever erotic same-sex images flashed on a screen. Other "treatments" were lobotomy, a surgical procedure in which an ice-pick-like instrument was poked into the prefrontal lobe of the brain to render patients "morally sane"; prayer and religious counseling; and "beauty therapy" to enhance one's appeal to the opposite sex.[40]

The problem was not that gay people were Communists; nobody knew how many—or, indeed, if any—gay government workers were Party members. (The CPUSA was leery about gays; it did not knowingly recruit them and expelled those it detected.) Nevertheless, a 1950 Senate report titled *Employment of Homosexuals and Other Sex Perverts in Government* detailed the risks of employing "sexual deviants." Homosexuality, the authors warned, was highly contagious. Like a flu virus, they said, "one homosexual can pollute an entire government office." Additionally, gays and lesbians allegedly lacked emotional stability; they had weak "moral fiber," which made them "easy prey to the blackmailer." Conclusion: "Persons who indulge in such degraded activity are committing not only illegal and immoral acts, but they also constitute security risks in

Cover of the *Employment of Homosexuals and Other Sex Perverts in Government* report. (1950)

positions of public trust." In other words, as author Arthur G. Matthews notes, homosexuality was the equivalent in destructive power to "Stalin's atom bomb."[41]

McCarthy agreed, insisting that gays "must not be handling top secret materials." So did the president. In April 1953, Eisenhower issued Executive Order 10450, banning anyone with a "sexual perversion"

(his term) from the federal workforce. Investigators tracked suspected homosexuals, interviewing their neighbors, opening their mail, and subjecting them to lie-detector tests. Postal inspectors set up a watch list of recipients of bodybuilding magazines and put tracers on targets' mail so as to locate other gays. By 1960, more than five thousand federal employees had been fired on suspicion of "immoral conduct," a thousand of them from the State Department alone. The military discharged thousands more because of their "disorder," including some with valuable skills in electronics and code breaking. In Europe, embassy staffs underwent "hellish grilling"; several people committed suicide, jumping out of windows. "Each time somebody would disappear," a staffer recalled, "I thought 'Oh God! What's going on?' We were all scared." The anti-gay hunt bled into the private sector as well. The American Red Cross "summarily dismissed" employees suspected of homosexual leanings. As in the film industry, these individuals were blacklisted and found it difficult to find work in keeping with their education and skills.[42]

The Lavender Scare intensified the climate of fear in the country. It sowed distrust, shattering personal relationships.

"Everybody was suspicious because everyone was squealing on everybody else," recalled Raymond Mailloux. "You were afraid to make friends with anybody." In Washington, at least one State Department employee broke under the strain: Andrew Ference killed himself with gas from the kitchen stove. Another federal employee shot himself after a grilling by investigators. The State Department tried to cover up the suicide, saying he died of an "inactive lung lesion," whatever that is.[43]

All the suffering was for nothing. Senate investigators found no evidence of gay people's involvement in espionage. This makes sense, for scientists today do not think that sexual preference determines other human qualities. No gene has been found for political affiliation, let alone loyalty and courage. History records cowardly straight warriors and courageous gay ones; we need only think of T. E. Lawrence— "Lawrence of Arabia"—the English colonel who fought alongside the Arabs against Turkish rule during World War I. Neither race nor religion nor sexual preference makes a person prone to betray their country. Despite all the effort and heartache, no American has ever been shown to have stolen state secrets because of sexual preference or being blackmailed over it.

With the passage of time, attitudes changed. After much debate, in 1973 the American Psychiatric Association reversed itself by removing homosexuality from its list of mental disorders. It went on to urge civil rights legislation to ensure gays and lesbians the same rights as other citizens. In 2012, the CIA began to actively recruit gay, lesbian, bisexual, and transgender people. Explaining that it was no longer an issue for holding security clearance, a CIA official said, "We want the best and the brightest regardless of your sexual orientation." That, after all, is the American way.[44]

AT WAR WITH THE ARMY

As head of a Senate subcommittee, Joe McCarthy extended its reach while making himself a force in both the Republican Party and the nation at large. Yet without intending to, he was sailing into dangerous waters. The Bible says, "Pride goeth before destruction, and a haughty spirit before a fall" (Proverbs 16:18). This is a counsel of wisdom and a rule of life, for power breeds pride, which leads to arrogance, which leads to disaster. The senator's war with the U.S. Army would teach him that lesson in spades.

During the summer of 1953, McCarthy's investigators heard about supposed security lapses at Fort Monmouth, New Jersey. Located sixty miles south of New York City, this sprawling military base hosted laboratories doing cutting-edge research on radar and missile guidance systems. Julius Rosenberg had often visited it during the war, and his spies Joel Barr and Alfred Sarant had worked there for a time.

In October, McCarthy, who had recently married a staffer named Jean Kerr, vowed to uncover the remnants of the "Rosenberg spy ring," which he felt certain were still active at Fort Monmouth. It would be a wild-goose chase, as futile as anything he'd poked into thus far. Nevertheless, for several weeks he held public hearings in New York, questioning people who'd met Rosenberg at the base. The senator had no patience with anyone invoking the Fifth Amendment. For him, "a witness's refusal to answer whether or not he is a Communist on the ground that his answer would tend to incriminate him is the most positive proof obtainable that the witness is a Communist." Aggressive as always, he and Roy Cohn treated witnesses as defendants, bombarding them with pointed questions. "What have you got against this country?" they'd ask, and "Do you feel that if Rosenberg was properly executed, you deserve the same fate?"

When witnesses seemed puzzled, they were branded "sleazy characters."[45]

Having failed to get the information he sought, McCarthy turned up the heat. But when he sent investigators to the base, they found no evidence of espionage, let alone remnants of the Rosenberg ring. Still not satisfied, he pressed ahead with charges of guilt by association—that is, holding a person guilty not on evidence, but because of a connection to an alleged offender. Thus, engineer "John Doe" was accused of Communist leanings since his brother "William Doe" favored "leftist policies." Others were accused of Communist sympathies because they once attended a rally at which Paul Robeson sang, or had belonged to a front group. Though no spies were found at Fort Monmouth, the army fired forty-three civilian employees, largely to placate the senator. McCarthy's badgering had a negative effect. "The morale problem," stated an internal report, "has hit in the area most directly affected—the smaller but key groups of highly trained physicists, engineers, and technicians." In his zeal, the senator committed an unforced error. The immediate effects of his efforts were to slow work on key defense projects, a gift to the Soviet military.[46]

Undeterred, McCarthy moved on. In

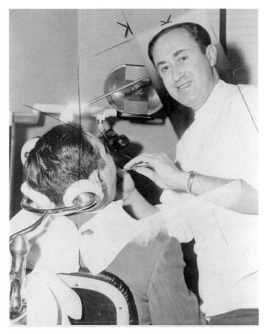

Irving R. Peress. (1955)

discharge, effective March 31, 1954. McCarthy smelled a rat. Rather than treat the case as what it was, a bureaucratic slipup, he charged that dark forces in high places were working to conceal disloyalty. Overnight, "Who promoted Peress?" became the battle cry of millions of McCarthy's supporters.

McCarthy summoned Brigadier General Ralph W. Zwicker, Camp Kilmer's commandant, to explain the Peress matter. The hearing went badly. Under questioning, the general refused to give a straight answer; he simply would not say if he knew who authorized the dentist's promotion or his honorable discharge. Roy Cohn thought superiors in the Pentagon had ordered Zwicker not to cooperate. That may indeed have been the case. As the general later said, with a wink and a nod, "Perhaps I was holding back, and perhaps I wasn't too cooperative." Frustrated, McCarthy raked Zwicker over the coals. One nasty exchange went like this:

November 1953, an anonymous army officer brought to his attention the case of Irving R. Peress, a thirty-six-year-old dentist stationed at Camp Kilmer, New Jersey. Despite Peress's refusal to answer questions on the loyalty form signed by all draftees, he had been promoted from captain to major. The dentist had in fact been a Communist before, though not during, his time in the army, or so he claimed in a 2005 interview. Soon after McCarthy learned about Peress, the army caught up with its backlog of paperwork. Pentagon officials then tried to cover up the error by giving the major a quickie

McCARTHY: Don't be coy with me, General. . . . Don't give me double-talk, General. . . . General, let's try to be truthful. I am going to keep you here as long as you keep hedging and hawing.

Brigadier General Ralph W. Zwicker.
(Date unknown)

ZWICKER: I am not hedging.

MCCARTHY: Or hawing.

ZWICKER: I am not hawing, and I don't like to have anyone impugn my honesty, which you just about did.

MCCARTHY: Either your honesty or your intelligence; I can't help impugning one or the other.

After more back-and-forth like this, the chairman declared Zwicker unfit to wear the uniform of an American soldier. Roy Cohn noted: "McCarthy's control over himself had broken. He should never have uttered those words." This time, Cohn knew, his boss had gone too far. By disrespecting the general, he'd also disrespected the United States Army, effectively signing his political death warrant.[47]

For the man in the Oval Office, the attack on Zwicker was an unforgivable sin. Dwight Eisenhower had given most of his adult life to the army, and admired men who'd served with equal dedication. Though he'd ignored McCarthy's treatment of George C. Marshall out of political expediency, as president he had no intention of letting this latest insult pass. "I'm not going to take this one lying down," Ike fumed to aides. He especially liked Zwicker, a born leader, brave and smart. During the war, as a colonel, he'd landed on D-Day, June 6, 1944, ahead of the first wave of assault troops in Normandy. As head of an advance intelligence unit, Zwicker radioed information on German positions to Allied headquarters. For these actions, he received the Bronze Star and the Silver Star and Britain's Distinguished Service Order. McCarthy's bullying the general was the last straw. Ike now saw the senator as a definite menace, not an asset, in the Cold War battle for hearts and minds. America, above all, stood for fair play, the rule of law, and personal integrity, the values and ideals at the bedrock of the nation's identity in the world. Thus, he said, "we cannot defeat Communism by destroying the things in which we believe." Ike vowed to destroy the senator by using Roy Cohn as his lever.[48]

There was plenty to work with. In the fall of 1953, David Schine was drafted into the army. When he began basic training at Fort Dix, New Jersey, Cohn used his position on McCarthy's staff to demand special treatment for his friend. No peeling potatoes, no scrubbing latrines, no guard duty for Private G. David Schine! Cohn browbeat the brass at Fort Dix into excusing him from these and "other disagreeable tasks." Hence, Schine was the only draftee able to use the telephone whenever he pleased; records show that he was released from drill to make or take several hundred long-distance calls. One rainy day, an officer found him asleep in a truck while the rest of his company wallowed in the mud on the rifle range. On weekends, Schine got passes so he could catch up on "committee work" in his penthouse atop New York's ritzy Waldorf-Astoria Hotel. When word of Schine's privileges leaked to the press, the Pentagon ordered them revoked. To make matters worse, upon learning that his friend might be sent overseas, Cohn threw a temper tantrum. Spluttering with rage, he warned John Adams, the army's chief lawyer, not to cross him and McCarthy—ever. "We'll wreck the army," Cohn snarled. "The army will be ruined . . . if you pull a dirty, lousy, stinking, filthy, shitty double cross like that."[49]

Eisenhower now had his lever. In January 1954, he ordered John Adams to prepare a secret report detailing Cohn's actions on behalf of Schine. When it was completed, Adams leaked the thirty-four-page document to reporters. In the uproar that followed, senators from both parties agreed to schedule televised public hearings. Known as the Army-McCarthy hearings, these were to begin in April and would focus on two questions: (1) Did Cohn and his boss behave improperly in seeking special treatment for Schine? (2) Was the army, as McCarthy charged, holding Schine "hostage" to derail further investigations?

Meanwhile, the Washington press corps sharpened its knives. Stories about McCarthy's aides appeared almost on a daily basis—true, exaggerated, and outright false. Columnists portrayed Private

Cohn whispering in McCarthy's ear during a subcommittee session. (1954)

Schine as a pampered, coddled, sissified, and oh-so-delicate rich kid. This "dream boy," this "golden boy," this "gilded private" supposedly wore "tailor-made" uniforms and a fur-lined hood. What's more, he paid ordinary grunts to clean his rifle and make his bed. The private, according to *Life* magazine, "often rubbed his hands with lotion before going out in the morning." On days off, he "left post spectacularly in a chauffeur-driven Cadillac."[50]

Roy Cohn raised more profound questions. Even before the scheduled hearings, a photograph of the senator and his aide became iconic; to this day, it appears in books, including this one, about the McCarthy era. It shows Cohn whispering into his boss's ear during a subcommittee session, while McCarthy holds his hands over the microphones. For many viewers, this image showed who was really in charge: not the senator, but his underling, a mere twenty-seven-year-old who'd helped "railroad" the Rosenbergs. As one critic explained, McCarthy was little more than a "transmitter" for Cohn, the true power behind the throne.

Nevertheless, McCarthy's relations with his aides were side issues. The chief target of the Army-McCarthy hearings, left unsaid, was the Wisconsin senator's credibility and, thus, his political future. Little did he dream that television would prove to be his undoing.

THE POWER OF TELEVISION

"This is London!" Most Americans of a certain age were familiar with this phrase from the darkest days of World War II. It was the sign-on of Edward R. Murrow, a legendary radio broadcaster who described the Nazi air raids live from his perch on a rooftop in Britain's capital. Murrow's deep baritone voice and his attention to the human details of war captivated American listeners, boosting support for lend-lease at a time when the CPUSA opposed aiding the beleaguered democracy.

After the war, Murrow pioneered in the new medium of television. *See It Now,* his weekly half-hour program on CBS, drew millions of viewers. While the vast majority of programs were devoted to entertainment, Murrow saw TV's amazing power for good and evil. TV, he insisted, should do more than broadcast sitcoms and deodorant commercials; it should enlighten people about big, important issues. "This

Radio broadcaster Edward R. Murrow. (1947)

instrument can teach," he declared, "it can illuminate; yes, and even it can inspire. But it can do so only to the extent that humans are determined to use it to those ends. Otherwise, it's nothing but wires and lights in a box."[51]

In 1954, the overriding issue for Ed Murrow was McCarthyism. The broadcaster loathed its namesake. "He felt," as a friend put it, "that we were in the presence of a man who would turn America around, who had so much power just in terms of being a destroyer. He feared the beginning of a Nazi-like mass movement." Murrow also thought he knew how to check this evil. One day, over lunch with cartoonist Walt Kelly, creator of the comic strip *Pogo,* he said: "You know, the best man to destroy McCarthy is Joe himself." In other words, Murrow meant to use TV as a sword against the man he saw as a would-be Hitler. The result would be what historian Stephen J. Whitfield calls "the most important single show in the history of television."[52]

Murrow and his staff viewed fifteen thousand feet of film in search of damning material. Aired on the evening of March 9, the program, titled "A Report on Senator Joseph R. McCarthy," was not a direct attack on the senator. Instead, it showed the supposed "real" man speaking for himself in carefully edited snippets. What viewers saw was a crude, rude, bullying, blustering fraud. There, before their eyes, was McCarthy "belching and picking his nose," disheveled, giggling, clowning, and berating witnesses like the heroic Ralph Zwicker. In his comments between film clips, Murrow described this combination of thug and clown "terrorizing" fellow Americans and "demoralizing" the State Department. In the closing sequence, Murrow looked directly into the camera and spoke about American values in words that resonate in our own time of fear:

We must not confuse dissent with disloyalty. We must remember always that accusation is not proof and that conviction depends upon evidence and due process of law. We will not walk in fear, one of another. We will not be driven by fear into an age of unreason, if we dig deep in our history and our doctrine, and remember that we are not descended from fearful men—not from men who feared to write, to speak, to associate and to defend the causes that were, for the moment, unpopular.

This is no time for men who oppose Senator McCarthy's methods to keep silent. . . . We proclaim ourselves, as indeed we are, the defenders of freedom, wherever it continues to exist in the world, but we cannot defend freedom abroad by deserting it at home.

The actions of the junior Senator from Wisconsin have caused alarm and dismay amongst our allies abroad, and given considerable comfort to our enemies. And whose fault is that? Not really his. He didn't create this situation of fear; he merely exploited it—and rather successfully. Cassius was right. "The fault, dear Brutus, is not in our stars, but in ourselves."

Good night, and good luck.[53]

For the rest of that night and all the next day, phone calls and telegrams praising Murrow flooded CBS headquarters. When pedestrians saw him on the street, shouts of "Attaboy, Ed" greeted him. A pregnant woman ran up and grabbed his hand. "Ed, if it's a boy, I'm gonna name him after you!" Approval came from the White House, too. Asked by reporters if he saw Murrow as a "loyal and patriotic American," the president replied: "I have known that man for many years. He has been one of the men I consider my friend among your profession."[54]

Yet Eisenhower's was not the last word. Equally thoughtful people wondered if the McCarthy program was honest reporting. Visual images are powerful—more powerful, perhaps, than bare facts presented coolly and without comment. This raises questions for our own time, dominated as it is by the Internet and social media. How ethical is it for a trusted journalist, whose duty it is to present the facts as they are, to manipulate images and words to shape his audience's unconscious responses? Can journalists rightly employ the techniques of propaganda? What right did Murrow have to use television's awesome power to attack a man, however vile he thought him to be? Besides, by airing another set of film clips, one could just as easily have shown McCarthy in a favorable light. As film journalist John Cogley wrote at the time, "A totally different selection . . . would turn Senator McCarthy into a man on a shining steed—infinitely reasonable, burdened with the onus of single-handedly cleaning out subversives in the face of violent criticism." Cogley feared that Murrow might have set an evil precedent. He ended with a warning all too true: "Television is dynamite; combined with selectivity it could explode in any person's or any group's face." Nonetheless, Murrow had achieved his purpose: He'd tarnished McCarthy's image in the eyes of millions of TV viewers. The senator would finish the job on his own.[55]

THE ARMY-McCARTHY HEARINGS

The Army-McCarthy hearings lasted from April 22 to June 17, 1954. Held in a room in the Senate Office Building, they took place under glaring klieg lights and the unblinking eyes of television cameras. Literally nothing like them had ever been seen in America before. On any given day, the viewing audience numbered at least twenty million, more than five times the nation's population when George Washington became president in 1789.

From the outset, the senator's physical appearance, body language, and tone gave offense. Roy Cohn sensed trouble ahead. As he later recalled, McCarthy "was verbally brutal where he should have been dexterous and light. . . . With his erupting temper, his menacing monotone, his unsmiling mien, and his perpetual 5 o'clock shadow, he did seem the perfect stock villain. Central casting could not have come up with a better one." Senator William Jenner used more graphic language. McCarthy, he noted, acted like "the kid who came to the party and peed in the lemonade." During sessions, McCarthy constantly interrupted witnesses, trying to rattle them or waste time until the session ended. But when he wanted to make a speech, he'd bellow, "Point of order! Point of order!" The senator broke in so often that viewers dubbed him "Point of Disorder."[56]

The critical moment came on June 9. Everyone knew that Joseph Nye Welch,

the army's counsel, would question Roy Cohn about his efforts on David Schine's behalf. Welch was not a man to trifle with. The tall, soft-spoken sixty-three-year-old Boston trial lawyer had a knack for demolishing an opponent with his wit. Two days earlier, he'd taken Cohn aside for a few minutes. Welch said he'd just sent an assistant, Fred Fisher, back to Boston after he admitted to having once belonged to the National Lawyers Guild, allegedly a Communist front group; Welch wished to protect Fisher by keeping him out of the spotlight at the hearings. Cohn had his own reason for avoiding exposure, which Welch knew all about. He had flunked the physical exam for admission to West Point and joined the National Guard instead, thus avoiding active duty in Korea. Welch proposed a trade: If McCarthy did not mention Fisher, he would keep mum about Cohn's lackluster military record. Cohn agreed, gratefully. That night, he told McCarthy about the deal, and the senator promised not to bring up Fisher's name. But Cohn had not reckoned on his boss's lack of self-discipline. On the critical day, as Welch questioned Cohn, McCarthy lost his temper, growling that the army's counsel had a Communist named Fisher on his staff. Stunned, Cohn could hardly believe his ears. His lips silently formed the words "No! No!"[57]

The wily Bostonian, expecting McCarthy to break his promise, had prepared his reply in advance. His face grim, his voice harsh, Welch verbally cut his opponent to shreds. He said: "Until this moment, Senator, I think I never really gauged your cruelty or your recklessness. Fred Fisher is a young man who went to the Harvard Law School and came into my firm and is starting what looks to be a brilliant career with us. . . . Little did I dream you would be so reckless and so cruel as to do an injury to that lad. . . . Let us not assassinate this lad further, Senator. You have done enough. Have you no sense of decency, sir, at long last? Have you left no sense of decency?" With that, the hearing room burst into applause. In our living room, my father could only say, "This guy is cooked!" McCarthy, Dad knew, had destroyed himself.[58]

The next day, newspapers across America bore headlines such as "Have You No Sense of Decency?" Editorials condemned

Boston Herald front page reporting on McCarthy's dramatic confrontation with Joseph Nye Welch at the hearings. (1954)

McCarthy's "destructive personality," his "fanaticism," his "implacable cruelty," his "utter nastiness" and "utter viciousness." The senator's poll numbers crashed. In January, his ratings had been 50 percent favorable and 29 percent unfavorable; in June, they were 34 percent favorable and 45 percent unfavorable. Yet die-hard supporters still loved their hero. Observers noted, "Even if it were known that McCarthy had killed five innocent children, they would probably still go along with him." Some said the senator was doing God's work, likening his ordeal to Christ's agony on the cross.[59]

Though the Army-McCarthy committee's report faulted Roy Cohn for seeking special treatment for his friend Schine, it found McCarthy blameless on that count. It added that army brass had, indeed, tried to block certain aspects of the senator's probes into disloyalty in the military. That was no consolation for McCarthy. Once the Republicans' prize vote getter, he'd become political poison. In December, the Senate voted 67–22 to condemn him for acting "contrary to senatorial ethics" and "impairing its dignity." Every Democrat voted for the censure resolution except John F. Kennedy, who did not vote at all. JFK happened—some thought conveniently—to be hospitalized with back problems at the time. He never said how he would have voted and never spoke an unkind word about McCarthy in public. Indeed, when a speaker at a banquet criticized the senator, JFK reprimanded him, calling McCarthy "a great American."[60]

President Eisenhower savored McCarthy's downfall. At a gathering of Republican congressmen, he repeated a saying that was making the rounds in the capital. "It's no longer McCarthyism," Ike said, smiling broadly. "It's McCarthywasm." The humiliated senator had become a has-been, a pariah shunned by colleagues in both parties. Alone among

President Dwight D. Eisenhower. (1959)

congressional couples, he and his wife, Jean, never received invitations to White House receptions. When he rose to speak in the Senate, there was a rush to the door. At lunch in the Senate dining room, colleagues hurriedly finished eating and left without speaking to him. Handouts from his office landed in wastebaskets. Reporters, who used to trail him everywhere, dropped him like a hot potato. Joe McCarthy was no longer news. And his life was ebbing away.[61]

McCarthy had been troubled by health problems throughout his Senate career. Time and again, sinus infections put him in the hospital. Worse, he was drinking himself to death. While he'd been a heavy drinker before entering the Senate, his crusade against communism put him under terrific stress, increasing his craving for whiskey. By 1954, McCarthy was a bottle-a-day man, downing a water glass of Scotch in one swallow. Nothing his wife or friends said could get the confirmed alcoholic to seek treatment or change his behavior—not even the couple's adoption of a baby girl. As a result, he spoke with a boozy slur, his hands trembled, and he had visions of snakes leaping at him. When tormented by an upset stomach, he'd swallow a quarter-pound stick of butter to line

it, explaining, "Oh, this helps me hold my liquor better." He'd wake up screaming from nightmares, terrifying Jean. With his liver failing, McCarthy entered Bethesda Naval Hospital, where he died of acute hepatitis on May 2, 1957. He was forty-eight years old. McCarthy's family and the friends he still had mourned his passing. Enemies were gleeful, saying his death was clear "proof for the existence of God!"[62]

DARK LEGACY

Joe McCarthy was at once a failure and a destructive force. He unmasked zero traitors, and nobody he accused served a day in prison for espionage. To be sure, his knowledge of Communist ideology was shallow; he had never read the key Marxist works, let alone the writings of Lenin and Stalin. Newsman George Reedy observed, "Joe couldn't find a Communist in Red Square—he didn't know Karl Marx from [comedian] Groucho [Marx]." Because of him, however, loyal civil servants were forced out of government or left in disgust. FBI agents groused that investigating his charges increased their caseload, resulting "in a waste of manpower." Robert Lamphere had no use for the senator whatsoever. The FBI veteran was certain that "McCarthy's . . . lies and overstatements hurt our counterintelligence efforts" by scaring away potential sources.[63]

As was the case with the Rosenberg trial, normally friendly Europeans saw McCarthyism as a blot on America, a sign of its unfitness to lead the free world. In Vienna, newspapers compared the senator's methods to those of Hitler's Gestapo and Stalin's NKVD—an overstatement, to put it mildly. A leading London newspaper asked, "How long will the Americans stand for this?" The British journalist Rebecca West wrote to a friend from Paris: "YOU CANNOT BELIEVE THE EFFECT OF McCARTHY ON THE FRENCH POPULACE. They do not see why Eisenhower does not take him by the scruff of the neck and throw him into the Potomac." Jean-Paul Sartre called McCarthy "this blood-stained imbecile" who'd helped "murder" the Rosenbergs, though the senator had had nothing to do with their case.[64]

During the Army-McCarthy hearings, Ike said the Kremlin ought to put McCarthy on its payroll. Though made in jest, the remark contained a large grain of truth. Wisconsin's junior senator likely did more to further Soviet interests than to damage them. He addressed a real concern—Communist infiltration of the federal government—but his wild charges further divided Americans at a time of high anxiety. To make matters worse, they cast doubt on the legitimacy of reputable anti-Communists, thus giving the CPUSA a handy argument against its critics. For years to come, the comrades would simply denounce critics as "McCarthyites," frenzied followers of a bully and a charlatan. As the *Daily Worker* (April 4, 1954) put it, McCarthy's "Big Lie" (its term) was that Communists spied for a hostile foreign power. But, the paper continued, "the Communist menace and the spy menace is a fake," which was another of the Party's own big lies. Nevertheless, that lie allowed true believers to dismiss the truth as propaganda by "home-grown Hitlerites." This was no legacy to be proud of.[65]

BRUTAL FANTASIES

We had fed the heart on fantasies,
The heart's grown brutal from the fare.
—William Butler Yeats, "Meditations in Time of Civil War" (1922)

By the time Joe McCarthy was laid to rest, the CPUSA had become a hollow shell. This was due not to anything the senator had done, but to forces beyond his control. True, the Party had been battered by HUAC, which conducted wide-ranging investigations on subjects beyond the film industry, among them Soviet espionage. President Truman's loyalty program and a host of other measures, heavy-handed as they were, also impacted its membership rolls. Nevertheless, the Party's long-term members carried on, faithful to its ideology and accepting of its discipline. Ideologies are like addictions, and it is never easy to break their grip.

For many Party faithful, however, Stalin's death at age seventy-four from a cerebral hemorrhage on March 5, 1953, came as a profound shock. At last it was the tyrant's turn to undergo torture. He was found by bodyguards speechless and lying in a puddle of his own urine, and over the course of three days, the muscles that controlled his breathing gradually became paralyzed. Lack of oxygen turned his lips black, and his features twisted in agony as he slowly suffocated. His daughter, Svetlana, thought this a fitting end for a man without pity or remorse, who'd never "suffered any pangs of conscience." She wrote: "My father died a difficult and terrible death. . . . God grants an easy death only to the just." Even so, Stalin left this life surrounded by physicians fearful of their own lives, trying to save him, an end denied to the millions of his victims. This was a kind of poetic justice. Stalin despised physicians, distrusting their abilities and loyalty. He once had his personal doctor, a professor of medicine, tortured in the Lubyanka for saying he looked tired and should rest![1]

Russians were stunned when Radio Moscow announced his passing. Wherever people gathered, even strangers embraced and wept together. Their sorrow was genuine. For nearly three decades, Stalin's propaganda machine had glorified him as an infallible, all-wise, all-good friend of working people. To be sure, he was the only ruler the young had ever known, the Mighty Helmsman who'd steered Mother Russia to victory in the Great Patriotic War against Hitler's Germany.

There were tears in the Gulag, too—tears of sadness and joy. Stalin's passing lifted a weight from slaves' minds, replacing dread with a glimmer of hope for eventual freedom, or at least more humane treatment. Eugenia Ginzburg, sent to the Gulag as an "enemy of the people," sobbed upon learning that "the blood-stained graven idol of our century had breathed his last." She sobbed not only for his victims, "but most of all for myself. What this man had done to me, to my spirit, to my children." In an Arctic camp, prisoners openly prayed, "May the devil take his soul today!" In a mine shaft, a wizened man dropped to his knees in a puddle of muddy water, shouting, "Thank God someone still looks after the wretched." Elsewhere, lines of slaves marching to work under guard passed the news in whispers: "He's croaked! He's croaked!" A group of men, living skeletons in rags, held a midnight party and celebrated with grain alcohol stolen from a warehouse. Hollow-cheeked and lice-ridden women "set down their tools and began to sing and dance when they heard the news." Slaves of both sexes threw their caps in the air and greeted one another: "I wish you great joy on this day of resurrection!" Elsewhere, slaves knocked the head off his marble statue and rolled it in the dirt. It was said that he'd "departed for hell, to report to the devil." In factories, ordinary workers exclaimed, "A dog dies a dog's death. It's good that he died." One man raised his head, sniffed the air, and said, "Smell that? His corpse is already stinking."[2]

Across the Atlantic, Communists and fellow travelers mourned their fallen idol. "I remember how we cried when Stalin died," longtime Communist Richard Healey wrote. "He was my greatest hero. The whole family cried. It was a major, scary thing. For me as a little kid, he was more than a hero, he was a protector." Adults spoke of the tyrant with reverence.

Cartoon by Jimmy Friell, published in the *Daily Worker* the day after Stalin's death. (1953)

For years Paul Robeson, holder of the 1952 Stalin Peace Prize, had doggedly followed the Party line, exalting the USSR, "that land of love and happiness." Upon hearing the news, the singer responded with a eulogy titled "To You Beloved Comrade." In it, Robeson gushed about the genius "who was wise and good," about "his deep humanity," about "his wise understanding" and his "deep kindness and wisdom." Robeson ended with this paean to the Kremlin's resident monster: "Slava—slava—slava Stalin, Glory to Stalin. Forever will his name be honored and beloved in all lands. . . . How consistently, how patiently, he labored for peace and ever-increasing abundance, and with what deep kindness and wisdom. He leaves tens of millions all over the earth bowed in heart-aching grief." Labor organizer and CPUSA activist Elizabeth Gurley Flynn was also grief-stricken. To her, Stalin was "the best loved man on earth of our time. . . . No dictator would be so loved by the people." Mrs. S., who lived down the hall from us, buried her face in her hands, sobbing, "There died a man who never hurt anyone."[3]

The fantasy of Great Stalin was like a delicate soap bubble floating on wisps of propaganda and the will to believe. That

Nikita Khrushchev. (1961)

Stalin is the beacon which guides all
  progressive mankind.
Stalin is our banner.
Stalin is our will.
Stalin is our hope.

bubble burst on February 24, 1956, when Nikita Khrushchev addressed a closed session of the Twentieth Congress of the CPSU in Moscow. While Khrushchev, the USSR's new ruler, titled his speech "The Crimes of the Stalin Era," he lacked the moral authority to accuse anyone of criminality. An obedient Stalinist thug, he'd "worshiped" (his word) the tyrant; at a mass meeting in Moscow, he'd led the chant:

Stalin is our hope.
Stalin is our expectation.

Over the years, to please Stalin, he'd signed death warrants for close friends, men he knew to be innocent. During the 1930s, he'd ordered the shooting of 55,741 Soviet government and CPSU officials on suspicion of disloyalty. "My arms are up to the elbows in blood," he'd later admit. "That is the most terrible thing that lies in my soul." But we may wonder how heavily the guilt truly lay, for Khrushchev never rejected terror as an instrument of state control. Stalin's sin, he thought, was using terror when unnecessary. Like Stalin, too, he hated Jews, calling them "crooks" and "shylocks" who preyed on society.[4]

Khrushchev attacked his late master in order to destroy his image as an infallible leader and solidify his own position as the nation's ruler. The audience listened for nearly four hours as the pudgy, balding man recited a litany of Stalin's crimes. As he spoke, many delegates wept; others held their heads in despair, and one kept popping nitroglycerin tablets to ward off a heart attack. Stalin had abused his power,

Khrushchev charged, creating a "cult of personality" that portrayed him as god-like. However, the real Stalin was petty, spiteful, and "sickly suspicious." Audience members gasped as he accused Stalin of being a bloodthirsty fiend who killed indiscriminately, without qualms, the good with the bad. The tyrant's victims, including Lenin's old comrades, had been forced to confess to crimes that existed only in his diseased imagination. "How," Khrushchev asked, "is it possible that a person confesses to crimes which he has not committed? Only in one way—because of applications of physical methods of pressuring him, tortures, bringing him to a state of unconsciousness, depriving him of his judgment, taking away his human dignity. In this manner were the 'confessions' obtained." Moreover, the speaker insisted, correctly, Stalin had ignored warnings about the coming invasion of the USSR in June 1941 and had even had officers who'd reported German troop movements shot for spreading disinformation. As for the Doctors' Plot, it was a hoax aimed at murdering innocents for no reason other than to soothe Stalin's morbid fears. Stalin had urged their torturers on, warning, "If you do not obtain confessions from the doctors, we will shorten you by a head."

Khrushchev naively ended with a plea for secrecy, because he did not want to give ammunition to the USSR's enemies.[5]

"The truth hurts," my grandma used to say, and now it hurt more than ever. Somehow, copies of the "secret" speech reached the West. On April 30, 1956, an English translation was read aloud at a national committee meeting of 120 CPUSA leaders; the chairman, veteran activist Steve Nelson, called them "the collective backbone of the Party." Afterward, Nelson

Khrushchev's "secret" speech to the Twentieth Congress of the Communist Party of the Soviet Union (CPSU) in Moscow. (1956)

expressed what most senior comrades were thinking and feeling:

> The words of the speech were like bullets, and each found its place in the hearts of veteran Communists. Tears streamed down the faces of men and women who had spent . . . their whole adult lives in the movement. I looked into the faces of people who had been beaten up and jailed with me, and . . . I thought . . . 'There's no longer one seat of wisdom. . . . We're on our own.' . . . I said simply, 'This is not why I joined the Party.' . . . Above all, I was angry, not with the Russians . . . or even Stalin, but with myself and others who had been so blind in our adherence to Soviet policy. . . . I, and I'm sure, many others who were at the meeting, vowed that our Party would change in order that nothing like this could ever happen again.[6]

But it was too late to change the Party in any meaningful way. Rank-and-filers reacted to Khrushchev's speech with anguish and disgust. A common thread runs through their responses: "We believed and were lied to by those we trusted." CPUSA

Copies of Khrushchev's speech were distributed throughout the world, despite his plea for it to be kept secret, eventually reaching the West. (1956)

old-timers groaned, "There are no more gods"—no more infallible authorities to believe in. A woman screamed at her aunt: "Lies! Lies and treachery and murder. A maniac has been sitting there in Moscow! A maniac has been sitting there in the name of socialism. In the name of *socialism*! And all of you—all these years—have undone yourselves over and over again in the service of this maniac. Millions of Russians have been destroyed! Millions of Communists have betrayed themselves and each other." Letters written in a similar vein flooded the *Daily Worker,* which published many of them. A typical letter: "The American CP repeated as gospel truth which it sincerely believed, every lie told by the Soviet Union about its living standards . . . about the Moscow Trials, about the electoral system, about the doctors' case, [and] the stamping out of Jewish culture in Russia."[7]

Why should this have come as a surprise? The crimes Khrushchev cited were hardly "revelations" or "shocking disclosures." In researching this book, I was struck by the variety and abundance of materials available to anyone willing to look at them. Since Lenin's day, the Western press, academic journals, and popular works had given lengthy accounts of the Soviet tyranny, often by refugees, fugitives, and keen-eyed foreign visitors. Take the Gulag: There was plenty of information about its existence and horrors in the years just prior to Khrushchev's speech. The best of these accounts are historian David J. Dallin's *Forced Labor in Soviet Russia* (1947) and the bombshell *Slave Labor in Russia: The Case Presented by the American Federation of Labor to the United Nations* (1949). There are also the writings of several lucky survivors, men and women who'd been released after serving their time in the camps, made it to the West, and wrote about their experiences. Among the best known was Elinor Lipper's heart-wrenching *Eleven Years in Soviet Prison Camps* (1951), an account of her lost years.

Yet it was as if the brains of the CPUSA faithful were wired to accept whatever came from official Moscow. Evidently, their need to believe overrode their reason, as did their emotional investment in the Soviet experiment. In this regard, Peggy Dennis showed keen insight. A Communist since her early teens, she'd always accepted the Moscow line "as an act of faith in the infallibility of the Soviet leadership . . . [who] are always wiser than we. . . . It was the ingrained habit of the membership to say, even when it had doubts, 'Our leaders know best.'" To be sure, "it was as though each of us knew we could not trust ourselves to open the lid of that Pandora's box," in which the truth lay. But now Stalin's heir, the anointed leader of the CPSU, had spoken. Whatever he said, the faithful comrade was obliged to believe, because *he* said it.[8]

A statue of Stalin toppled in the Hungarian Revolution. (1956)

Khrushchev soon discredited himself as well as Stalin. In November 1956, nine months after his damning speech, the people of Hungary rebelled against Soviet domination. Unyielding, the Kremlin's master sent troops and tanks to Budapest, the capital; perhaps thirty thousand civilians died in the fighting that ensued, and two hundred thousand fled to the West, fearing Soviet reprisals. That was too much even for Jean-Paul Sartre. In a stunning turnaround, the philosopher, who had bashed the United States over the Rosen-bergs' fate, accused the French Communist Party of "thirty years of lies." A fellow traveler, famed actor Yves Montand, who had co-starred in films with Marilyn Monroe and Barbra Streisand, also saw the light; he declared that he'd "been exploited, used to advertise an idea, just like a shampoo or drink" by "Red Nazis." In effect, Montand admitted to having stood in that long line of dupes and useful idiots.[9]

Thoughtful Soviet observers well understood Moscow's lies, having lived with them since Lenin's day. In 1957,

Boris Pasternak's novel *Doctor Zhivago,* the manuscript of which had been smuggled out of the USSR, was published in the West. Named after its main character, Yuri Zhivago, a physician and poet, the novel is set between the years prior to World War I and the Russian Revolution and Civil War. Such terrible years—years in which a great nation had been subjugated by the "inhuman reign of the lie." Pasternak felt the power of the lie himself. When the Swedish Academy awarded him the Nobel Prize in Literature, Khrushchev's Kremlin ordered him to refuse the honor—or else.[10]

Meanwhile, in America, people abandoned the Party in droves. John Gates, a member of its central committee, saw the rot all around. "We are isolated almost entirely from the labor movement, the Negro people, and the farmers," he wrote in despair. For nearly two decades, novelist Howard Fast had been the nation's foremost Communist author, a darling of the Kremlin and a winner of the Stalin Peace Prize. Yet, upon reading Khrushchev's speech, his dreamworld turned into a nightmare. Communism became for the author a false god, a pagan idol worshipped by fanatics. "I was," Fast wrote, "filled with loathing and disgust. I felt a sense of unmitigated mental nausea at the revelation that I had supported and defended this murderous bloodbath and I felt . . . a sense of being a victim of the most incredible swindle in modern times." In order to understand communism properly, Fast later wrote, it must be seen as an ideology of "naked terror, awful brutality, and frightening ignorance." Though Fast's colleague Dalton Trumbo resigned for business reasons, the screenwriter continued to support CPUSA causes whenever he could. In 1958, he doubted that five members were left in all of Hollywood.[11]

The Party that Fast and Trumbo had known all but shriveled away. Its national membership tumbled from an all-time high of around eighty thousand in 1945 to twenty thousand within weeks of the publication of Khrushchev's speech; perhaps three thousand remained in 1958, the same year in which the *Daily Worker* ceased publication. Yet a large proportion of these "members" were not Communists at all; an estimated one in three was a paid FBI informer, as was half the Chicago branch. In 1961, the Party was being kept alive by contributions from Moscow and dues payments from members on J. Edgar Hoover's payroll! In 1971, eleven members of the CPUSA's national committee were reporting to the FBI, including Morris

Childs, a Soviet spy who was also a double agent for the FBI.[12]

By then, the process of "de-Stalinization" was well under way in the USSR. The Jewish doctors—those who'd survived the torture cells—were cleared, freed, and allowed to resume their careers. But even before Khrushchev's speech, Russians had begun clamoring for change. In response, Stalin's heirs drastically reduced the number of slaves in the Gulag. Of the over 2.5 million prisoners, more than a million were pardoned and allowed to return to their families, though without any apology for their sufferings or compensation for their lost years. Worse, nobody was held to account for the injustices they'd suffered—not their NKVD torturers, not the heads and guards of the camps or hellholes like the Lubyanka. Although the Gulag system gradually faded as camps were closed, it was not completely abolished until 1987, when Soviet leader Mikhail Gorbachev, a grandson of Gulag prisoners, gave the order.[13]

As for Stalin, his body had been mummified to preserve it for the ages and placed beside Lenin's in the mausoleum on Red Square. After Khrushchev's speech, however, some Party leaders, echoing public opinion, began saying it did not belong in that hallowed place. As one delegate, an eighty-year-old Bolshevik who worshipped Lenin's memory, put it in a speech to the Twenty-Second Congress in October 1961, her idol did not want Stalin beside him. The Bolshevik hero had come to her in a dream, she announced with a straight face: "He was standing there before me as if he were alive, and he said: 'It is unpleasant to be next to Stalin, who did so much harm to the party.' "[14]

On October 31—coincidentally Halloween, the day of ghosts, ghouls, and goblins—Stalin's body was quietly removed and buried beside the Kremlin wall. Officials placed a marble bust of the mass murderer over the grave and a stone slab with a simple inscription: "J. V. Stalin 1879–1953." Today, the gravesite is a place of pilgrimage for those who pine for the days when Moscow was the center of a vast and feared empire, among them Vladimir Putin, the current president of the Russian Federation. Putin has found the image of Stalin a useful tool in solidifying his image as Russia's strongman. However, in certain parts of Russia, up to 39 percent of young people do not even know who Stalin was. Yet there is more to the story. For many Russians, Stalin and his legacy still represent the high point in their country's modern history. Accordingly, his reputation and popularity have experienced an uptick since the early 2000s.

The year 1989 saw the end of Soviet domination in Eastern Europe. A series of rebellions in Iron Curtain countries, particularly Poland and Hungary, triggered a chain reaction in East Germany, the western spearhead of Soviet power. What happened in Berlin began the unraveling of the USSR itself. In May 1961, Nikita Khrushchev approved construction of a wall to prevent East Berliners from fleeing to West Berlin. On June 12,

1987, President Ronald Reagan, who often spoke of the USSR as the "Evil Empire," stood in front of the Berlin Wall and called upon Mikhail Gorbachev, the then Soviet leader: "Mr. Gorbachev, tear down this wall." On November 9, 1989, people in the divided city gathered at the Berlin Wall and began tearing it down after the East German Communist Party buckled to popular demand, announcing that East Germans could freely cross the border.

By the end of 1989, the USSR, weakened by decades of corruption, economic

Germans protest in front of the Berlin Wall a few days before its fall. (1989)

stagnation, and wasteful armaments expenditures, began withdrawing its troops from Eastern Europe. The regime had reached the end of the line. On Christmas Day 1991, the red hammer-and-sickle flag was lowered from the Kremlin and the Soviet Union ceased to exist, giving way to fifteen separate countries, the largest being the Russian Federation. Across the former USSR, Stalin's remaining portraits were removed from public buildings. His statues were toppled and broken with sledgehammers, or just left for children to play on. Places named in his honor were renamed. Stalingrad, for example, became Volgograd, and Stalino became Donetsk. So ended the Cold War.

Though Moscow, desperately hard up for cash, ended funding for the CPUSA in 1989, it survives nevertheless. Like the Party in its heyday, this younger version still aims at achieving "the communist society, the ending of all class divisions, [and] a society of equality." Unlike the old-timers, however, members say they reject revolutionary violence and the overthrow of the United States government. This being the case, they saw no reason to cling to the Moscow-tainted past. So, in 2007, they donated twelve thousand cartons of documents, dating from the CPUSA's formation eighty-eight years earlier, to New York University's Tamiment Library. A treasure trove that will take many years to catalog and evaluate, the archive contains everything from a complete run of the *Daily Worker* and its million-plus file of photos to pamphlets, personal letters, confidential minutes of central committee and branch meetings, secret code words, and directives from Moscow. It is unclear—so far—if the files are complete, or if they were purged of sensitive materials before being turned over. What is clear is that, as of 2014, the Party claimed to have a mere two thousand to three thousand members.[15]

That same year, 2014, the prominent Russian actor Leonid Bronevoy, whose father had been a Cheka torturer, only to wind up in the Gulag himself as a supposed traitor, described the Soviet experiment as "an absurd horror film stretching over 70 years." Exactly! Rule by terror, government-caused famine, mass arrests, torture, obscene show trials, state-sponsored atheism, slave-labor camps, bald-faced lies told as gospel truth: All were the legacy of a ruthless regime committed to an ideology.[16]

Finally, I write this shortly after the centenary of Red October. An ancient Chinese curse says, "May you live in interesting times," for these are dangerous and tumultuous times, times of woe and confusion. The twentieth century was one of the most interesting times humanity has ever experienced. But if it has taught us anything, it is that ideologies claiming to explain everything, and to hold the key to achieving paradise on earth, never deliver. This is due to the crucial fact that they simply do not describe the reality of an endlessly complex world, and also fail to appreciate human nature. Human beings are not merely material objects capable of being fashioned by master craftsmen like Lenin and Stalin into a preconceived form. People do not neatly fall into categories and think, feel, and act alike. Individuals have their own thoughts, beliefs, outlooks, ways, wills, desires, aspirations, and interests, as well as spiritual needs that seek fulfillment in ways materialists cannot understand. So, when an ideology is empowered, as Marxism was in Soviet Russia and racism was in Nazi Germany, its believers invariably turn to violence, resulting in tyranny, misery, and death.

On the other hand, as we learn from the American experience, fear is a powerful emotion—perhaps the most powerful of all. Humans tend to react to stressful times such as economic crises, political upheavals, costly wars, and threats of annihilation in extreme ways. When this happens, as we see from the history of the CPUSA, there is a strong backlash. At such times, those whose professed democratic values have been swept away by fear are not above persecuting "the Other" in the name of security and resistance to tyranny.

Humans seem also to have an innate capacity for wishful thinking and clinging to fantasies. Yet there is hope. As Langston Hughes said in his 1934 poem "History":

The past has been a mint
Of blood and sorrow.
That must not be
True of tomorrow.[17]

History is not destiny. This is a truth that bears repeating, for, being human, we are capable of rational thought, mastering fear, and learning through experience.

NOTES

PROLOGUE: LENIN'S JOURNEY

1. John Ellis, *Eye Deep in Hell: Trench Warfare in World War I* (New York: Pantheon Books), 5.

2. Walter LaFeber, *The Clash: U.S.-Japanese Relations Throughout History* (New York: Norton, 1998), 82.

3. Winston S. Churchill, *The World Crisis: The Aftermath* (London: Thornton Butterworth, 1929), 73.

4. Simon Sebag Montefiore, *Young Stalin* (New York: Knopf, 2007), 314–315; "Lenin Arrives at Finland Station," wsws.org/en/articles/2017/04/10/twrr-a10.html.

5. Aleksandr I. Solzhenitsyn, *The Gulag Archipelago, 1918–1956: An Experiment in Literary Investigation* (New York: Harper & Row, 1974), 103–104.

6. Wolfgang Leonhardt, quoted in Stephen Kotkin, *Stalin: Waiting for Hitler, 1929–1941* (New York: Penguin Press, 2017), 671.

7. Karl Marx and Friedrich Engels, *Manifesto of the Communist Party,* 22, 23, marxists.org.

8. Ibid., 34.

9. Ralph Raico, "Marxist Dreams and Soviet Realities," mises.org/library/marxist-dreams-and-realities; Stéphane Courtois et al., *The Black Book of Communism: Crimes, Terror, Repression* (Cambridge, MA: Harvard University Press, 1999), 4.

I. FRIGHTENED VICTORS

1. Sean McMeekin, *The Russian Revolution: A New History* (New York: Basic Books, 2017), 132–135.

2. Dmitri Volkogonov, *Autopsy for an Empire: The Seven Leaders Who Built the Soviet Regime* (New York: Free Press, 1998), 9; Orlando Figes, *A People's Tragedy: A History of the Russian Revolution* (New York: Viking, 1996), 391, 630.

3. V. I. Lenin, "The Tasks of the Youth Leagues," October 2, 1920, marxists.org/archive/lenin/works/1920/oct/02.htm; *Department of State Bulletin* 85 (June 1989), 86.

4. Richard Pipes, *Russia Under the Bolshevik Regime* (New York: Knopf, 1993), 401; Lenin, "The Tasks of the Youth Leagues"; Max Eastman, *Reflections on the Failure of Socialism* (New York: Devin-Adair, 1955), 87.

5. Richard Pipes, *Communism: A History* (New York: Modern Library, 2001), 95; Dmitri Volkogonov, *Lenin: A New Biography* (New York: Free Press, 1994), 236–237.

6. W. Bruce Lincoln, *Red Victory: A History of the Russian Civil War* (New York: Simon & Schuster, 1989), 132; Richard Pipes, *A Concise History of the Russian Revolution* (New York: Knopf, 1995), 224; Lenin, "Hanging Order," November 8, 1918, loc.gov/exhibits/archives/as2kulak.html.

7. Courtois, *The Black Book of Communism,* 102, italics added; Pipes, *Russia Under the Bolshevik Regime,* 512. See also George Leggett, *The Cheka: Lenin's Political Police* (New York: Oxford University Press, 1986).

8. Figes, *A People's Tragedy,* 534–535; Pipes, *A Concise History of the Russian Revolution,* 224.

9. Courtois, *The Black Book of Communism,* xviii.

10. Figes, *A People's Tragedy,* 732, 743; Alexander N. Yakovlev, *A Century of Violence in Soviet Russia* (New Haven, CT: Yale University Press, 2002), 156, 161; McMeekin, *The Russian Revolution,* 331. Daniel Peris's *Storming the Heavens: The Soviet League of the Militant Godless* (Ithaca, NY: Cornell University Press, 1998) is a scholarly account of this important subject.

11. Rene Fulop-Miller, *The Mind and Face of Bolshevism: An Examination of Cultural Life in Russia* (New York: Knopf, 1928), 104–105; Pipes, *A Concise History of the Russian Revolution,* 406; Yakovlev, *A Century of Violence in Soviet Russia,* 106.

12. Volkogonov, *Autopsy for an Empire,* 3; Donald Rayfield, *Stalin and His Hangmen: The Tyrant and Those Who Killed for Him* (New York: Random House, 2004), 119, 121.

13. Leon Trotsky, *Literature and Revolution,* 1924, marxists.org/archive/trotsky/1924/lit_revo/ch08.htm.

14. Paul Kengor, *Dupes: How America's Adversaries Have Manipulated Progressives for a Century* (Wilmington, DE: ISI Books, 2010), 16; Rafael Medoff, *Los Angeles Times,* "What FDR Said About Jews in Private," April 7, 2013.

15. William E. Leuchtenburg, *The Perils of Prosperity, 1914–32* (Chicago: University of Chicago Press, 1958), 13; John Milton Cooper Jr., *The Warrior and the Priest: Woodrow Wilson and Theodore Roosevelt* (Cambridge, MA: Harvard University Press, 1999), 273.

16. George M. Cohan, "Over There," encyclopedia.com/history/dictionaries-thesauruses-pictures-and-press-releases/lyrics-over-there-1917-george-m-cohan.

17. Edward Robb Ellis, *Echoes of Distant Thunder: Life in the United States, 1914–1918* (New York: Coward, McCann & Geohegan, 1975), 423, 428–429, 439; David T. Morgan, "The Revivalist as Patriot: Billy Sunday and World War I," *Journal of Presbyterian History* 51, no. 2 (Summer 1973), 209, 214.

18. "The Military Collapse of the Central Powers," encyclopedia.1914–1918-online.net/article/the_military_collapse_of_the_central_powers.

19. Ted Morgan, *Reds: McCarthyism in Twentieth-Century America* (New York: Random House, 2003), 68; V. I. Lenin, "Letter to American Workers," marxists.org/archive/lenin/works/1918/aug/20.htm.

20. Robert K. Murray, *Red Scare: A Study in National Hysteria, 1919–1920* (New York: McGraw-Hill, 1964), 39.

21. Ibid., 36.

22. Overman Committee, *Bolshevik Propaganda: Hearings Before a Subcommittee of the United States Senate, February 11, 1919, to March 10, 1919* (Washington, DC: Government Printing Office, 1919), 246–247. The historian S. P. Melgunov's 1924 book *"Red Terror" in Russia, 1918–1923* has many eyewitness accounts of the Red Terror.

23. *Revolutionary Radicalism: Its History, Purpose, and Tactics with an Exposition and Discussion of the Steps Being Taken and Required to Curb It, Being the Report of the Joint Legislative Committee Investigating Seditious Activities, Filed April 24, 1920, in the Senate of the State of New York,* 2 vols. (Albany, NY: J. B. Lyon, 1920), 1:878–881.

24. Federal Bureau of Investigation, *Membership of the Communist Party, USA, 1919–1954* (Washington, DC: Federal Bureau of Investigation, 1955), figure 1.

25. Ann Hagedorn, *Savage Peace: Hope and Fear in America, 1919* (New York: Simon & Schuster, 2007), 86, 351; Stanley Coben, "A Study in Nativism: The American Red Scare of 1919–20," *Political Science Quarterly* 79, no. 1 (March 1964), 66–67.

26. Murray B. Levin, *Political Hysteria in America: The Democratic Capacity for Repression* (New York: Basic Books, 1971), 40.

27. Regin Schmidt, *Red Scare: FBI and the Origins of Anitcommunism in the United States, 1919–1943* (Copenhagen, Denmark: Museum Tusculanum Press, University of Copenhagen, 2000), 36; Levin, *Political Hysteria in America,* 133.

28. Murray, *Red Scare,* 81.

29. Walter Nelles, *Seeing Red: Civil Liberty and the Law in the Period Following the War* (New York: American Civil Liberties Union, 1920), 3; F. G. Franklin, "Anti-Syndicalist Legislation," *American Political Science Review* 14, no. 2 (1920), 294.

30. Levin, *Political Hysteria in America,* 28–29; Tom Copeland, "Wesley Everest, IWW Martyr," *Pacific Northwest Quarterly* 77, no. 4 (October 1986), 125.

31. Levin, *Political Hysteria in America,* 28, 65; Morgan, *Reds,* 90.

32. Murray, *Red Scare,* 90–91, 178.

33. Anthony Read, *The World on Fire: 1919 and the Battle with Bolshevism* (New York: Norton, 2008), 189.

34. Hagedorn, *Savage Peace,* 222.

35. Read, *The World on Fire,* 185; Murray, *Red Scare,* 194.

36. Tim Weiner, *Enemies: A History of the FBI* (New York: Random House, 2012), 23; Murray, *Red Scare,* 194.

37. Murray, *Red Scare,* 207–208.

38. David M. Oshinsky, *A Conspiracy So Immense: The World of Joe McCarthy* (New York: Free Press, 1983), 87.

39. Morgan, *Reds,* 81; *To the American People: Report upon the Illegal Practices of the United States Department of Justice* (Washington, DC: National Popular Government League, 1920).

40. Murray, *Red Scare,* 277; Schmidt, *Red Scare,* 300.

41. Ronald Kessler, *The Secrets of the FBI* (New York: Crown, 2012), 38.

II. TRUE BELIEVERS: A PARTY LIKE NONE OTHER

1. Orlando Figes, *The Whisperers: Private Life in Stalin's Russia* (New York: Metropolitan Books, 2007), 34.

2. Peggy Dennis, *The Autobiography of an American Communist: A Personal View of a Political Life, 1925–1975* (Westport, CT: Lawrence Hill, 1977), 64, 70; Orlando Figes, *Revolutionary Russia, 1891–1991: A History* (New York: Metropolitan Books, 2014), 199.

3. McMeekin, *The Russian Revolution,* 302–303; John Earl Haynes and Harvey Klehr, "'Moscow Gold,' Confirmed at Last?" *Labor History* 33, no. 2 (Spring 1992); John Earl Haynes and Harvey Klehr, *In Denial: Historians, Communists & Espionage* (San Francisco: Encounter Books, 2003), 96.

4. *New York Times,* November 17, 1931.

5. George Charney, *A Long Journey* (Chicago: Quadrangle Books, 1968), 29; Vivian Gornick, *The Romance of American Communism* (New York: Basic Books, 1977), 64.

6. Howard Fast, *The Naked God: The Writer and the Communist Party* (New York: Praeger, 1957), 38.

7. Federal Bureau of Investigation, *Membership of the Communist Party, USA,* figure 1; Irving Howe and Lewis Coser, *The American Communist Party: A Critical History* (New York: Da Capo Press, 1974), 404; J. Peters, *The Communist Party: A Manual on Organisation* (New York: Workers Library Publishers, 1935), 104, marxists.org/history/usa/parties/cpusa /1935/07/organisers-manual/ch04.htm.

8. Benjamin Gitlow, *I Confess: The Truth About American Communism* (New York: Dutton, 1940), 218–219.

9. James T. Patterson, "The Enemy Within," *Atlantic,* October 1998, theatlantic.com/magazine/archive/1998/10/the-enemy -within-9810/377272/.

10. Fast, *The Naked God,* 38; Gornick, *The Romance of American Communism,* 233.

11. Judy Kaplan and Linn Shapiro, eds., *Red Diapers: Growing Up in the Communist Left* (Urbana: University of Illinois Press, 1998), 126; Irving Howe, "Some Romance!," *New York Review of Books,* April 16, 1978; Aileen S. Kraditor, *"Jimmy Higgins": The Mental World of the Rank-and-File Communist, 1930–1958* (New York: Greenwood Press, 1988), 90.

12. Vera Buch Weisbord, *A Radical Life* (Bloomington: University of Indiana Press, 1977), 116.

13. Dorothy Ray Healey and Maurice Isserman, *California Red: A Life in the American Communist Party* (Urbana: University of Illinois Press, 1993), 67.

14. Gil Green, *The Truth About Soviet Russia* (New York: New Age Publishers, 1938), 9–15.

15. Earl Browder, *Traitors in American History: Lessons of the Moscow Trials* (New York: Workers Library Publishers, 1938), 28.

16. *The Communist International, 1919–1943: Documents,* ed. Jane Degras, vol. 2, *1923–1928,* marxists.org/history /international/comintern/documents/volume2-1923-1928.pdf.

17. Dmitri Volkogonov, *Stalin: Triumph and Tragedy* (New York: Grove Weidenfeld, 1991), 155; Nikolai Tolstoy, *Stalin's Secret War* (New York: Holt, Rinehart and Winston, 1981), 26.

18. Ta-Nehisi Coates, "Grappling with Holodomor," *Atlantic,* January 3, 2014, theatlantic.com/international /archive/2014/01/grappling-with-holodomor/282816/. Anne Applebaum's *Red Famine: Stalin's War on Ukraine* (New York: Doubleday, 2017) is the standard work on this grisly subject.

19. Norman M. Naimark, *Stalin's Genocides* (Princeton, NJ: Princeton University Press, 2010), 107.

20. Figes, *Revolutionary Russia*, 191, 195; Anne Applebaum, *Gulag: A History* (New York: Doubleday, 2003), 175; Tolstoy, *Stalin's Secret War,* 11, 30.

21. Robert Conquest, *Kolyma: The Arctic Death Camps* (New York: Viking Press, 1978), 227.

22. John Steinbeck, *A Russian Journal* (New York: Penguin Books, 1999), 48.

23. Edvard Radzinsky, *Stalin* (New York: Doubleday, 1996), 540; Figes, *The Whisperers,* 252.

24. Maurice Isserman, *Which Side Were You On? The American Communist Party During the Second World War* (Middletown, CT: Wesleyan University Press, 1982), 64; Louis Francis Budenz, *Men Without Faces: The Communist Conspiracy in the U.S.A.* (New York: Harper & Brothers, 1950), 139, 140, 143; Alan Wood, *Stalin and Stalinism* (New York: Routledge, 2004), 60; Anton Antonov-Ovseyenko, *The Time of Stalin: Portrait of a Tyranny* (New York: Harper, 1983), 229; Mikhail Heller, *Cogs in the Wheel: The Formation of Soviet Man* (New York: Knopf, 1988), 195, 204.

25. Browder, *Traitors in American History,* 27, 31; William Z. Foster, *Questions & Answers on the Piatakov-Radek Trial* (New York: Workers Library Publishers, 1936), 54–55; Earl Browder, "Lessons of the Moscow Trials," *Communist,* April 1938, 306, 313; Alex De Jonge, *Stalin and the Shaping of the Soviet Union* (New York: William Morrow, 1986), 339.

26. Richard Reuss, "American Folklore and Left-Wing Politics: 1927–1957" (PhD diss., Indiana University, 1971), 58; "The Internationale," marxists.org/history/ussr/sounds/lyrics/international.htm.

27. "Which Side Are You On?," unionsong.com/u015.html.

28. *Working Class Against Capitalist Class Is the Main Election Issue of the Communist Party: Election Platform of the Communist Party USA* (New York: CPUSA, 1929), 18, 20; Grace Hutchins, *Women Who Work* (New York: International Pamphlets, 1932), 11.

29. Van Gosse, "'To Organize in Every Neighborhood, in Every Home': The Gender Politics of American Communists Between the Wars," *Radical History Review* 50 (Spring 1991), 110, 127; Daniel Opler, "Monkey Business in Union Square: A Cultural Analysis of the Klein's-Ohrbach's Strikes of 1934–5," *Journal of Social History* 36, no. 1 (Autumn 2002), 156.

30. Gosse, "'To Organize in Every Neighborhood,'" 113.

31. Ludwig von Mises, *Human Action: A Treatise on Economics* (Auburn, AL: Ludwig von Mises Institute, 1998), 714.

32. Kengor, *Dupes,* 113–119; Harry Haywood, *The South Comes North in Detroit's Own Scottsboro Case* (New York: National Office of League of Struggles for Negro Rights, 1934), 13; Gil Green, *Youth Confronts the Blue Eagle* (New York: Youth Publishers, 1933), 23; "The Red Army," spartacus-educational.com/RUSred.htm.

33. William Z. Foster, *Toward Soviet America: The United States of Soviet America* (New York: Coward-McCann, 1932), chapter 5.

34. Alexander Berkman, *The Bolshevik Myth (Diary 1920–22)* (New York: Boni & Liveright, 1925), 171, in Anarchist Archives, dwardmac.pitzer.edu. See also Emma Goldman, *My Further Disillusionment with Russia* (New York: Doubleday, Page, 1924), 70.

35. William Henry Chamberlin, "Making the Collective Man in Soviet Russia," *Foreign Affairs* 10, no. 2 (January 1932), 284; Vladimir Gsovski, *Elements of Soviet Labor Law: Penalties Facing Russian Workers on the Job* (Washington, DC: Department of Labor, 1951), 7–8.

36. Goldman, *My Further Disillusionment with Russia,* 105.

37. Dennis, *The Autobiography of an American Communist,* 63; Figes, *The Whisperers,* 252.

38. Eugene Lyons, *Workers' Paradise Lost: Fifty Years of Soviet Communism; A Balance Sheet* (New York: Funk & Wagnalls, 1967), 63–64; Sheila Fitzpatrick, *The Russian Revolution* (New York: Oxford University Press, 1994), 97.

39. Pipes, *A Concise History of the Russian Revolution,* 297.

40. Foster, *Toward Soviet America,* 273, 314.

41. Gosse, "'To Organize in Every Neighborhood,'" 121.

42. P. D. Stachura, "The Ideology of the Hitler Youth in the Kampfzeit," *Journal of Contemporary History* 8, no. 3 (July 1973), 158; Figes, *The Whisperers,* 20.

43. Fulop-Miller, *The Mind and Face of Bolshevism,* 319.

44. Chamberlin, "Making the Collective Man in Soviet Russia," 280; Catriona Kelly, "Riding the Magic Carpet: Children and the Leader Cult in the Stalin Era," *Slavic and East European Journal* 49, no. 2 (Summer 2005), 215. Lee Hockstader, "From a Ruler's Embrace to a Life in Disgrace," *Washington Post,* March 10, 1995, washingtonpost.com/archive/politics /1995/03/10/from-a-rulers-embrace-to-a-life-in-disgrace/6df151d2-82c3-4589-85b3-2015c802258f/; Oleg Yegorov, "'Children's Friend': The Dark Story Behind Stalin's Popular Photo with a Soviet Girl," *Russia Beyond,* June 15, 2018, rbth.com/history/328538-stalin-children-gelya-markizova.

45. Figes, *The Whisperers,* 130, 301, 309.

46. Anne Applebaum, *Gulag,* 102, 324–325; Alan M. Ball, *And Now My Soul Is Hardened: Abandoned Children in Soviet Russia, 1918–1930* (Berkeley: University of California Press, 1994). I have also found useful Deborah Hoffman's *The Littlest Enemies: Children in the Shadow of the Gulag* (Bloomington, IN: Slavica, 2009).

47. Eugenia Ginzburg, *Within the Whirlwind* (New York: Harcourt Brace Jovanovich, 1981), 3–4; Margaret K. Stolee, "Homeless Children in the USSR, 1917–1957," *Soviet Studies* 40, no. 1 (January 1988), 74, 76; Fitzpatrick, *The Russian Revolution,* 151; Ball, *And Now My Soul Is Hardened,* 30–32, 72.

48. Kaplan and Shapiro, *Red Diapers,* 88; Figes, *The Whisperers,* 11; Figes, *A People's Tragedy,* 747; Oleg Khlevniuk, *The History of the Gulag: From Collectivization to the Great Terror* (New Haven, CT: Yale University Press, 2004), 24.

49. "Radical Children's Literature," literature.oxfordre.com/view/10.1093/acrefore/9780190201098.001/acrefore -9780190201098-e-89; Julia L. Mickenberg and Philip Nel, eds., *Tales for Little Rebels: A Collection of Radical Children's Literature* (New York: New York University Press, 2008), 18.

50. Kraditor, *"Jimmy Higgins,"* 81.

51. Martha Campion, *Who Are the Young Pioneers?* (New York: New Pioneer, 1934), 26–27; "Pioneers Fight Boy Scouts," *Young Pioneer,* July–August 1929, 2.

52. Dennis, *The Autobiography of an American Communist*, 126.

53. Kaplan and Shapiro, *Red Diapers*, 21; "Young Reds in New York City," *Journal of Education* 111, no. 3 (January 20, 1930), 82; "Forward to the Soviet Union," *Young Pioneer*, June 3, 1929, 9; Morgan, *Reds*, 117, 118; "Defend the Soviet Union!," *Young Comrade*, March 1930, 2; "To All Central High School Cadets," January 1930, loc.gov/resource/rbpe .20804800/?st=text.

54. Paul C. Mishler, *Raising Reds: The Young Pioneers, Radical Summer Camps, and Communist Political Culture in the United States* (New York: Columbia University Press, 1999), 58.

55. Campion, *Who Are the Young Pioneers?*, 2–3.

56. "Program of the Young Communist League of America: Adopted by the First National Convention, Early May 1922," marxisthistory.org/history/usa/parties/ycl/1922/0500-ycla-program.pdf.

III. BLACK COMRADES AWAKEN!

1. Robin D. G. Kelley, " 'Comrades, Praise Gawd for Lenin and Them!': Ideology and Culture Among Black Communists in Alabama, 1930–1935," *Science & Society* 52, no. 1 (Spring 1988), 69.

2. Gilbert Osofsky, *The Burden of Race: A Documentary History of Negro-White Relations in America* (New York: Harper & Row, 1966), 409; Nicholas D. Kristof, "Is Race Real?" *New York Times*, July 11, 2003.

3. Ida B. Wells-Barnett, *The Red Record: Tabulated Statistics and Alleged Causes of Lynching in the United States* (1895), archive.org/stream/theredrecord14977gut/14977.txt; "History of Lynchings," naacp.org/history-of-lynchings.

4. V. J. Jerome, *The Negro in Hollywood Films* (New York: Masses & Mainstream, 1952), 16; Harry Alan Potamkin, *The Eyes of the Movie* (New York: International Pamphlets, 1934), 21; Mark E. Benbow, "Birth of a Quotation: Woodrow Wilson and 'Like Writing History with Lightning,' " *Journal of the Gilded Age and Progressive Era* 9, no. 4 (October 2010), 509–533; Mel Watkins, "What Was It About 'Amos 'n' Andy'?," *New York Times*, July 7, 1991.

5. Kate Smith, "That's Why Darkies Were Born," genius.com/Kate-smith-thats-why-darkies-were-born-lyrics.

6. Virginia Gardner, *The Rosenberg Story* (New York: Masses & Mainstream, 1954), 192; Charles H. Martin, "The International Labor Defense and Black America," *Labor History* 26, no. 2 (Spring 1985), 169.

7. Joy Gleason Carew, "Black in the USSR: African Diasporan Pilgrims, Expatriates and Students in Russia, from the 1920s to the First Decade of the Twenty-First Century," *African and Black Diaspora: An International Journal* 8, no. 2 (2015), 210; Harry Haywood, *Black Bolshevik: The Autobiography of an African-American Communist* (San Francisco: Encounter Books, 2003), 193; Maxim Matusevich, "An Exotic Subversive: Africa, Africans and the Soviet Everyday," *Race & Class* 49, no. 4 (April 2008), 66; Anthony Cave Brown and Charles B. MacDonald, *On a Field of Red: The Communist International and the Coming of the First World War* (New York: Putnam, 1981), 362.

8. Paul Robeson, "I Am at Home," in *Paul Robeson Speaks: Writings, Speeches, Interviews, 1918–1974*, ed. Philip S. Foner (New York: Kensington, 1978), 95; "Exploiting His Race: Paul Robeson," thelibertyconservative.com/exploiting-race-paul -robeson; *Daily Worker*, January 15, 1935, revolutionarydemocracy.org/rdv4n2/USSRpr.htm; Paul Kenger, "Death of a Communist," *American Spectator*, June 11, 2014, spectator.org/death-of-a-communist/.

9. Hughes's Soviet poems are in "The Poetry of Langston Hughes," revolutionarydemocracy.org/rdv16n1/hughes.htm; Vera M. Kutzinski, *The Worlds of Langston Hughes: Modernism and Translation in the Americas* (Ithaca, NY: Cornell University

Press, 2012), 191. Hughes later disowned his pro-Soviet poetry. In an appearance before Senator Joseph McCarthy's investigating committee in 1953, he explained that those poems, written when he was very young, no longer reflected his views.

10. Woodford McClellan, "Africans and Black Americans in Comintern Schools, 1925–1934," *International Journal of African Historical Studies* 26, no. 2 (1993), 384–385; Linda Feldman, "American Describes His 44-Year Soviet Odyssey," *Christian Science Monitor,* August 9, 1998, csmonitor.com/1988/0809/arob.html.

11. Theodore Bilbo, *Take Your Choice: Separation or Mongrelization* (Poplarville, MS: Dream House, 1947).

12. Wilson Record, *The Negro and the Communist Party* (Chapel Hill: University of North Carolina Press, 1951), 78; August Meier and Elliott Rudwick, *Along the Color Line* (Urbana: University of Illinois Press, 1976), 332–335.

13. Haywood, *Black Bolshevik,* 361; League of Struggle for Negro Rights, *Equality, Land, and Freedom: A Program for Negro Liberation* (New York: League of Struggle for Negro Rights, 1933), 7–9.

14. Committee on Un-American Activities, U.S. House of Representatives, *The American Negro in the Communist Party* (Washington, DC: Government Printing Office, 1954), 4–5.

15. Nathan Glazer, *The Social Basis of American Communism* (New York: Harcourt, Brace, 1961), 170–171; Landon R. Y. Storrs, "Attacking the Washington 'Femmocracy': Antifeminism in the Cold War Campaign Against 'Communists in Government,'" *Feminist Studies* 33, no. 1 (Spring, 2007), 131; Mark Naison, "Historical Notes on Blacks and American Communism: The Harlem Experience," *Science & Society* 42, no. 3 (Fall 1978), 339; Melech Epstein, *The Jew and Communism: The Story of Early Communist Victories and Ultimate Defeats in the Jewish Community, 1919–1941* (New York: Trade Union and Sponsoring Committee, 1959), 246–247.

16. Haywood, *Black Bolshevik,* 354, 357; Howe and Coser, *The American Communist Party,* 210; Mark Naison, *Communists in Harlem During the Depression* (New York: Grove Press, 1985), 48.

17. Mary Heaton Vorse, "How Scottsboro Happened," *New Republic,* May 10, 1933, marxists.org/subject/women/authors /vorse/scotts.html.

18. Hollace Ransdall, "Report on the Scottsboro, Ala., Case," American Civil Liberties Union, New York, May 27, 1931, 18–19, famous-trials.com/scottsboroboys/1563-firsttrial; Vorse, "How Scottsboro Happened."

19. Ransdall, "Report on the Scottsboro, Ala., Case," 20.

20. James S. Allen, *Organizing in the Depression South: A Communist's Memoir* (Minneapolis: MEP Publications, 2001), 9; Michael J. Klarman, "Scottsboro," scholarship.law.marquette.edu/cgi/viewcontent.cgi?article=4.

21. David M. Oshinsky, "Only the Accused Were Innocent," *New York Times,* April 3, 1994; Jay Bellamy, "The Scottsboro Boys: Injustice in Alabama," *Prologue,* Spring 2014, 28; Dan T. Carter, *Scottsboro: A Tragedy of the American South* (Baton Rouge: Louisiana State University Press), 18–19, 22; Hugh Murray, "The NAACP Versus the Communist Party: The Scottsboro Rape Cases, 1932–1933," anthonyflood.com/murraynaacpvscp.htm.

22. Carter, *Scottsboro,* 27–28.

23. Langston Hughes, *Scottsboro Limited: Four Poems and a Play in Verse* (New York: Golden Stair Press), 1932.

24. Martin, "The International Labor Defense and Black America," 77, 167.

25. Moissaye J. Olgin, *Why Communism? Plain Talks on Vital Problems* (New York: Workers Library Publishers, 1935); International Labor Defense, *Under Arrest! Workers' Self-Defense in the Courts* (New York: International Labor Defense, c. 1930), 7, 16.

26. Allen, *Organizing in the Depression South,* 98.

27. Ibid., 94, 98.

28. Carter, *Scottsboro*, 232; John L. Spivak, "Ruby Bates: Symbol of 'White Supremacy,'" *Labor Defender,* May 1933, 46.

29. Carter, *Scottsboro*, 235–236; Allen, *Organizing in the Depression South,* 114.

30. "Samuel Leibowitz," famoustrials.com/scottsboroboys/1559-leibowitz.

31. Allen, *Organizing in the Depression South,* 91; James S. Allen, *Smash the Scottsboro Lynch Verdict* (New York: Workers Library Publishers, 1933)*,* 5; Klarman, "Scottsboro," 385.

32. Cecil S. Hope, "Halt Lynch Terror!," *Labor Defender,* February 1932, 26; League of Struggle for Negro Rights, *Equality, Land, and Freedom,* 14; Haywood, *Black Bolshevik,* 394; William Michael Goldsmith, "The Theory and Practice of the Communist Front" (PhD diss., Columbia University, 1971), 192; Angelo Herndon, *The Scottsboro Boys: Four Freed! Five to Go!* (New York: Workers Library Publishers, 1937), 14; Harry Haywood, "NAACP—Assistant Hangman," *Labor Defender,* February 1932, 27; Goldsmith, "The Theory and Practice of the Communist Front," 192; R. D. Amis, "They Shall Not Die!," *Labor Defender,* May 1932, 80.

33. Troy Kickler, "George S. Schuyler: Black Conservative, Intellectual, and Iconoclast," lewrockwell.com/2007/02/troy -kickler/george-s-schuyler-black-conservative-intellectual-andiconoclast/; Richard Gid Powers, *Not Without Honor: The History of American Anticommunism* (New York: Free Press, 1995), 101.

34. Joseph North, *Lynching Negro Children in Southern States* (New York: International Labor Defense, 1931).

35. Paul D'Amato, "The Communist Party and Black Liberation in the 1930s," *International Socialist Review* 1 (Summer 1997), isreview.org/issues/01/cp_blacks_1930s.html.

36. Louise Thompson, "We March on Washington!," *Labor Defender,* June 1933, 65; Haywood, *Black Bolshevik,* 393; Carter, *Scottsboro,* 249.

37. catalog.archives.gov/id/7856849; Osofsky, *The Burden of Race,* 408.

38. Carter, *Scottsboro,* 144.

39. Reuss, "American Folklore and Left-Wing Politics," 61; Kelley, "'Comrades, Praise Gawd for Lenin and Them!,'" 74–75.

40. Hugh T. Murray Jr., "Aspects of the Scottsboro Campaign," *Science & Society* 35, no. 2 (Summer 1971), 179.

41. James A. Miller, Susan D. Pennybacker, and Eve Rosenhaft, "Mother Ada Wright and the International Campaign to Free the Scottsboro Boys, 1931–1934," *American Historical Review* 106, no. 2 (April 2001), 413, 423, 426.

42. Ibid., 415; Murray, "Aspects of the Scottsboro Campaign," 179; Maxim Gorky, "The World Looks at Scottsboro," *Labor Defender,* February 1932, 23; Haywood, *Black Bolshevik,* 385.

43. Herbert Romerstein, "The Communist Assault on Hawaii," archive.org/stream/CommunismInHawaiiAndTheObama Connection-RomersteinAndKincaid/CommunismInHawaiiAndTheObamaConnection-RomersteinAndKincaid_djvu.txt.

44. Carter, *Scottsboro,* 310–311.

IV. THE PARTY AND STALIN'S WAR

1. "Stalin's Speech to the Politburo on 19 August 1939," theeasternfront.org/mein_sozialismus/downloads/article.pdf.

2. Robert C. Tucker, *Stalin in Power: The Revolution from Above, 1928–1941* (New York: Norton, 1990), 596–597.

3. Victor Kravchenko, *I Chose Freedom: The Personal and Political Life of a Soviet Official* (London: Robert Hale, 1947), 333; Tucker, *Stalin in Power,* 599; Roger Moorhouse, *The Devils' Alliance: Hitler's Pact with Stalin, 1939–1941* (New York: Basic Books, 2014), 119; Richard Overy, *Russia's War: Blood upon the Snow* (New York: TV Books, 1997), 778.

4. Harvey Klehr, *The Heyday of American Communism: The Depression Decade* (New York: Basic Books, 1984), 390; Kenneth Lloyd Billingsley, *Hollywood Party: How Communism Seduced the American Film Industry in the 1930s and 1940s* (Rocklin, CA: Forum, 1998), 72; William Z. Foster, *The War Crisis: Questions and Answers* (New York: Workers Library Publishers, 1940), 5–6.

5. Henry F. Srebrnik, "'The Jews Do Not Want War!': American Jewish Communists Defend the Hitler-Stalin Pact, 1939–1941," *American Communist History* 8, no. 1 (2009), 62; Epstein, *The Jew and Communism,* 355.

6. Srebrnik, "'The Jews Do Not Want War!,'" 60; Epstein, *The Jew and Communism,* 372, 373.

7. Brendan McGeever, "Revolution and Antisemitism: The Bolsheviks in 1917," *Patterns of Prejudice* 51 (2017), 245.

8. Irving Howe, *World of Our Fathers* (New York: Harcourt Brace Jovanovich, 1976), 346; Howe and Coser, *The American Communist Party,* 401–402; Ilene Philipson, *Ethel Rosenberg: Beyond the Myths* (New Brunswick, NJ: Rutgers University Press, 1992), 16.

9. Srebrnik, "'The Jews Do Not Want War!,'" 66; Nikita Khrushchev, *Khrushchev Remembers* (Boston: Little, Brown, 1990), 141; Moorhouse, *The Devils' Alliance,* 54; Epstein, *The Jew and Communism,* 374; Earl Browder, *The Jewish People and the War* (New York: Workers Library Publishers, 1940), 16.

10. Tolstoy, *Stalin's Secret War,* 113; William L. Shirer, *Berlin Diary: The Journal of a Foreign Correspondent, 1934–1941* (New York: Knopf, 1941), 436, 438; David Wingate Pike, "Between the Junes: The French Communists from the Collapse of France to the Invasion of Russia," *Journal of Contemporary History* 28, no. 3 (July 1993), 470, 472, 480; De Jonge, *Stalin and the Shaping of the Soviet Union,* 360.

11. Moorhouse, *The Devils' Alliance,* 59–60; Overy, *Russia's War,* 778; Antonov-Ovseyenko, *The Time of Stalin,* 262.

12. Budenz, *Men Without Faces,* 82, 151; William Z. Foster, *History of the Communist Party of the United States* (New York: International Publishers, 1952), 388.

13. Elizabeth Gurley Flynn, *I Didn't Raise My Boy to Be a Soldier—for Wall Street* (New York: Workers Library Publishers, 1940), 3, 8, 9, 15.

14. Paul Kengor, *Red Herring: The Great Depression and the American Communist Party; A White Paper* (Grove City, PA: Grove City College, Center for Vision & Values, Fall 2008), 8–9; Guenter Lewy, *The Cause That Failed: Communism in American Political Life* (New York: Oxford University Press, 1990), 180; Budenz, *Men Without Faces,* 151; Moorhouse, *The Devils' Alliance,* 109; Browder, *The Jewish People and the War,* 19; Theodore S. Hamerow, *Why We Watched: Europe, America, and the Holocaust* (New York: Norton, 2008), 221–222; James Roosevelt, *My Parents: A Differing View* (Chicago: Playboy Press, 1976), 241–242.

15. Howe and Coser, *The American Communist Party,* 393; Eugene Lyons, *The Red Decade: The Classic Work on Communism in America During the Thirties* (New Rochelle, NY: Arlington House, 1972), 383; Allan H. Ryskind, *Hollywood Traitors: Blacklisted Screenwriters—Agents of Stalin, Allies of Hitler* (Washington, DC: Regnery History, 2015), 66.

16. Isserman, *Which Side Were You On?*, 99; Howe and Coser, *The American Communist Party*, 398.

17. Moorehouse, *The Devils' Alliance*, 257; Rayfield, *Stalin and His Hangmen*, 415.

18. Ronald Radosh and Allis Radosh, *Red Star over Hollywood: The Film Colony's Long Romance with the Left* (San Francisco: Encounter Books, 2005), 80; Matthew Dower Blake, "Woody Sez: Woody Guthrie in the *People's World* Newspaper" (PhD diss., University of Florida, 2006), 102.

19. Bernard Bellush and Jewel Bellush, "A Radical Response to the Roosevelt Presidency: The Communist Party, 1933–1945," *Presidential Studies Quarterly* 10, no. 4 (Fall 1980), 656; Tim Tzouliadis, *The Forsaken: An American Tragedy in Stalin's Russia* (New York: Penguin Press, 2008), 207–209; Howe and Coser, *The American Communist Party*, 411; Judith Stepan-Norris and Maurice Zeitlin, *Left Out: Reds and America's Industrial Unions* (New York: Cambridge University Press, 2003), 146.

20. Committee on Un-American Activities, *The American Negro in the Communist Party*, 8.

21. Kengor, *Dupes*, 159; "The Negro March on Washington Movement in the First World War," anarkismo.net.article/24786.

22. Howe and Coser, *The American Communist Party*, 415; Bellush and Bellush, "A Radical Response to the Roosevelt Presidency," 656.

23. Ellen Wright and Michel Fabre, eds., *Richard Wright Reader* (New York: Da Capo Press, 1997), 71; Richard Crossman, ed., *The God That Failed* (New York: Harper & Brothers, 1949), 140–141. The only Communist protest came from the Party unit in Cuyahoga County, Ohio, which passed a resolution condemning the Red Cross action as "Barbarian Hitlerism" (Thomas A. Guglielmo, "'Red Cross, Double Cross': Race and America's First World War–Era Blood Donor Service," *Journal of American History* 97, no. 1 [June 2010], 81). The Red Cross finally rescinded its blood-segregation policy in 1950. But only in the late 1960s and early 1970s did Southern states like Arkansas and Louisiana follow suit.

24. Lewy, *The Cause That Failed*, 73–74; Patti Iiyama, "Recalling U.S. Detention of Japanese Americans," *Militant*, January 17, 2011; James Gilbert Ryan, *Earl Browder: The Failure of American Communism* (Tuscaloosa: University of Alabama Press, 1997), 210.

25. Les K. Adler and Thomas G. Paterson, "Red Fascism: The Merger of Nazi Germany and Soviet Russia in the American Image of Totalitarianism, 1930's–1950's," *American Historical Review* 75, no. 4 (April 1970), 1051; Tolstoy, *Stalin's Secret War*, 257; Erik Bruce, "Dangerous World, Dangerous Liberties: Aspects of the Smith Act Prosecutions," *American Communist History* 13, no. 1 (2014), 29.

26. Paul Willen, "Who 'Collaborated' with Russia?," *Antioch Review* 14, no. 3 (Autumn 1954), 262, 264; Bruce, "Dangerous World, Dangerous Liberties," 29; Howe and Coser, *The American Communist Party*, 433–434.

27. Melvin Small, "Buffoons and Brave Hearts: Hollywood Portrays the Russians, 1939–1944," *California Historical Quarterly* 52, no. 4 (Winter 1973), 326, 330.

28. Clayton R. Koppes and Gregory D. Black, *Hollywood Goes to War: How Politics, Profits, and Propaganda Shaped World War II Movies* (New York: Free Press, 1987). Davies is quoted in William Henry Chamberlin, "Khrushchev's War with Stalin's Ghost," *Russian Review* 21, no. 1 (January 1962), 8.

29. Kravchenko, *I Chose Freedom*, 466, 467.

30. Richard Rhodes, *The Making of the Atomic Bomb* (New York: Simon & Schuster, 1986), 719.

31. Howe and Coser, *The American Communist Party*, 433; Willen, "Who 'Collaborated' with Russia?," 275.

32. Tolstoy, *Stalin's Secret War,* 329.

33. Arthur M. Schlesinger Jr., "Origins of the Cold War," *Foreign Affairs* 46, no. 1 (October 1967), 47; Milovan Djilas, *Conversations with Stalin* (New York: Harcourt, Brace, 1962), 114–115; Sergo Beria, quoted at cnn.com/SPECIALS/cold .war/episodes/01/interviews/beria.

34. Dmitri Shostakovich, *Testimony: The Memoirs of Dmitri Shostakovich* (New York: Harper & Row, 1979), 138; Tzouliadis, *The Forsaken,* 261.

35. "February 9, 1946 Speech Delivered by Stalin at a Meeting of Voters of the Stalin Electoral District, Moscow," digitalarchive.wilsoncenter.org/document/116179.

36. Willen, "Who 'Collaborated' with Russia?," 274; Winston Churchill, "The Sinews of Peace ('Iron Curtain Speech')," winstonchurchill.org/resources/speeches/1946-1963-elder-statesman/the-sinews-of-peace/.

V. NIGHTMARE YEARS

1. Hans Doenecke, *Storm on the Horizon: The Challenge to American Isolation, 1939–1941* (New York: Rowman & Littlefield, 2000), 217.

2. David McCullough, *Truman* (New York: Simon & Schuster, 1992), 376.

3. "Truman Doctrine," avalon.law.yale.edu/20th_century/trudoc.asp.

4. Ben Steil, *The Marshall Plan: Dawn of the Cold War* (New York: Simon & Schuster, 2018), 15–16.

5. Thomas Powers, "Inside the Department of Dirty Tricks," *Atlantic,* August 1979, theatlantic.com/magazine/archive /1979/08/inside-the-department-of-dirty-tricks/305460/.

6. McCullough, *Truman,* 630.

7. Anne Applebaum, *Iron Curtain: The Crushing of Eastern Europe, 1944–1956* (New York: Doubleday, 2012), 254.

8. "How NATO's Article 5 Works," *Economist,* March 9, 2015, economist.com/blogs/economist-explains/2015/03 /economist-explains-6. NATO's founding members were Belgium, Canada, Denmark, France, Great Britain, Iceland, Italy, Luxembourg, the Netherlands, Norway, Portugal, and the United States. In 1952, Greece and Turkey joined; West Germany became a member in 1955, and Spain in 1982.

9. Ellen Schrecker, "McCarthyism: Political Repression and the Fear of Communism," *Social Research* 71, no. 4 (Winter 2004), 1049.

10. Griffin Fariello, *Red Scare: Memories of the American Inquisition; An Oral History* (New York: Norton, 1995), 81; Geoffrey R. Stone, "Free Speech in the Age of McCarthy: A Cautionary Tale," *California Law Review* 93 (October 2005), 1392–1393.

11. Schrecker, "McCarthyism," 1064.

12. Stone, "Free Speech in the Age of McCarthy," 1393; Schrecker, "McCarthyism," 1064, 1066, 1067; David Caute, *The Great Fear: The Anti-Communist Purge Under Truman and Eisenhower* (New York: Simon & Schuster, 1978), 282.

13. Morgan, *Reds,* 521.

14. Storrs, "Attacking the Washington 'Femmocracy,'" 122, 127–128, 140.

15. Caute, *The Great Fear,* 275; Schrecker, "McCarthyism," 1048, 1049.

16. Fariello, *Red Scare,* 42; Schrecker, "McCarthyism," 1068; "How to Spot a Communist," alphahistory.com.coldwar/how-to-spot-a-communist-1947/.

17. Robert L. Dahlgren, "Red Scare in the Sunshine State: Anti-Communism and Academic Freedom in Florida Public Schools, 1945–1960," *Cogent Education* 3, no. 1 (2016), 5; Fariello, *Red Scare,* 42.

18. Richard Frank, "The Schools and the People's Front, *Communist,* May 1937, 432–433, 440.

19. "Supreme Court Rules on Communist Teachers," history.com/this-day-in-history/supreme-court-rules-on-communist-teachers.

20. Albert E. Kahn, *The Game of Death: Effects of the Cold War on Our Children* (New York: Cameron & Kahn, 1953), 62–63; Clarence Taylor, *Reds at the Blackboard: Communism, Civil Rights, and the New York City Teachers Union* (New York: Columbia University Press, 2013), 126–129.

21. Kahn, *The Game of Death,* 60.

22. Fariello, *Red Scare,* 420.

23. Ellen Schrecker, "Political Tests for Professors: Academic Freedom During the McCarthy Years" (lecture, University Loyalty Oath Symposium, Universiy of California, Berkeley, October 7, 1999), www.lib.berkeley.edu/uchistory/archives_exhibits/loyaltyoath/symposium/schrecker.html; Fariello, *Red Scare,* 422.

24. Stone, "Free Speech in the Age of McCarthy," 1392, 1400–1401; Elsie McCurties, "Red Roots, Radical Fruit: Children of the Old Left in the Civil Rights Movement and the New Left" (PhD diss., Michigan State University, 2011), 88; Leslie A. Rose, *The Cold War Comes to Main Street: America in 1950* (Lawrence: University Press of Kansas, 1999), 38; Patterson, "The Enemy Within."

25. "Un-American Activities Committee (HUAC)," spartacus-educational.com/USAhuac.htm.

26. John Cogley, *Report on Blacklisting,* vol. 1, *Movies* (New York: Fund for the Republic, 1956), 2–3.

27. Billingsley, *Hollywood Party,* 170; Special Committee on Un-American Activities, House of Representatives, *Investigation of Un-American Propaganda Activities in the United States* (Washington, DC: Government Printing Office, 1938), 1123, 1124.

28. Billingsley, *Hollywood Party,* 170; Rose, *The Cold War Comes to Main Street,* 29.

29. E. S. Shapiro, "Anti-Semitism Mississippi Style," in David A. Gerber, ed., *Anti-Semitism in American History* (Urbana: University of Illinois Press, 1986), 133, 134, 135; "Jackie Robinson and the House Un-American Activities Committee," blogs.weta.org/boundarystones/2016/04/08/jackie-robinson-and-house-un-american-activities-committee.

30. Potamkin, *The Eyes of the Movie,* 3; Billingsley, *Hollywood Party,* 20; Simon Sebag Montefiore, "Why Stalin Loved Tarzan and Wanted John Wayne Shot," *Daily Telegraph,* June 4, 2004, telegraph.co.uk/culture/3618319/Why-Stalin-loved-Tarzan-and-wanted-John-Wayne-shot.html.

31. Billingsley, *Hollywood Party,* 45.

32. Ibid., 58.

33. Lyons, *The Red Decade,* 284, 285, 286; Radosh and Radosh, *Red Star over Hollywood,* 40, 49.

34. Lewy, *The Cause That Failed,* 93.

35. Kaplan and Shapiro, *Red Diapers,* 57; Ryskind, *Hollywood Traitors,* 352; Arthur Eckstein, "The Hollywood Ten in History and Memory," *Film History* 16, no. 4 (2004), 429; Cogley, *Report on Blacklisting,* 29, 31, 35, 38–39, 42.

36. Committee on Un-American Activities, House of Representatives, *Hearings Regarding the Communist Infiltration of the Motion Picture Industry* (Washington, DC: Government Printing Office, 1947), 111–112; "Salaries of Hollywood in 1937," stuffnobodycaresabout.com/2014/08/30/salaries-hollywood-1937/; Cogley, *Report on Blacklisting,* 42.

37. Cogley, *Report on Blacklisting,* 32–33.

38. John Howard Lawson, *Film in the Battle of Ideas* (New York: Masses & Mainstream, 1953), 104; Eckstein, "The Hollywood Ten in History and Memory," 430; Arthur M. Eckstein, "Not Just Another Political Party," *American Communist History,* 5, no. 1 (2006), 123, 124.

39. Radosh and Radosh, *Red Star over Hollywood,* 72; Albert Maltz, "What Shall We Ask of Writers?," *New Masses,* February 12, 1946, 19–22.

40. Alan Casty, *Communism in Hollywood: The Moral Paradoxes of Testimony, Silence, and Betrayal* (Lanham, MD: Scarecrow Press, 2009), 7, 11; Victor S. Navasky, *Naming Names* (New York: Viking Press, 1980), 298; Eckstein, "Not Just Another Political Party," 242.

41. Cogley, *Report on Blacklisting,* 4.

42. HUAC, *Hearings Regarding the Communist Infiltration of the Motion Picture Industry,* 10; Caute, *The Great Fear,* 493.

43. Bob Spitz, *Reagan: An American Journey* (New York: Penguin Press, 2018), 217; Peter Schweitzer, *Reagan's War: The Epic Story of His Forty-Year Struggle and Final Triumph over Communism* (New York: Doubleday, 2002), 11; Radosh and Radosh, *Red Star over Hollywood,* 115–116; Stephen Vaughn, *Ronald Reagan in Hollywood: Movies and Politics* (New York: Cambridge University Press, 1994), 125, 148; HUAC, *Hearings Regarding the Communist Infiltration of the Motion Picture Industry,* 217.

44. Dorothy B. Jones, "Communism and the Movies: A Study of Film Content," in Cogley, *Report on Blacklisting,* 213–214.

45. Eckstein, "The Hollywood Ten in History and Memory," 425; Ron Radosh, "Red Star Falling: The Trumbo Train Wreck," pjmedia.com/ronradosh/2015/11/26/trumbo-train-wreck/.

46. "A Statement by John Howard Lawson," historymatters.gmu.edu/d/6441; HUAC, *Hearings Regarding the Communist Infiltration of the Motion Picture Industry,* 294.

47. Vaughn, *Ronald Reagan in Hollywood,* 127; Billingsley, *Hollywood Party,* 82; Ronald Radosh, "Will the New *Trumbo* Movie Rehash Old Myths?" *National Review,* November 2, 2013; HUAC, *Hearings Regarding the Communist Infiltration of the Motion Picture Industry,* 334.

48. HUAC, *Hearings Regarding the Communist Infiltration of the Motion Picture Industry,* 598–600; "When Bogie and Bacall Were Duped by Hollywood Communists," *American Spectator,* August 15, 2014, spectator.org/60253_when-bogie-and-bacall-were-duped-by-hollywood-communists/.

49. Vaughn, *Ronald Reagan in Hollywood,* 153; "Waldorf Statement," cobbles.com/simpp_archive/huac_nelson1947.htm; "Red Scare Filmography," guides.lib.uw.edu/c.php?341346&p=2303736.

50. Raymond Gram Swing, "Speech to the Radio Executives Club," spartacus-educational.com/USAredC.htm.

51. "Red Channels," spartacus-educational.com/USAredC.htm; Cogley, *Report on Blacklisting,* 477.

52. Aviva Kempner, "How an Actor Died of the Blacklist," *Forward,* September 1, 2010, forward.com/schmooze/130897 /how-an-actor-died-of-the-blacklist/.

53. Swing, "Speech to the Radio Executives Club"; Richard A. Schwartz, "How the Film and Television Blacklists Worked," comptalk.fiu.edu/blacklist.htm.

54. Susan King, "How Dalton Trumbo and Other Blacklisted Writers Quietly Racked Up '50s Oscar Wins," *Los Angeles Times,* January 4, 2016, latimes.com/entertainment/envelope/la-en-oscar-archives-20160105-story.html.

55. John Meroney and Sean Coons, "How Kirk Douglas Overstated His Role in Breaking the Hollywood Blacklist," *Atlantic,* July 5, 2012, theatlantic.com/entertainment/archive/2012/07/how-kirk-douglas-overstated-his-role-in-breaking-the -hollywood-blacklist/259111/.

56. Eckstein, "Not Just Another Political Party," 237; "Hollywood Remembers Its Red Scare Victims," CNN, October 28, 1997, edition.cnn.com/SHOWBIZ/9710/28/blacklist.remembered/; Allan H. Ryskind, "The Stalin Ten—a True Story About Communists in the Movie Industry," cnsnews.com/commentary/allan-h-ryskind/stalinist-ten-true-story-about -communists-movie-industry.

VI. OF ATOMIC BOMBS AND SPIES

1. Hugh Thomas, *Armed Truce: The Beginnings of the Cold War, 1945–46* (New York: Atheneum, 1987), 465–466; Steil, *The Marshall Plan,* 10.

2. Rose, *The Cold War Comes to Main Street,* 313.

3. Jim Green, "Albert Einstein on Nuclear Weapons," *Nuclear Monitor,* April 23, 2015, wiseinternational.org/nuclear -monitor/802/albert-einstein-nuclear-weapons.

4. *Survival Under Atomic Attack* (Washington, DC: Government Printing Office, 1950), 4, 16, 17, 26.

5. Sam Roberts, *The Brother: The Untold Story of the Rosenberg Case* (New York: Simon & Schuster, 2014), 241.

6. "Bert the Turtle" ("The 'Duck and Cover' Song"), vimeo.com/166955340.

7. Rose, *The Cold War Comes to Main Street,* 311; Kahn, *The Game of Death,* 15, 16.

8. John Earl Haynes and Harvey Klehr, *Venona: Decoding Soviet Espionage in America* (New Haven, CT: Yale University Press, 1999), 21; John Earl Haynes, Harvey Klehr, and Alexander Vassiliev, *Spies: The Rise and Fall of the KGB in America* (New Haven, CT: Yale University Press, 2009), 303, 546; John Earl Haynes, James G. Ryan, and Harvey Klehr, "Helen Lowry and Earl Browder: The Genealogy of a KGB Agent and Her Relationship to the Chief of the CPUSA," *American Communist History* 6, no. 2 (2007), 320; Allen Weinstein and Alexander Vassiliev, *The Haunted Wood: Soviet Espionage in America—the Stalin Era* (New York: Random House, 1999), 310, 304; James G. Ryan, "Socialist Triumph as a Family Value: Earl Browder and Soviet Espionage," *American Communist History* 1, no. 2 (2002), 131, 138–141; Katherine A. S. Sibley, *Red Spies in America: Stolen Secrets and the Dawn of the Cold War* (Lawrence: University Press of Kansas, 2004), 96.

9. Haynes, Klehr, and Vassiliev, *Spies,* 541.

10. Ibid.

11. Kravchenko, *I Chose Freedom,* 443, 465.

12. Sibley, *Red Spies in America,* 94; Committee on Un-American Activities, House of Representatives, *Hearings Regarding Shipment of Atomic Material to the Soviet Union During World War II* (Washington, DC: Government Printing Office, 1950), 1185.

13. "Igor Gouzenko," spartacus-educational.com/SSgouzenko.htm; "This Was My Choice," spyinggame.wordpress.com /2012/09/18/this-was-my-choice.

14. Morgan, *Reds,* 253; Katherine A. S. Sibley, "Soviet Military-Industrial Espionage in the United States and the Emergence of an Espionage Paradigm in U.S.-Soviet Relations, 1941–45," *American Communist History* 2, no. 1 (2003), 43; Katherine A. S. Sibley, "Soviet Industrial Espionage Against American Military Technology and the U.S. Response, 1939–1945," *Intelligence and National Security* 14, no. 2 (Summer 1999), 108; Weinstein and Vassiliev, *The Haunted Wood,* 105, 106; Harvey Klehr, *The Communist Experience in America: A Political and Social History* (New Brunswick, NJ: Transaction Publishers, 2010), 145. Kathryn S. Olmsted's *The Red Spy Queen: A Biography of Elizabeth Bentley* (Chapel Hill: University of North Carolina Press, 2002) has also been useful.

15. Svetlana Alliluyeva, *Only One Year* (New York: Harper & Row, 1969), 392.

16. Morgan, *Reds,* 227.

17. Sibley, "Soviet Military-Industrial Espionage in the United States," 28; Haynes and Klehr, *Venona,* 16.

VII. THE ROSENBERG SPY RING

1. Michael Gold, *Jews Without Money* (New York: Horace Liveright, 1930), 1–2.

2. Philipson, *Ethel Rosenberg,* 79.

3. Ibid., 86–87.

4. Irving Howe, *A Margin of Hope: An Intellectual Biography* (New York: Harcourt Brace Jovanovich, 1982), 26; Opler, "Monkey Business in Union Square," 154; Philipson, *Ethel Rosenberg,* 86; "The Red Flag," marxists.org/subject/art/music /lyrics/en/red-flag.htm; Ruth R. Wisse, "Why It's Necessary to Bring Jewish Communism into Full View," *Mosaic Magazine,* June 17, 2019.

5. Philipson, *Ethel Rosenberg,* 93.

6. Irving Kristol, "Memoirs of a Trotskyist," *New York Times,* January 23, 1977; Steven T. Usdin, "The Rosenberg Ring Revealed: Industrial-Scale Conventional and Nuclear Espionage," *Journal of Cold War Studies* 11, no. 3 (Summer 2009), 97; Steven T. Usdin, *Engineering Communism: How Two Americans Spied for Stalin and Founded the Soviet Silicon Valley* (New Haven, CT: Yale University Press, 2005), 11; Michael Dobbs, "Julius Rosenberg Spied, Russian Says," *Washington Post,* March 16, 1997, washingtonpost.com/archive/politics/1997/03/16/julius-rosenberg-spied-russian-says/f6ae1ead -f8d4-4485-83c6-ec460b5ed4da/.

7. Philipson, *Ethel Rosenberg,* 31.

8. Roberts, *The Brother,* 45; Philipson, *Ethel Rosenberg,* 108, 134.

9. Ronald Radosh and Joyce Milton, *The Rosenberg File: A Search for Truth* (New York: Holt, Rinehart & Winston, 1983), 496; Philipson, *Ethel Rosenberg,* 124.

10. Philipson, *Ethel Rosenberg,* 123; Alexander Feklisov, *The Man Behind the Rosenbergs* (New York: Enigma Books, 2001), 119.

11. Haynes and Klehr, *Venona,* 295; Haynes, Klehr, and Vassiliev, *Spies,* 338; Feklisov, *The Man Behind the Rosenbergs,* 17.

12. Feklisov, *The Man Behind the Rosenbergs,* 109, 120, 122; Dobbs, "Julius Rosenberg Spied, Russian Says."

13. Feklisov, *The Man Behind the Rosenbergs,* 293; Haynes, Klehr, and Vassiliev, *Spies,* 338; Haynes and Klehr, *Venona,* 295; Usdin, "The Rosenberg Ring Revealed," 92–93, 140–141.

14. "New York 1657 to Moscow, 27 November 1944," Central Intelligence Agency, cia.gov/library/center-for-the-study-of -intelligence/csi-publications/books-and-monographs/venona-soviet-espionage-and-the-american-response-1939-1957 /b73.gif/image.gif; Mark Kramer, "Why Ethel Rosenberg Should Not Be Exonerated," wbur.org.cognoscenti/2017/01/05 /julius-rosenberg-soviet-spying-mark-kramer.

15. Usdin, "The Rosenberg Ring Revealed," 115, 122.

16. Dobbs, "Julius Rosenberg Spied, Russian Says"; John Earl Haynes and Harvey Klehr, *Early Cold War Spies: The Espionage Trials That Shaped American Politics* (New York: Cambridge University Press, 2006), 159; Ronald Radosh, "Cold Case: Ethel and Julius Rosenberg," *Tablet,* March 29, 2011, tabletmag.com/jewish-news-and-politics/62998/cold-case. A comprehensive catalog of the Rosenberg ring's thefts is in Usdin, "The Rosenberg Ring Revealed," 119–120; Feklisov, *The Man Behind the Rosenbergs,* 116; David Evanier, "The Death of Morton Sobell and the End of the Rosenberg Affair," *Mosaic,* June 3, 2019, mosaicmagazine.com/essay/history-ideas/2019/06/the-death-of-morton-sobell-and-the-end-of-the -rosenberg-affair/.

17. Dobbs, "Julius Rosenberg Spied, Russian Says"; Feklisov, *The Man Behind the Rosenbergs,* 128.

18. Roberts, *The Brother,* 56, 59.

19. Ibid., 71, 104.

20. Radosh and Milton, *The Rosenberg File,* 67; Richard Rhodes, *Dark Sun: The Making of the Hydrogen Bomb* (New York: Simon & Schuster, 1995), 138–139; Weinstein and Vassiliev, *The Haunted Wood,* 198; Feklisov, *The Man Behind the Rosenbergs,* 153. The declassified original of Venona cable 1340 is at "New York KGB Station—Moscow Cables, 1944," wilsoncenter.org/sites/default/files/Venona-New-York-KGB-1944.pdf.

21. Haynes, Klehr, and Vassiliev, *Spies,* 242; Steven T. Usdin, "Tracking Julius Rosenberg's Lesser Known Associates," cia.gov /library/center-for-the-study-of-intelligence/csi-publications/csi-studies/studies/vol49no3/html_files/Rosenberg_2.htm.

22. "Rosenberg Grand Jury Transcripts," 9099, 9102–9103, National Archives, archives.gov/research/court-records/rosenberg .jury; Allen M. Hornblum, *The Invisible Harry Gold: The Man Who Gave the Soviets the Atom Bomb* (New Haven, CT: Yale University Press, 2010), 140–141, 272.

23. "Interview with Alexander Feklisov," pbs.org/redfiles/kgb/deep/intervik_int_alexander_feklisov.htm.

24. Haynes and Klehr, *Early Cold War Spies,* 155. Klaus Fuchs was convicted of espionage and sentenced to fourteen years in prison. Moscow, of course, denied all knowledge of his existence, let alone his spying. Released in 1959 after serving only nine years, he left Britain and took a top science position in East Germany.

25. Roberts, *The Brother,* 188.

26. Robert J. Lamphere and Tom Shachtman, *The FBI-KGB War: A Special Agent's Story* (New York: Random House, 1986), 184; Radosh and Milton, *The Rosenberg File,* 81; Rhodes, *Dark Sun,* 433.

27. Radosh and Milton, *The Rosenberg File,* 98, 99.

28. Ibid., 173; Rosemary Serino, "Espionage Prosecutions in the United States," *Catholic University Law Review* 4 (1954), 47–48.

29. Feklisov, *The Man Behind the Rosenbergs,* 303. David Greenglass bragged to historian Ronald Radosh that he and his brother-in-law saw themselves as "soldiers for Stalin" (Radosh, "Cold Case: Ethel and Julius Rosenberg").

30. Rakesh Krishnan Simha, "Korean War: How the MiG-15 Put an End to American Mastery over the Skies," *Russia Beyond,* April 27, 2017, rbth.com/blogs/continental_drift/2017/04/27/korean-war-how-mig-15-put-end-american-mastery-over -skies-751633.

31. Rose, *The Cold War Comes to Main Street,* 234; Ryskind, *Hollywood Traitors,* 3; "The Korean War: Barbarism Unleashed," peacehistory-usfp.org/korean-war/.

32. "FBI File: Emanuel Bloch," accessed through the Wikipedia article "Emanuel Hirsch Bloch"; Curt Gentry, *J. Edgar Hoover: The Man and the Secrets* (New York: Norton, 1991), 422; Alan M. Dershowitz, "Rosenbergs Were Guilty—and Framed: Justice Department and Judiciary Conspired to Convict a Couple Accused of Espionage," *Los Angeles Times,* July 19, 1995, articles.latimes.com/print/1995-07-19/local/me-25407_1_julius-rosenberg.

33. Roberts, *The Brother,* 268.

34. Ronald Radosh, "To the Mainstream Media, Ethel Rosenberg Was Completely Innocent," hudson.org/research/13104-to -the-mainstream-media-ethel-rosenberg-was-completely-innocent.

35. Roberts, *The Brother,* 480–491; Rebecca Leung, "The Traitor: David Greenglass Testified Against His Own Sister," cbsnews.com/news/the-traitor/.

36. Philipson, *Ethel Rosenberg,* 284–285; Radosh and Milton, *The Rosenberg File,* 245.

37. Sheila M. Brennan, "Popular Images of American Women in the 1950's and Their Impact on Ethel Rosenberg's Trial and Conviction," *Women's Rights Law Reporter* 14 (Winter 1992), 55; Betty Friedan, *The Feminine Mystique* (New York: Norton, 1963), 43–44; Kathryn S. Olmsted, "Blond Queens, Red Spiders, and Neurotic Old Maids: Gender and Espionage in the Early Cold War," *Intelligence and National Security* 19, no. 1 (Spring 2004), 88–89; Ari Kelman, " 'Julius Is the Slave and His Wife, Ethel, the Master,' " *Chronicle of Higher Education,* June 19, 2008, chronicle.com /blognetwork/edgeofthewest/2008/06/19/julius-is-the-slave-and-his-wife-ethel-the-master/.

38. "Judge Kaufman's Statement Upon Sentencing the Rosenbergs for Atomic Espionage," digitalhistory.uh.edu/disp _textbook.cfm?smtID=3&psid=1118.

39. Rhodes, *Dark Sun,* 480–481; Hornblum, *The Invisible Harry Gold,* 284–285.

40. S. Andhil Feinberg, *The Rosenberg Case: Fact and Fiction* (New York: Oceana Publications, 1953), 149; Carol Jochnowitz, "The Rosenbergs: What Is Left to Say?," *Jewish Currents,* January 11, 2011, jewishcurrents.org/articles/the-rosenbergs -what-is-left-to-say?; Harrison E. Salisbury, "The Strange Correspondence of Morris Ernst and John Edgar Hoover, 1939–1964," *Nation,* December 1, 1984; Radosh and Milton, *The Rosenberg File,* 391.

41. Elizabeth Schulte, "The Trial of Ethel and Julius Rosenberg," *International Socialist Review* 29 (May–June 2003), isreview .org/issues/29/rosenbergs.shtml; Ronald Radosh, "A Tale of Two Trials: Soviet Propaganda at Home and Abroad," *World*

Affairs 175, no. 1 (May/June 2012), 84, worldaffairsjournal.org/article/tale-two-trials-soviet-propaganda-home-and -abroad.

42. Pavel Sudoplatov and Anatoli Sudoplatov, *Special Tasks: The Memoirs of an Unwanted Witness—a Soviet Spymaster* (Boston: Little, Brown, 1994), 216, 217; Radosh, "A Tale of Two Trials."

43. Radosh and Milton, *The Rosenberg File,* 270.

44. Figes, *The Whisperers,* 521; Radzinsky, *Stalin,* 551; Robert Gellately, *Stalin's Curse: Battling for Communism in War and Cold War* (New York: Knopf, 2013), 372.

45. *A Decade of Destruction: Jewish Culture in the USSR, 1948–1958* (New York: Congress of Jewish Culture, 1958), 7; Joshua Rubinstein, "The Night of the Murdered Poets," *New Republic,* August 25, 1997, 25–30; Radosh, "Cold Case"; "Anticosmopolitan Campaign," *YIVO Encyclopedia of Jews in Eastern Europe,* yivoencyclopedia.org/article.aspx /Anticosmopolitan_Campaign.

46. Jonathan Brent and Vladimir P. Naumov, *Stalin's Last Crime: The Plot Against the Jewish Doctors, 1948–1953* (New York: HarperCollins, 2003), 289; A. Mark Clarfield, "The Soviet 'Doctors' Plot'—50 Years On," *BMJ: British Medical Journal* 325, no. 7378 (December 21–28, 2002), 1487–1489. See also Louis Rapoport, *Stalin's War Against the Jews: The Doctors' Plot and the Soviet Solution* (New York: Free Press, 1990).

47. Edward S. Shapiro, "Ethel and Julius Rosenberg: When the Rosenbergs Were Charged with Spying, American Jews Feared an Anti-Semitic Backlash," myjewishlearning.com/article/julius-and-ethel-rosenberg/; Julie Wiener, "From the Archive: Julius and Ethel Rosenberg—and the Rabbis," jta.org/2014/10/15/culture/from-the-archive-julius-and-ethel-rosenberg -and-the-rabbis.

48. Radosh and Milton, *The Rosenberg File,* 353; Robert B. Glynn, "L'Affaire Rosenberg in France," *Political Science Quarterly* 70, no. 4 (December 1955), 510; Lori Clune, "Executing the Rosenbergs: A Transnational History" (PhD diss., University of California, Davis, 2010), 137; Howard Fast, "Save the Rosenbergs!," *Masses & Mainstream,* April 1952, 48–50.

49. Clune, "Executing the Rosenbergs," 54, 274; Don Whitehead, *The FBI Story: A Report to the People* (New York: Random House, 1956), 320; David Evanier, "The Death of Morton Sobell and the End of the Rosenberg Affair."

50. S. Andhil Feinberg, *The Rosenberg Case,* 45–46; "Mrs. Rosenberg Hits Political Frameup," *Daily Worker,* April 13, 1951.

51. Clune, "Executing the Rosenbergs," 274.

52. Radosh, "A Tale of Two Trials."

53. "Letter by Mrs. Rosenberg to the President," *New York Times,* June 20, 1953.

54. "Statement by the President Declining to Intervene on Behalf of Julius and Ethel Rosenberg," June 19, 1953, presidency .ucsb.edu/ws/?pid=9617.

55. Philipson, *Ethel Rosenberg,* 248, 258, 345; Radosh and Milton, *The Rosenberg File,* 376.

56. "The Final Letter from the Rosenbergs to Their Children," famous-trials.com/rosenberg/2232-finalletter. The original letter, in Ethel's handwriting, may be seen at archives.bu.edu/web/rosenberg-archive. It is catalog number JERA-1953-06 -19b.

57. Lamphere and Shachtman, *The FBI-KGB War,* 265–266; "Interview with Robert Lamphere," pbs.org/redfiles/kgb/deep /interv/k-int-robert-lamphere.htm; "Rabbi Irving Koslowe, 80; Gave the Rosenbergs Last Rites," *New York Times,* December 7, 2000.

58. Radosh and Milton, *The Rosenberg File,* 419; Committee on Un-American Activities of the U.S. House of Representatives. *Trial by Treason: The National Committee to Secure Justice for the Rosenbergs and Morton Sobell.* Washington, DC, August 25, 1956, 11; Healey and Isserman, *California Red,* 117.

59. Jochnowitz, "The Rosenbergs."

60. "FBI—the Vault," 91, vault.fbi.gov/rosenberg-case-ethel-rosenberg-part-02-of.

61. Leslie A. Fiedler, "A Postscript to the Rosenberg Case," *Encounter,* October 1953, 18; Jean-Paul Sartre, "Animals Sick with Rabies," *Trial by Treason,* 56; John V. Fleming, *The Anti-Communist Manifestos: Four Books That Shaped the Cold War* (New York: Norton, 2009), 285; Courtois, *The Black Book of Communism,* 750; Mona Charen, *Useful Idiots: How Liberals Got It Wrong in the Cold War and Still Blame America First* (Washington, DC: Regnery Publishing, 2003), 55; Billingsley, *Hollywood Party,* 251.

62. Fariello, *Red Scare,* 193; Lamphere and Shachtman, *The FBI-KGB War,* 275–276; Doug Linder, "Tale of the Rosenbergs: An Account," law2.umkc.edu/faculty/projects/ftrials/rosenb/ROS_ACCT.HTM; Sam Roberts, "Figure in Rosenberg Case Admits to Soviet Spying," *New York Times,* September 11, 2008; David Evanier, " 'I Bet on the Wrong Horse,' Says an Unrepentant 101-Year-Old Spy," *Wall Street Journal,* June 22, 2018; Evanier, "The Death of Morton Sobell and the End of the Rosenberg Affair."

63. *Khrushchev Remembers: The Glasnost Tapes,* trans. and ed. by Jerrold L. Schecter with Vyacheslav V. Luchkov (Boston: Little, Brown, 1990), 193–194.

64. J. Edgar Hoover, "The Crime of the Century," *Reader's Digest,* May 1951.

65. "The Truth After 26 Years," *New Republic,* June 3, 1979.

VIII. A LITTLE LIST: JOE McCARTHY INVESTIGATES

1. Oshinsky, *A Conspiracy So Immense,* 3, 6, 8.

2. Ibid., 10.

3. Ibid., 9–11, 15, 17.

4. Ibid., 25.

5. Ibid., 32.

6. Ibid., 48; Morgan, *Reds,* 348, 352.

7. Oshinsky, *A Conspiracy So Immense,* 59; Roy Cohn, *McCarthy* (New York: New American Library, 1958), 16.

8. Arthur Herman, *Joseph McCarthy: Reexamining the Life and Legacy of America's Most Hated Senator* (New York: Free Press, 2000), 53; Rose, *The Cold War Comes to Main Street,* 121.

9. Oshinsky, *A Conspiracy So Immense,* 76, 78; Morgan, *Reds,* 363, 371; Thomas C. Reeves, *The Life and Times of Joseph McCarthy: A Biography* (New York: Stein and Day, 1982), 161–185.

10. Oshinsky, *A Conspiracy So Immense,* 107; Herman, *Joseph McCarthy,* 81.

11. Reeves, *The Life and Times of Joseph McCarthy,* 202; Richard H. Rovere, *Senator Joe McCarthy* (New York: Harcourt, Brace, 1959), 122–123.

12. "'Enemies from Within': Senator Joseph R. McCarthy's Accusations of Disloyalty," historymatters.gmu.edu/d/6456.

13. Reeves, *The Life and Times of Joseph McCarthy,* 224; Rovere, *Senator Joe McCarthy,* 127–128.

14. "'Enemies fom Within'"; "Truman's Reply to McCarthy," https://commons.wikimedia.org/wiki/File:Truman%27s_reply _to_McCarthy.gif.

15. Conquest, *Kolyma,* 208–209.

16. Herman, *Joseph McCarthy,* 120.

17. Margaret Chase Smith, "Classic Senate Speeches" and "A Declaration of Conscience," senate.gov.

18. Eric Pace, "Owen Lattimore, Far East Scholar Accused by McCarthy, Dies at 88," *New York Times,* June 1, 1989; Owen Lattimore, *Ordeal by Slander* (London: MacGibbon & Kee, 1950), 89.

19. *Congressional Record—Senate,* August 20, 1951, 10325; Oshinsky, *A Conspiracy So Immense,* 29; Adolf Hitler, *Mein Kampf,* trans. Ralph Manheim (Boston: Houghton Mifflin, 1999), 231–232. McCarthy's campaign manager was one of his oldest friends, the judge Urban Van Susteren.

20. Stone, "Free Speech in the Age of McCarthy," 1395–1396; Oshinsky, *A Conspiracy So Immense,* 158–159.

21. Richard Hofstadter, *The Paranoid Style in American Politics and Other Essays* (New York: Vintage Books, 2008), 3–4; "Dr. Strangelove," archiviokubrick.it/opere/film/ds/script/ds-script.pdf.

22. William G. McLoughlin, *Revivals, Awakenings, and Reform: An Essay on Religion and Social Change in America, 1607–1977* (Chicago: University of Chicago Press, 1978), 189.

23. Glen Gendzel, "Pride, Wrath, Glee, and Fear: Emotional Responses to Senator Joseph McCarthy in the Catholic Press, 1950–1954," *American Catholic Studies* 120, no. 2 (Summer 2009), 38–39.

24. Oshinsky, *A Conspiracy So Immense,* 178.

25. Joseph R. McCarthy, *America's Retreat from Victory: The Story of George Catlett Marshall* (New York: Devin-Adair, 1951), 79, 92, 94, 95–96.

26. Oshinsky, *A Conspiracy So Immense,* 260.

27. Rovere, *Senator Joe McCarthy,* 181–182.

28. Herman, *Joseph McCarthy,* 10.

29. Rovere, *Senator Joe McCarthy,* 188–189.

30. Herman, *Joseph McCarthy,* 217–218; Robert Sherrill, "King Cohn," *Nation,* August 12, 2009; Ken Auletta, "Don't Mess with Roy Cohn," *Esquire,* December 1978.

31. William K. Klingaman, *Encyclopedia of the McCarthy Era* (New York: Facts on File, 1966), 215.

32. Morgan, *Reds,* 429; G. David Schine, *Definition of Communism,* vault.fbi.gov/; Lately Thomas, *When Even Angels Wept: The Senator Joe McCarthy Affair—a Story Without a Hero* (New York: William Morrow, 1973), 309.

33. Richard Gid Powers, *Secrecy and Power: The Life of J. Edgar Hoover* (New York: Free Press, 1987), 321; Rovere, *Senator Joe McCarthy,* 25–26; Oshinsky, *A Conspiracy So Immense,* 256–257.

34. Rovere, *Senator Joe McCarthy,* 26; Oshinsky, *A Conspiracy So Immense,* 181, 183.

35. Reeves, *The Life and Times of Joseph McCarthy,* 485; "McCarthy's Achilles Heel," thelibertyconservative.com/mccarthys-achilles-heel/.

36. "The Horrible, Oppressive History of Book Burning in America," *New Republic,* June 28, 1953, newrepublic.com/article/119516/report-book-burning-under-huac-and-eisenhower; Cohn, *McCarthy,* 78, 80.

37. Cohn, *McCarthy,* 81, 82; Thomas, *When Even Angels Wept,* 327; Oshinsky, *A Conspiracy So Immense,* 277–278; Morgan, *Reds,* 444; "Ike, Milton, and the McCarthy Battle," web.archive.org/web/20060615173752/http://eisenhowermemorial.org/stories/Ike-Milton-McCarthy.htm.

38. Morgan, *Reds,* 433; K. A. Cuordileone, "Politics in an Age of Anxiety: Cold War Political Culture and the Crisis of American Masculinity, 1949–1960," *Journal of American History* 87, no. 2 (September 2000), 539–540; Judith Adkins, " 'These People Are Frightened to Death': Congressional Investigations and the Lavender Scare," *Prologue,* Summer 2016, archives.gov/publications/prologue/2016/summer/lavender.html.

39. "The Gay 50's," archives.evergreen.edu/webpages/curricular/2007-2008/fifties/index-34917.php.html; Jamie Scot, "Shock the Gay Away: Secrets of Early Gay Aversion Therapy Revealed," June 28, 2013, huffingtonpost.com/entry/shock-the-gay-away-secrets-of-early-gay-aversiontherapy-revealed_b_3497435.

40. David K. Johnson, *The Lavender Scare: The Cold War Persecution of Gays and Lesbians in the Federal Government* (Chicago: University of Chicago Press, 2004), 37, 116; *Employment of Homosexuals and Other Sex Perverts in Government*, 81st Congress, Document No. 241 (Washington, DC: Government Printing Office, 1950), 4, 5, 19.

41. "The U.S. Government Once Purged Gay Employees Saying They Were a Threat to National Security," timeline.com/government-purged-gay-employees-ea274b33fbd0; "Executive Order 10450—Security Requirements for Government Employment, archives.gov/federal-register/codification/executive-order/10450html; Williams Institute, "The Legacy of Discriminatory State Laws, Policies," williamsinstitute.law.ucla.edu/wp-content/uploads/5_History.pdf; Johnson, *The Lavender Scare,* 166–167.

42. Johnson, *The Lavender Scare,* 151; "The U.S. Government Once Purged Gay Employees."

43. Johnson, *The Lavender Scare,* 115.

44. Ellen Schrecker, "Congressional Committees and Unfriendly Witnesses," english.illinois.edu/maps/mccarthy/schrecker4.htm; Oshinsky, *A Conspiracy So Immense,* 339; Caute, *The Great Fear,* 480; "Mission Diversify: CIA Begins LGBT Recruiting," npr.org/2012/12/02/166238287/mission-diversify-cia-begins-lgbt-recruiting.

45. Murrey Marder, "The Fort Monmouth Story," *Bulletin of the Atomic Scientists* 10, no. 1 (January 1954), 23, 24; Shirley Horner, "McCarthy's 'Purge' at Fort Is Recalled," *New York Times,* July 3, 1983.

46. Reeves, *The Life and Times of Joseph McCarthy,* 543; Morgan, *Reds,* 472, 473; Cohn, *McCarthy,* 104, 106.

47. William I. Hitchcock, *The Age of Eisenhower: America and the World in the 1950s* (New York: Simon & Schuster, 2018), 139.

48. Rovere, *Senator Joe McCarthy,* 211; Oshinsky, *A Conspiracy So Immense,* 363, 404; Herman, *Joseph McCarthy,* 245; Morgan, *Reds,* 468.

49. Andrea Friedman, "The Smearing of Joe McCarthy: The Lavender Scare, Gossip, and Cold War Politics," *American Quarterly,* 57, no. 4 (December 2005), 1117–1118.

50. Ibid., 1121–1122.

51. Edward R. Murrow, "Wires and Lights in a Box," rtdna.org/content/edward_r_murrow_s_1958_wires_lights_in_a_box _speech.

52. A. M. Sperber, *Murrow: His Life and Times* (New York: Fordham University Press, 1998), 433; Joseph E. Persico, *Edward R. Murrow: An American Original* (New York: McGraw-Hill, 1988), 7; Stephen J. Whitfield, *The Culture of the Cold War* (Baltimore: Johns Hopkins University Press, 1991), 165.

53. "Edward R. Murrow: A Report on Senator Joseph R. McCarthy, See It Now (CBS-TV, March 9, 1954)," lib.berkeley.edu /MRC/murrowmccarthy.html.

54. Sperber, *Murrow,* 439; Persico, *Edward R. Murrow,* 383, 391.

55. Thomas, *When Even Angels Wept,* 466.

56. Cohn, *McCarthy,* 208; Morgan, *Reds,* 489.

57. Cohn, *McCarthy,* 200–203; Oshinsky, *A Conspiracy So Immense,* 461.

58. Herman, *Joseph McCarthy,* 275–276.

59. Reeves, *The Life and Times of Joseph McCarthy,* 631; Cohn, *McCarthy,* 207; Oshinsky, *A Conspiracy So Immense,* 464, 465.

60. "Senate Resolution 301: Censure of Senator Joseph McCarthy (1954)," ourdocuments.gov/doc.php?doc=86&page =transcript; Joyce Milton, *John F. Kennedy* (London: DK Publishing, 2003), 89–90.

61. David S. Nichols, "Eisenhower and McCarthy: How the President Toppled a Reckless Senator," *Prologue,* Fall 2015, archives.gov/files/publications/prologue/2015/fall/ike-mccarthy.pdf; Morgan, *Reds,* 504; Rovere, *Senator Joe McCarthy,* 238, 240.

62. Oshinsky, *A Conspiracy So Immense,* 231–232; Morgan, *Reds,* 508; Herman, *Joseph McCarthy,* 1.

63. David Halberstam, *The Fifties* (New York: Villard Books, 1993), 35; Rose, *The Cold War Comes to Main Street,* 214; Schrecker, "McCarthyism," 1073; Lamphere and Shachtman, *The FBI-KGB War,* 137.

64. Herbert S. Parmet, *Eisenhower and the American Crusades* (New York: Macmillan, 1972), 249; Oshinsky, *A Conspiracy So Immense,* 299; Alice Citron, "The International Reaction," *Jewish Life,* August 1953, 24; Fleming, *The Anti-Communist Manifestos,* 285.

65. Halberstam, *The Fifties,* 251; *Daily Worker,* quoted in *Congressional Record,* November 8, 1954, 15, 879. Paul Robeson echoed the Party paper, saying: "We must reject the Big Lie on which McCarthyism thrives. The big lie is the fairy tale that the American people are somehow threatened by 'communism'" (*Paul Robeson Speaks,* 377).

EPILOGUE: BRUTAL FANTASIES

1. Svetlana Alliluyeva, *Twenty Letters to a Friend* (New York: Harper & Row, 1967), 10.

2. Ginzburg, *Within the Whirlwind,* 356; Tzouliades, *The Forsaken,* 308; Figes, *The Whisperers,* 529; Applebaum, *Gulag,* 477; Yakovlev, *A Century of Violence in Soviet Russia,* 32; Oleg V. Khlevniuk, *Stalin: New Biography of a Dictator,* trans. by Nora Seligman Favorov (New Haven: Yale University Press, 2015), 319.

3. Healey and Isserman, *California Red,* 149; Kraditor, *"Jimmy Higgins,"* 82; Paul Robeson, "To You Beloved Comrade," in *Paul Robeson Speaks,* 328, 347–349.

4. Chamberlin, "Khrushchev's War with Stalin's Ghost," 5; William Taubman, *Khrushchev: The Man and His Era* (New York: Norton, 2002), 99, 103, 106; Simon Sebag Montefiore, *Stalin: The Court of the Red Tsar* (New York: Knopf, 2004), 249; Robert Payne, *The Rise and Fall of Stalin* (New York: Simon & Schuster, 1965), 491; Arkady Vaksberg, *Stalin Against the Jews* (New York: Knopf, 1994), 285.

5. Nikita S. Khrushchev, *The Crimes of the Stalin Era,* trans. by Boris I. Nicolaevsky (New York: New Leader, 1962); Claire Bigg, "Russia: Khrushchev's 'Secret Speech' Remembered After 50 Years," Radio Free Europe, rferl.org/a/1065804.html.

6. Steve Nelson, James R. Barrett, and Rob Ruck, *Steve Nelson, American Radical* (Pittsburgh: University of Pittsburgh Press, 1981), 386–388.

7. Isserman, *Which Side Were You On?,* 250; Gornick, *The Romance of American Communism,* 11; Howe and Coser, *The American Communist Party,* 492.

8. Kraditor, *"Jimmy Higgins,"* 84–85; Dennis, *The Autobiography of an American Communist,* 117, 118, 136, 137.

9. "November 9, 1956: Jean-Paul Sartre Denounces Communists," history.com/this-day-in-history/sartre-renounces -communists; Billingsley, *Hollywood Party,* 288.

10. Boris Pasternak, *Doctor Zhivago* (New York: Pantheon Books, 1958), 809.

11. Morgan, *Reds,* 546; Fast, *The Naked God,* 3; Billingsley, *Hollywood Party,* 258; Phillip Deery, "Finding His Kronstadt: Howard Fast, 1956 and American Communism," *Australian Journal of Politics and History* 58, no. 2 (2012), 186. When the sailors at the Kronstadt naval base rebelled against Communist rule in 1921, the Red Army slaughtered them, causing scores of CPUSA members to resign in protest.

12. Gornick, *The Romance of American Communism,* 10; Howe and Coser, *The American Communist Party,* 419, 560, 563; Fariello, *Red Scare,* 82, 92; Schrecker, "McCarthyism," 1069; Harvey Klehr, "Few American Jews Were Communists, and Many Fewer Were Spies," *Mosaic,* June 11, 2019, mosaicmagazine.com/response/history-ideas/2019/06/few-american -jews-were-communists-and-many-fewer-were-spies/?print.

13. Roy Medvedev and Zhores Medvedev, *The Unknown Stalin: His Life, Death, and Legacy* (Woodstock, NY: Overlook Press, 2003), 116–117; Applebaum, *Gulag,* 556.

14. Payne, *The Rise and Fall of Stalin,* 712–713; Maria Lipman, Lev Gudkov, and Lasha Bakradze, *The Stalin Puzzle: Deciphering Post-Soviet Public Opinion* (Washington, DC: Carnegie Endowment for International Peace, 2013). Doug Bandow, "Who Gets Buried at the Kremlin? Time for a Post-Revolutionary Purge," cato .org>publications>commentary>who-gets-buried-kremlin-time-post-revolutionary-purge.

15. Aidan Lewis, "The Curious Survival of the U.S. Communist Party," bbc.com/news/magazine-26126325; Patricia Cohen, "Communist Party USA Gives Its History to N.Y.U.," *New York Times,* March 20, 2007.

16. Alexandra Popoff, *Vasily Grossman and the Soviet Century* (New Haven, CT: Yale University Press, 2019), 319.

17. "History Is a Weapon: A Selection of the Poetry of Langston Hughes (1902–1967)," historyisaweapon.com/defcon1 /langston.html.

SELECTED SOURCES

Adkins, Judith. "'These People Are Frightened to Death': Congressional Investigations and the Lavender Scare," *Prologue,* Summer 2016, archives.gov/publications/prologue/2016/summer/lavender.html.

Allen, James S. *Organizing in the Depression South: A Communist's Memoir.* Minneapolis: MEP Publications, 2001.

Andrew, Christopher, and Oleg Gordievsky. *KGB: The Inside Story of Its Foreign Operations from Lenin to Gorbachev.* New York: HarperCollins, 1990.

Antonov-Ovseyenko, Anton. *The Time of Stalin: Portrait of a Tyranny.* New York: Harper, 1983.

Applebaum, Anne. *Gulag: A History.* New York: Doubleday, 2003.

Billingsley, Kenneth Lloyd. *Hollywood Party: How Communism Seduced the American Film Industry in the 1930s and 1940s.* Rocklin, CA: Forum, 1998.

Blakely, Alison. *Russia and the Negro: Blacks in Russian History and Thought.* Washington, DC: Howard University Press, 1986.

Brent, Jonathan, and Vladimir P. Naumov. *Stalin's Last Crime: The Plot Against the Jewish Doctors, 1948–1953.* New York: HarperCollins, 2003.

Camp, Helen C. *Iron in Her Soul: Elizabeth Gurley Flynn and the American Left.* Pullman: Washington State University Press, 1995.

Carter, Dan T. *Scottsboro: A Tragedy of the American South.* Baton Rouge: Louisiana State University Press, 1979.

Casty, Alan. *Communism in Hollywood: The Moral Paradoxes of Testimony, Silence, and Betrayal.* Lanham, MD: Scarecrow Press, 2009.

Caute, David. *The Fellow-Travellers: A Postscript to the Enlightenment.* New York: Macmillan, 1973.

———. *The Great Fear: The Anti-Communist Purge Under Truman and Eisenhower.* New York: Simon & Schuster, 1978.

Ceplair, Larry, and Steven Englund. *The Inquisition in Hollywood: Politics in the Film Community, 1930–60.* Urbana: University of Illinois Press, 1979.

Ceplair, Larry, and Christopher Trumbo. *Dalton Trumbo: Blacklisted Hollywood Radical.* Lexington: University Press of Kentucky, 2015.

Charen, Mona. *Useful Idiots: How Liberals Got It Wrong in the Cold War and Still Blame America First.* Washington, DC: Regnery Publishing, 2003.

Churchill, Allen. *Over Here: An Informal Re-creation of the Home Front in the First World War.* New York: Dodd, Mead, 1968.

Cogley, John. *Report on Blacklisting.* Vol. 1, *Movies.* New York: Fund for the Republic, 1956.

Cohn, Roy. *McCarthy.* New York: New American Library, 1968.

Courtois, Stéphane, et al. *The Black Book of Communism: Crimes, Terror, Repression.* Cambridge, MA: Harvard University Press, 1999.

Dennis, Peggy. *The Autobiography of an American Communist: A Personal View of a Political Life, 1925–1975.* Westport, CT: Lawrence Hill, 1977.

Draper, Theodore. *American Communism and Soviet Russia: The Formative Period.* New York: Viking Press, 1963.

———. *The Roots of American Communism.* New York: Viking Press, 1957.

Dray, Philip. *At the Hands of Persons Unknown: The Lynching of Black America.* New York: Random House, 2002.

Duberman, Martin Bauml. *Paul Robeson.* New York: Knopf, 1988.

Eckstein, Arthur. "The Hollywood Ten in History and Memory." *Film History* 16, no. 4 (2004), 424–436.

Ellis, Edward Robb. *Echoes of Distant Thunder: Life in the United States, 1914–1918.* New York: Coward, McCann & Geohegan, 1975.

Evans, M. Stanton, and Herbert Romerstein. *Stalin's Secret Agents: The Subversion of Roosevelt's Government.* New York: Threshold Editions, 2012.

Fariello, Griffin. *Red Scare: Memories of the American Inquisition; An Oral History.* New York: Norton, 1995.

Fast, Howard. *Being Red.* Boston: Houghton, Mifflin, 1990.

Feklisov, Alexander. *The Man Behind the Rosenbergs.* New York: Enigma Books, 2001.

Feldman, Jay. *Manufacturing Hysteria: A History of Scapegoating, Surveillance, and Secrecy in Modern America.* New York: Pantheon Books, 2011.

———. *The Naked God: The Writer and the Communist Party.* New York: Praeger, 1957.

Figes, Orlando. *Revolutionary Russia, 1891–1991: A History.* New York: Metropolitan Books, 2014.

———. *The Whisperers: Private Life in Stalin's Russia.* New York: Metropolitan Books, 2007.

Fitzpatrick, Sheila. *Everyday Stalinism: Ordinary Life in Extraordinary Times: Soviet Russia in the 1930s.* New York: Oxford University Press, 1999.

Foner, Philip S., and Herbert Shapiro. *American Communism and Black Americans: A Documentary History.* Philadelphia: Temple University Press, 1991.

Fried, Albert, ed. *Communism in America: A History in Documents.* New York: Columbia University Press, 1997.

———. *McCarthyism: The Great American Red Scare; A Documentary History.* New York: Oxford University Press, 1997.

Fried, Richard M. *Nightmare in Red: The McCarthy Era in Perspective.* New York: Oxford University Press, 1990.

Gaddis, John Lewis. *The Cold War: A New History.* New York: Penguin Press, 2005.

Gardner, John L. "African Americans in the Soviet Union in the 1920s and 1930s: The Development of Transcontinental Protest." *Western Journal of Black Studies* 23, no. 3 (1999), 190–200.

Gardner, Virginia. *The Rosenberg Story.* New York: Masses & Mainstream, 1954.

Gentry, Curt. *J. Edgar Hoover: The Man and the Secrets.* New York: Norton, 1991.

Gerber, Marjorie, and Rebecca L. Walkowitz. *Soviet Agents: The Rosenberg Case, McCarthyism, and Fifties America.* New York: Routledge, 1995.

Glazer, Nathan. *The Social Basis of American Communism.* New York: Harcourt, Brace, 1961.

Goldman, Eric C. *The Crucial Decade—and After: America, 1945–1960.* New York: Vintage Books, 1960.

Goodman, Walter. *The Committee: The Extraordinary Career of the House Committee on Un-American Activities.* New York: Farrar, Straus & Giroux, 1968.

Gornick, Vivian. *The Romance of American Communism.* New York: Basic Books, 1977.

Griffith, Robert. *The Politics of Fear: Joseph R. McCarthy and the Senate.* Boston: University of Massachusetts Press, 1987.

Grogin, Robert C. *Natural Enemies: The United States and the Soviet Union in the Cold War, 1917–1991.* Lanham, MD: Lexington Books, 2001.

Hagedorn, Ann. *Savage Peace: Hope and Fear in America, 1919.* New York: Simon & Schuster, 2007.

Halberstam, David. *The Fifties.* New York: Villard Books, 1993.

Haynes, John Earl. *Red Scare or Red Menace? American Communism and Anti-Communism in the Cold War Era.* Chicago: Ivan R. Dee, 1995.

Haynes, John Earl, and Harvey Klehr. *The American Communist Movement: Storming Heaven Itself.* New York: Twayne Publishers, 1992.

———. *Early Cold War Spies: The Espionage Trials That Shaped American Politics.* New York: Cambridge University Press, 2006.

———. *In Denial: Historians, Communists and Espionage.* San Francisco: Encounter Books, 2003.

———. *Venona: Decoding Soviet Espionage in America.* New Haven, CT: Yale University Press, 1999.

Haynes, John Earl, Harvey Klehr, and Alexander Vassiliev. *Spies: The Rise and Fall of the KGB in America.* New Haven, CT: Yale University Press, 2009.

Haywood, Harry. *Black Bolshevik: Autobiography of an Afro-American Communist.* Chicago: Liberator Press, 1978.

Heale, M. J. *American Anticommunism: Combating the Enemy Within, 1830–1970.* Baltimore: Johns Hopkins University Press, 1990.

Healey, Dorothy Ray, and Maurice Isserman. *California Red: A Life in the American Communist Party.* Urbana: University of Illinois Press, 1993.

Heller, Mikhail, and Aleksandr M. Nekrich. *Utopia in Power: The History of the Soviet Union from 1917 to the Present.* New York: Summit Books, 1986.

Herman, Arthur. *Joseph McCarthy: Reexamining the Life and Legacy of America's Most Hated Senator.* New York: Free Press, 2000.

Hitchcock, William I. *The Age of Eisenhower: America and the World in the 1950s.* New York: Simon & Schuster, 2018.

Hofstadter, Richard. *The Paranoid Style in American Politics and Other Essays.* New York: Vintage Books, 2008.

Hornblum, Allen M. *The Invisible Harry Gold: The Man Who Gave the Soviets the Atom Bomb.* New Haven, CT: Yale University Press, 2010.

Horne, Gerald. *The Final Victim of the Blacklist: John Howard Lawson.* Berkeley: University of California Press, 2006.

Howard, William T., ed. *Black Communists Speak on Scottsboro: A Documentary History.* Philadelphia: Temple University Press, 2007.

Howe, Irving, and Lewis Coser. *The American Communist Party: A Critical History.* New York: Praeger, 1962.

Hunt, R. N. Carew. *A Guide to Communist Jargon.* London: Macmillan, 1957.

Johnson, David K. *The Lavender Scare: The Cold War Persecution of Gays and Lesbians in the Federal Government.* Chicago: University of Chicago Press, 2004.

Kahn, Albert E. *The Game of Death: Effects of the Cold War on Our Children.* New York: Cameron & Kahn, 1953.

Kaplan, Judy, and Linn Shapiro, eds. *Red Diapers: Growing Up in the Communist Left.* Urbana: University of Illinois Press, 1998.

Kelley, Robert D. G. *Hammer and Hoe: Alabama Communists During the Great Depression.* Chapel Hill: University of North Carolina Press, 1990.

Kengor, Paul. *The Crusader: Ronald Reagan and the Fall of Communism.* New York: Regan Books, 2006.

———. *Dupes: How America's Adversaries Have Manipulated Progressives for a Century.* Wilmington, DE: ISI Books, 2010.

Kennedy, David M. *Freedom from Fear: The American People in Depression and War, 1929–1945.* New York: Oxford University Press, 1999.

———. *Over There: The First World War and American Society.* New York: Oxford University Press, 1980.

Khrushchev, Nikita. *Khrushchev Remembers.* Boston: Little, Brown, 1990.

Klehr, Harvey. *The Communist Experience in America: A Political and Social History.* New York: Routledge, 2010.

———. *The Heyday of American Communism: The Depression Decade.* New York: Basic Books, 1984.

Knight, Amy. *How the Cold War Began: The Igor Gouzenko Affair and the Hunt for Soviet Spies.* New York: Carroll & Graf, 2005.

Koppes, Clayton R., and Gregory D. Black. *Hollywood Goes to War: How Politics, Profits, and Propaganda Shaped World War II Movies.* New York: Free Press, 1987.

Kraditor, Aileen S. *"Jimmy Higgins": The Mental World of the Rank-and-File Communist, 1930–1958.* New York: Greenwood Press, 1988.

Kunetka, James W. *City of Fire: Los Alamos and the Birth of the Atomic Age, 1943–1945.* Englewood Cliffs, NJ: Prentice-Hall, 1978.

Kutzinski, Vera M. *The Worlds of Langston Hughes: Modernism and Translation in the Americas.* Ithaca, NY: Cornell University Press, 2012.

Lamphere, Robert J., and Tom Shachtman. *The FBI-KGB War: A Special Agent's Story.* New York: Random House, 1986.

Leuchtenburg, William E. *The Perils of Prosperity, 1914–32.* Chicago: University of Chicago Press, 1958.

Levin, Murray B. *Political Hysteria in America: The Democratic Capacity for Repression.* New York: Basic Books, 1971.

Lewy, Guenter. *The Cause That Failed: Communism in American Political Life.* New York: Oxford University Press, 1990.

Lifton, Robert J. *Death in Life: Survivors of Hiroshima.* New York: Random House, 1967.

Lincoln, W. Bruce. *Red Victory: A History of the Russian Civil War.* New York: Simon & Schuster, 1989.

Lyons, Eugene. *The Red Decade: The Classic Work on Communism in America During the Thirties.* New Rochelle, NY: Arlington House, 1972. Reprint of a book originally published in 1941.

———. *Workers' Paradise Lost: Fifty Years of Soviet Communism; A Balance Sheet.* New York: Funk & Wagnalls, 1967.

McCullough, David. *Truman.* New York: Simon & Schuster, 1992.

McGilligan, Patrick, and Paul Buhle. *Tender Comrades: A Backstory of the Hollywood Blacklist.* New York: St. Martin's Press, 1997.

McMeekin, Sean. *The Russian Revolution: A New History.* New York: Basic Books, 2017.

Meeropol, Michael, ed. *The Rosenberg Letters: A Complete Edition of the Prison Correspondence of Julius and Ethel Rosenberg.* New York: Garland Reference Library of the Humanities, 1997.

Meeropol, Michael, and Robert Meeropol. *We Are Your Sons: The Legacy of Ethel and Julius Rosenberg.* Boston: Houghton Mifflin, 1975.

Mickenberg, Julia L., and Philip Nel, eds. *Tales for Little Rebels: A Collection of Radical Children's Literature.* New York: New York University Press, 2008.

Mishler, Paul C. *Raising Reds: The Young Pioneers, Radical Summer Camps, and Communist Political Culture in the United States.* New York: Columbia University Press, 1999.

Montefiore, Simon Sebag. *Stalin: The Court of the Red Tsar.* New York: Knopf, 2004.

Moorhouse, Roger. *The Devils' Alliance: Hitler's Pact with Stalin, 1939–1941.* New York: Basic Books, 2014.

Morgan, Ted. *Reds: McCarthyism in Twentieth-Century America.* New York: Random House, 2003.

Moss, Norman. *Klaus Fuchs: The Man Who Stole the Atom Bomb.* New York: St. Martin's Press, 1987.

Moynihan, Daniel Patrick. *Secrecy: The American Experience.* New Haven, CT: Yale University Press, 1999.

Murphy, Paul I. *World War I and the Origins of Civil Liberties in the United States.* New York: Norton, 1979.

Murray, Robert K. *Red Scare: A Study of National Hysteria, 1919–1920.* New York: McGraw-Hill, 1964.

Naison, Mark. *Communists in Harlem During the Depression.* Urbana: University of Illinois Press, 1983.

Navasky, Victor S. *Naming Names.* New York: Viking Press, 1980.

Nelson, Steve, James R. Barrett, and Rob Ruck. *Steve Nelson, American Radical.* Pittsburgh: University of Pittsburgh Press, 1981.

Neville, John F. *The Press, the Rosenbergs, and the Cold War.* Westport, CT: Praeger, 1995.

Nichols, David A. *Ike and McCarthy: Dwight Eisenhower's Secret Campaign Against Joseph McCarthy.* New York: Simon & Schuster, 2017.

O'Connor, John E. "Edward R. Murrow's Report on Senator McCarthy: Image as Artifact," *Film & History: An Interdisciplinary Journal of Film and Television Studies* 16, no. 3 (September 1986), 54–69.

Olmsted, Kathryn S. *The Red Spy Queen: A Biography of Elizabeth Bentley.* Chapel Hill: University of North Carolina Press, 2002.

O'Reilly, Kenneth. *Hoover and the Un-Americans: The FBI, HUAC, and the Red Menace.* Philadelphia: Temple University Press, 1983.

Oshinsky, David M. *A Conspiracy So Immense: The World of Joe McCarthy.* New York: Free Press, 1983.

Ottanelli, Fraser M. *The Communist Party of the United States: From the Depression to World War II.* New Brunswick, NJ: Rutgers University Press, 1991.

Packard, Jerrold M. *American Nightmare: The History of Jim Crow.* New York: St. Martin's Press, 2002.

Parmet, Herbert S. *Eisenhower and the American Crusades.* New York: Macmillan, 1972.

Persico, Joseph E. *Edward R. Murrow: An American Original.* New York: McGraw-Hill, 1988.

Philipson, Ilene. *Ethel Rosenberg: Beyond the Myths.* New Brunswick, NJ: Rutgers University Press, 1992.

Pipes, Richard. *Communism: A History.* New York: Modern Library, 2001.

———. *A Concise History of the Russian Revolution.* New York: Knopf, 1995.

———. *Russia Under the Bolshevik Regime.* New York: Knopf, 1993.

Powers, Richard Gid. *Not Without Honor: The History of American Anticommunism.* New York: Free Press, 1995.

Radosh, Ronald, and Joyce Milton. *The Rosenberg File: A Search for Truth.* New York: Holt, Rinehart & Winston, 1983.

Radosh, Ronald, and Allis Radosh. *Red Star over Hollywood: The Film Colony's Long Romance with the Left.* San Francisco: Encounter Books, 2005.

Rapoport, Louis. *Stalin's War Against the Jews: The Doctors' Plot and the Soviet Solution.* New York: Free Press, 1990.

Rayfield, Donald. *Stalin and His Hangmen: The Dictator and Those Who Killed for Him.* New York: Random House, 2004.

Read, Anthony. *The World on Fire: 1919 and the Battle with Bolshevism.* New York: Norton, 2008.

Record, Wilson. *The Negro and the Communist Party.* Chapel Hill: University of North Carolina Press, 1951.

Reeves, Thomas C. *The Life and Times of Joseph McCarthy: A Biography.* New York: Stein and Day, 1982.

Reynolds, Quentin. *Courtroom: The Story of Samuel S. Leibowitz.* New York: Farrar, Straus, 1950.

Rhodes, Richard. *Dark Sun: The Making of the Hydrogen Bomb.* New York: Simon & Schuster, 1995.

———. *The Making of the Atomic Bomb.* New York: Simon & Schuster, 1986.

Roberts, Sam. *The Brother: The Untold Story of the Rosenberg Case.* New York: Simon & Schuster, 2014.

Robeson, Paul. *Paul Robeson Speaks: Writings, Speeches, Interviews, 1918–1974.* Edited by Philip S. Foner. New York: Kensington Publishing, 1978.

Robinson, Robert. *Black on Red: My 44 Years Inside the Soviet Union.* Washington, DC: Acropolis Books, 1988.

Romerstein, Herbert, and Eric Brindel. *The Venona Secrets: Exposing Soviet Espionage and America's Traitors.* Washington, DC: Regnery Publishing, 2000.

Rose, Leslie A. *The Cold War Comes to Main Street: America in 1950.* Lawrence: University Press of Kansas, 1999.

Rovere, Richard H. *Senator Joe McCarthy.* New York: Harcourt, Brace, 1959.

Rubenstein, Joshua. *The Last Days of Stalin.* New Haven, CT: Yale University Press, 2016.

Ryan, James Gilbert. *Earl Browder: The Failure of American Communism.* Tuscaloosa: University of Alabama Press, 1997.

Ryskind, Allan H. *Hollywood Traitors: Blacklisted Screenwriters; Agents of Stalin, Allies of Hitler.* Washington, DC: Regnery History, 2015.

Schaffer, Richard. *America in the Great War.* New York: Oxford University Press, 1991.

Schmidt, Regin. *Red Scare: FBI and the Origins of Anticommunism in the United States, 1919–1943.* Copenhagen, Denmark: Museum Tusculanum Press, University of Copenhagen, 2000.

Schrecker, Ellen. *The Age of McCarthyism: A Brief History with Documents.* New York: Bedford/St. Martin's, 2002.

———. *Many Are the Crimes: McCarthyism in America.* Boston: Little, Brown, 1998.

———. "McCarthyism: Political Repression and the Fear of Communism." *Social Research* 71, no. 4 (Winter 2004), 1041–1086.

———. *No Ivory Tower: McCarthyism and the Universities.* New York: Oxford University Press, 1986.

Sebestyen, Victor. *Lenin: The Man, the Dictator, and the Master of Terror.* New York: Pantheon Books, 2017.

Shaw, Tony. *Hollywood's Cold War: The American and Soviet Struggle for Hearts and Minds.* Edinburgh: University of Edinburgh Press, 2017.

Sibley, Katherine A. S. *Red Spies in America: Stolen Secrets and the Dawn of the Cold War.* Lawrence: University Press of Kansas, 2004.

Solomon, Mark. *The Cry Was Unity: Communists and African Americans, 1917–1936.* Jackson: University of Mississippi Press, 1998.

Solzhenitsyn, Aleksandr I. *The Gulag Archipelago, 1918–1956: An Experiment in Literary Investigation.* New York: Harper & Row, 1974.

Sorin, Gerald. *Howard Fast: Life and Literature in the Left Lane.* Bloomington: University of Indiana Press, 2012.

Sperber, A. M. *Murrow: His Life and Times.* New York: Fordham University Press, 1998.

Starobin, Joseph R. *American Communism in Crisis, 1943–1957.* Cambridge, MA: Harvard University Press, 1972.

Steil, Ben. *The Marshall Plan: Dawn of the Cold War.* New York: Simon & Schuster, 2018.

Sudoplatov, Pavel, and Anatoli Sudoplatov. *Special Tasks: The Memoirs of an Unwanted Witness—a Soviet Spymaster.* Boston: Little, Brown, 1994.

Thomas, Hugh. *Armed Truce: The Beginnings of the Cold War, 1945–46.* New York: Atheneum, 1987.

Thomas, Lately. *When Even Angels Wept: The Senator Joseph McCarthy Affair—a Story Without Heroes.* New York: William Morrow, 1973.

Tolstoy, Nikolai. *Stalin's Secret War.* New York: Holt, Rinehart and Winston, 1981.

Tzouliadis, Tim. *The Forsaken: An American Tragedy in Stalin's Russia.* New York: Penguin Press, 2008.

Usdin, Steven T. *Engineering Communism: How Two Americans Spied for Stalin and Founded the Soviet Silicon Valley.* New Haven, CT: Yale University Press, 2005.

———. "The Rosenberg Ring Revealed: Industrial-Scale Conventional and Nuclear Espionage." *Journal of Cold War Studies* 11, no. 3 (Summer 2009), 91–143.

———. "Tracking Julius Rosenberg's Lesser Known Associates." cia.gov/library/center-for-the-study-of-intelligence/csi-publications/csi-studies/studies/vol49no3/html_files/Rosenberg_2.htm.

Vaksberg, Arkady. *Stalin Against the Jews.* New York: Knopf, 1994.

Vaughn, Robert. *Only Victims: A Study of Show Business Blacklisting.* New York: Limelight Editions, 1996.

Vaughn, Stephen. *Ronald Reagan in Hollywood: Movies and Politics.* New York: Cambridge University Press, 1994.

Volkogonov, Dmitri. *Autopsy for an Empire: The Seven Leaders Who Built the Soviet Regime.* New York: Free Press, 1998.

Weiner, Tim. *Enemies: A History of the FBI.* New York: Random House, 2012.

Weinstein, Allen, and Alexander Vassiliev. *The Haunted Wood: Soviet Espionage in America—the Stalin Era.* New York: Random House, 1999.

Whitehead, Don. *The FBI Story: A Report to the People.* New York: Random House, 1956.

Whitfield, Stephen J. *The Culture of the Cold War.* Baltimore: Johns Hopkins University Press, 1991.

Williams, Robert C. *Klaus Fuchs, Atomic Spy.* Cambridge, MA: Harvard University Press, 1987.

Wittner, Lawrence S. *Cold War America: From Hiroshima to Watergate.* New York: Praeger, 1974.

Yakovlev, Alexander N. *A Century of Violence in Soviet Russia.* New Haven, CT: Yale University Press, 2002.

Zangrando, Robert L. *The NAACP Campaign Against Lynching, 1909–1950.* Philadelphia: Temple University Press, 1980.

Zion, Sidney. *The Autobiography of Roy Cohn.* Secaucus, NJ: Lyle Stuart, 1988.

REFERENCE WORKS

Arms, Thomas S. *Encyclopedia of the Cold War.* New York: Facts on File, 1994.

Buhle, Mari Jo, Paul Buhle, and Dan Georgakas, eds. *Encyclopedia of the American Left.* New York: Oxford University Press, 1998.

Klingaman, William K. *Encyclopedia of the McCarthy Era.* New York: Facts on File, 1966.

Trahair, Richard C. S., and Robert Miller. *Encyclopedia of Cold War Espionage, Spies, and Secret Operations.* Westport, CT: Greenwood Press, 2004.

Tucker, Spencer C., ed. *The Encyclopedia of the Cold War: A Political, Social, and Military History.* 5 vols. Santa Barbara, CA: ABC-CLIO, 2007.

INTERNET SOURCES

The Internet is a gold mine of material on all aspects of the subjects covered in this book, and much more. The most useful websites are:

John Earl Haynes Historical Writings, johnearlhaynes.org.

"American Communism and Anticommunism: A Historian's Bibliography and Guide to the Literature" on this site is a comprehensive list of every important book and article on every aspect of American communism as of 2009.

The Julius and Ethel Rosenberg Archive at the Howard Gotlieb Archival Research Center, Boston University, archives.bu.edu/web /rosenberg-archive.

This site displays all the letters the couple wrote, in their own handwriting, during their years in prison.

Marxists Internet Archive, marxists.org.

This site contains digitized versions of most of the contemporary materials used in this book and includes all the classic works by Marx, Lenin, and Stalin.

PICTURE CREDITS

Alamy: 6, 20, 62, 130, 151, 183, 184 (bottom)

Archive Photos/Getty: 119

BArch (German Federal Archives): 205

Bettmann/Getty: 96, 147, 163, 187, 188, 192, 237

Boston Herald: 202, 242

CBS Radio/PD-US: 238

CCNY Archives: 173

Corbis Historical/Getty: 174

Cornell University Library: 81

Daily Worker/PD-US: 104, 248

Digital Public Library of America: 74

Federal Bureau of Investigation/PD-US: 35

FPG/Getty: 200

GraphicaArtis/Getty: 162

Harry S. Truman Presidential Library and Museum: 127

The Henry Ford Collections: 98

The Herb Block Foundation: 139 (bottom), 218

Heritage Images/Getty: 64

Imagno/Getty: 76

International Institute of Social History: 8

International Pamphlets/PD-US: 55

Jewish Women's Archive: 32

John F. Kennedy Presidential Library and Museum: 249

Keystone-France/Getty: 185

Library of Congress: 4, 22, 31, 78, 139 (top), 141, 166, 225, 226, 234

Library of Congress/Getty: 39

Los Alamos National Laboratory: 184 (top)

Manhattan District History, Manhattan Project/PD-US: 181

Morgan County Archives: 91

MPI/Getty: 93

MTI (Hungarian News Agency): 253

Museum of Political History of Russia/PD-US: 3

National Museum of African American History and Culture: 82

National Security Agency/Venona Documents: 177

Naval History and Heritage Command Archives: 179

New York Daily News Archive/Getty: 44, 193

Newman Library, Baruch College, CUNY: 27

PD-US: 13, 15, 23, 47, 49, 50, 52, 57, 65, 67, 75, 83, 85, 109, 110, 112, 121, 131, 137, 145, 149 (top), 149 (bottom), 152, 155, 159, 160, 170, 196, 223, 235, 243, 250, 251, 256

PhotoQuest/Getty: 215

Pittsburgh Courier: 115

Prozhektor magazine/PD-US: 19

Records of the U.S. Senate/PD-US: 231

Scheel: 57 (top)

Stars and Stripes: 128

Szépművészeti Múzeum/Museum of Fine Arts, Budapest: 199

UHM Library Digital Image Collections: 90

U.S. Copyright Office/PD-US: 220

U.S. Government/PD-US: 118

U.S. National Archives and Records Administration: 103, 191, 213

U.S. Office of War Information: 122

Virginia Tech Special Collections and University Archives: 88

Wisconsin Historical Society: 209, 210, 221

Woody Guthrie Archives: 113

Working Woman/PD-US: 54

Young Pioneer/PD-US: 69, 70

INDEX